Diaspora Christianities

Diaspora Christianities

*Global Scattering and Gathering
of South Asian Christians*

EDITOR

SAM GEORGE

FORTRESS PRESS

MINNEAPOLIS

DIASPORA CHRISTIANITIES

Global Scattering and Gathering of South Asian Christians

"Death in Diaspora: Reincarnation, Oblivion or Heaven?" is a summary of Bobby Bose's *Reincarnation, Oblivion or Heaven? A Christian Exploration*, published by Langham Global Library, Carlisle, UK, 2016 (used by permission, www.langhampublishing.org).

Cover design: Rob Dewey

Print ISBN: 978-1-5064-4704-9
eBook ISBN: 978-1-5064-4706-3

The paper used in this publication meets the minimum requirements of American National Standard for Information Sciences — Permanence of Paper for Printed Library Materials, ANSI Z329.48-1984.

Manufactured in the U.S.A.

Contents

Author Profiles

Sam George, PhD serves as a Global Catalyst for Diasporas of the Lausanne Movement and is the Executive Director of Parivar International. After a Bachelors in Engineering and Masters in Management, he worked in engineering design for nearly a decade. Later he did theological studies in US and UK, focusing on practical theology and missiology. He lives with his wife, and their two boys in the northern suburbs of Chicago, USA.

Danny Moses, PhD (Oxford) is the Director of Lanka Bible College, Centre for Graduate Studies in Colombo, Sri-Lanka. He did his BD at the Union Biblical Seminary, India and his MA in London Bible College. He did his doctorate in Biblical Studies at Wycliffe Hall, Oxford, UK. He is widely travelled and has taught in theological colleges in Australia, Canada, USA and Sri-Lanka.

Simon Samuel, PhD (University of Sheffield) is Professor of New Testament Studies and Christian Origins, and Principal of the New Theological College in Dehradun, India. He is a member of the Senate of Serampore College and president designate of Christian Evangelistic Assemblies. He is the author of *A Postcolonial Reading of Mark's Story of Jesus* (T & T Clark, 2007) and co-editor of *Remapping Mission Discourse* (ISPCK, 2008).

Prof. Rev. Daniel Jeyaraj, Dr. theol. Dr. Habil., Dr. phil., D.D. (h.c.) is a professor of World Christianity and Director of the Andrew Walls Center at Liverpool Hope University, UK. A leading historian and author of many publications. Serve as the Chief Editor of *Dharma Deepika* and an Associate Editor for the *International Bulletin of Missionary Research*. An ordained presbyter of the Church of South India and a licensed minister of the Church of England.

Prof. Rev. Godfrey Harold, PhD, ThD is a Senior Lecturer at Cape Town Baptist Seminary and Associate Researcher at the University of Pretoria. He is also a Distinguished Senior Fellow at BH Carroll Theological Institute (USA). He holds two earned doctorates and is presently enrolled for his third at the University of South Africa. He serves as the Executive Editor of The South African Baptist Journal of Theology.

John Lewis, MDiv. is the founder and director of The Grenada Institute for Theological Education and Caribbean director of EQUIP, leadership training ministry of John C. Maxwell. Earlier was director of Youth For Christ in St. Vincent and Grenadines and involved in various ministry initiatives in the Caribbeans.

George Joseph, MA is a Singapore-born journalist, administrator and business advisor. He is among the first generation of local born children of the Kerala pioneers of the Syrian Christian churches in Singapore and Malaysia. He graduated with honors in Political Science and Economics from Aligarh University, India.

Prema Kurien, PhD is Professor of Sociology and Robert D. McClure Professor of Teaching Excellence, as well as the founding director of the Asian/Asian American Studies program at Syracuse University. She is the author of two award-winning books, *Kaleidoscopic Ethnicity* and *A Place at the Multicultural Table*. Most recent book is *Ethnic Church Meets Mega Church: Indian American Christianity in Motion*. She is currently working on her next book, "Race, Religion, and Citizenship: Indian American Political Advocacy," and on a research project, "The Political Incorporation of Religious Minorities in Canada and the United States."

Rev. T.V. Thomas DMin is originally from Malaysia and now lives in Canada. He is the Director or the Centre for Evangelism & World Mission and for over three decades T.V. has enjoyed trans-denominational and trans-continental ministry of speaking, teaching and networking. He chairs the Board of Directors of Inter-Varsity Christian Fellowship of Canada, Lausanne Global Diaspora Network and Ethnic America Network. He also serves as a consultant for The Christian & Missionary Alliance in Canada.

Thomas Kulanjiyil, PsyD, PhD is a professor of Philosophy at College of DuPage, Glen Ellyn, Chicago, IL, and also a visiting professor of pastoral care and counseling at South Asia Institute of Advanced Christian Studies (SAIACS), Bangalore, India. He has written many Christian devotional songs in Malayalam and co-editor of *Caring for the South Asian Soul: Counseling South Asian in the Western World.*

Jonathan D James, PhD is a researcher in media, culture, politics and religion. He is currently the International Executive Director of AEF International, a mission organization with 200 missionaries in Asia and Adjunct professor at the School of Humanities at Edith Cowan University in Perth, Australia. Author of *Masala McGospel, Televangelism in Contemporary India*, and *Transnational Religious Movements.*

Joseph Paturi, PhD is Founder-President of TransWorld Ministries, and Co-founder and Vice-President of Global Telugu Christian Ministries. He is also the President Emeritus of Temple Baptist College, Cincinnati, Ohio and provides leadership to help establish Bible Colleges, Theological Seminaries and Christian Universities in different countries. He is an author of several books and articles. He lives in Cincinnati, Ohio with his wife Dr. Shobha.

Jamang Ngul Khan Pau, DMiss is a senior consultant with the Development Associates, based out of Guwahati, India and Colorado Springs, USA. He is a speaker, trainer and author of six books in Zomi language and two books in English.

Suneel Shivdasani and **Celia and Deepak Mahtani** are Hindu-background, diaspora-born Sindhis, who started following Christ over 30 years ago. They know and have visited Sindhi believers around the world including those in the Sindh, India and the Diaspora. They have played leadership roles in regional, national and international Christian events relating to South Asians both within South Asia and the Diaspora.

Rashid Gill, DMin is of Pakistani origin and now lives in Toronto, Canada. He is the pastor of the Light bearers of Christ Church International in Brampton, Ontario which offers services in Urdu, Punjabi and Hindi every Sunday and is one of the oldest South Asian Church in the Greater Toronto area in Canada.

Jeffery Jacob, PhD is the professor of Economics in Bethel University, Minneapolis, USA. His teaching and research is in the areas of international trade and development and applied econometrics. He enjoys working with data and teaches a course in business analytics. His current research is focused on empirically examining the role of institutions and values in economic development.

Reena Thomas has a PhD in Literature from the University of Arizona, specializing in postcolonial literature and criticism. Born and raised in the suburbs of New York, she currently teaches at Neosho County Community College in Chanute, Kansas, USA.

Bobby Bose, PhD is an adjunct Professor of World Missions and Urban Ministry at Gordon-Conwell Theological Seminary and President of Bengali Christian Ministry, USA. Born and raised in Kolkata, India, Dr. Bose has ministered for more than three decades in India, UK and US doing evangelism, discipleship and teaching.

Mathew Thomas, PhD is a Global Quality Process Manager with CNH Industrial in Burr Ridge, Illinois. He lives in Naperville, Illinois with his family and attends the Highpoint Church. Dr. Thomas immigrated to the US in 1998 and completed his doctorate in Industrial Engineering from Wayne State University, Detroit. Mathew has been an actively involved in student ministries in India and US as well as supports various diaspora ministries.

Foreword

Modern Migrations and the Christian Faith

Andrew E. Walls

Migration, the movement of peoples from one location to another, has throughout history been one of the most powerful influences in human affairs. This is as true in the sphere of religion as in that of politics or economics. The twentieth century saw the end of one major movement of peoples and the beginning of another. The religious effects of the first are only now beginning to be understood; serious calculation of the religious effects of the second has yet hardly begun.

The first of these movements, which came to an end in the middle of the twentieth century, began as early as the sixteenth century, when the trans-oceanic voyages of that period opened to Europeans vast areas – new worlds in effect in Asia, the Americas, had Africa that had hitherto been beyond their reach or knowledge. From that time on, people from different parts of Europe began to move to these territories, at first in small numbers, but eventually in millions. During the succeeding four centuries they created whole new nations by settlement, set up their rule over many others and brought about the migration of other peoples – forcibly moving, through the Atlantic slave trade, millions of Africans to North, Central and South America, not to mention bringing Asian peoples to the Americas, South Africa and the Pacific to meet their labour needs.

The Great European Migration that brought all this about lasted four and a half centuries. During that period the demographic and cultural base of the Christian faith changed dramatically. For long that base lay in Europe, and then among people of European descent. But by the end of the period of European migration it had begun to move elsewhere. By the end of the twentieth century, Christianity was in recession amongst Europeans, and most Christians were Africans, Asians or Latin Americans.

Soon after the middle of the twentieth century the Great European Migration ended. After the flow of European Jews that followed the creation of the state of Israel, Europeans moved out of Europe in much smaller numbers (though migration within Europe increased considerably). But another great migration movement began. In the period when the European empires were being dismantled, people from Asia, from Africa and from Latin America began to move to Europe, and to the lands in North America and Australasia which Europeans had once made their own.

We may call this development the Great Reverse Migration, for it was a sort of reflex of the Great European Migration and was in part an outcome of it. Its religious effects have already been huge: Buddhism, Hinduism, Islam, Sikhism, once thought of as characteristic of Asia, are now Western religions, with vast numbers of adherents in Europe and North America. Less noticed has been the movement of Christians from Africa, Asia and Latin America to those same Western nations, often bringing their own churches with an ethos of their own, and often coming into post-Christian settings where indigenous European or American Christianity has been in decline.

The Great Reverse Migration is in fact a movement full of hope for the future of Christian mission in the world. It is also full of challenge. Will the indigenous Christianity and the Christians from beyond the West truly share a life that displays the body of Christ to the world? The Great Reverse Migration raises the possibility of returning to the New Testament norm of the church, lost over centuries of mono-cultural Christianity. In the New Testament we meet two different styles of Christian living, reflecting two different forms of social reality, each converted to Christ. In the early chapters of Acts, we meet the thoroughly Jewish, Torah-keeping way of being disciples of Jesus; and we can recognize that this is what Jewish life looks like when turned to face Jesus as the Messiah. But the Council of Jerusalem described in Acts 15 agreed that this style was not to be required of Gentiles; and in Paul's letters we see another way of following Jesus being constructed, as Gentile (in this case, first century Hellenistic Mediterranean) social, family and intellectual life was turned to face Christ. But, as the Epistle to the Ephesians shows us, Jew and Gentile, with their respective styles of living converted to Christ, are complementary: both are building materials needed for the erection of the New Temple of the Holy Spirit. The Great Reverse Migration gives Christians in Europe and North America an opportunity to realize again the New Testament model of the Church.

This gives special significance of the rich collection of essays. that Dr Sam George has here brought together. Indian Christianity is itself diverse, with a history covering many centuries and a variety of cultural traditions. It now has a solid presence, as these essays show, in many parts of the world; it may, along with other Christian diasporas, have a part to play in the history of the re-evangelization of the post-Christian West. Further, while strongly represented in the Great Reverse Migration to the West, it is also present beyond the West because of earlier migrations, some of them caused by the Great European Migration.

Altogether, the book offers a feast of good things, opening new paths for study and reflection relating to one of the most potentially important movements of modern times; one in which, as in New Testament times, Christians are called by the Holy Spirit to be built together into a new Temple of God.

Introduction

Sam George

At the beginning of the twenty-first century, South Asians are omnipresent! One may find them in every nook and corner of the planet, literally in every time zone and probably in every country of the world. On account of their growing and widespread dispersion, it is popularly claimed that 'the Sun never sets on the South Asian diaspora akin to what was said of the British Empire in the past!'

South Asia comprises of several nations in the Indian subcontinent and includes seven countries namely Bangladesh, Bhutan, India, Mauritius, Nepal, Pakistan and Sri Lanka. This geographical region was knit together as a common entity during the British colonial rule despite its many differences. Some tend to include Myanmar (formerly known as Burma) and in recent times Afghanistan also into South Asia. The autonomous region of Tibet and China's interest in joining South Asian Association for Regional Cooperation (SAARC) has further complicated the definition of South Asia. Some categorization even includes Iran in Southern Asia. However, in this volume, we will confine the definition of South Asia to the original seven nations.

According to the United Nations assessment of the International migrant stock in 2015 from South Asia amounted to over 32 million and increased by five million in the last five years and near 11 million over the last ten years. By early 2018, according to some estimate the

South Asian diaspora population has swelled to cross 50 million people. The most populous countries in the region, namely India and Pakistan constitute the major share of displaced people from the region. It must be noted that these numbers do not include what is often called the old diaspora from the region – the dispersion of people from South Asia prior to their nationhood when millions were taken to work in the Colonial establishments around the world as indentured laborers and who lost links to their ancestral homelands. Even though some have amalgamated with native populations in their adopted countries, many still consider themselves as part of the Indian diaspora even if their ancestry is remotely traced to Sind or Ceylon. See appendix for latest data and infographics on the South Asian global diaspora.

Christianity had a continual presence in the South Asian region for nearly two thousand years, beginning with the witness of Apostle Thomas who was one of the twelve disciples of Jesus. The arrival of the Portuguese explorer Vasco da Gama began a new era in Indian Christianity with the introduction of Roman Catholic strand in the late fifteenth century. Subsequently, German, Dutch, French, English, Scottish, American and other foreign missionaries along with various established ecclesial entities made their distinctive contributions to Christianity in the region. The Bible translation activities of Bartholomew Ziegenbalg, William Carey, Claudius Buchannan and others provided a major impetus to South Asian Christianity. After gaining independence from Colonial powers in 1947, Christians became more nationalized as Indian, Pakistani or Ceylon Christians and the expulsion of foreign missionaries in 1977 forced the Indian church to take the onus of missionary task with indigenous human power and resources. Over the last seventy years, the churches in South Asia have experienced sustained vitality and growth, while some pockets have struggled and declined. According to the official census reports, Christians in India remains around 2.5 percent continuously of the population over many decades, while Christians populace in Pakistan have dwindled because of persecution against Christians, political instability, and war, whereas there has been an explosive growth of Christianity in Nepal.

In the last five decades or so, the South Asian Christians have spread out more globally through record migration out of the subcontinent to far corners of the globe and many from other faith backgrounds have embraced Christianity in diasporic locations. Because of the colonial links, English language proficiency, professional education and skills, strong work ethics, business savviness, community orientation, resilience and other characteristic features of South Asians, there has been a substantial emigration of people from the Indian subcontinent and they have successfully transplanted themselves all over the world. Christian devotional songs and liturgies are sung in South Asian languages in every continent every week. South Asians congregate for worship and sermons are preached with distinctive regional flavor in every time zone. They are involved in mission locally in their adopted country while they also send regular remittances to support family, churches and mission projects back in their ancestral homeland.

This book portrays the fascinating saga of Christians of South Asian origin who have pitched their tents to the furthest corners of the globe and showcases triumphs and challenges facing this scattered community. The chapters in this volume present historical and contemporary lived religious experiences of South Asian Christians from a plethora of discrete perspectives. It deals with issues such as community history, struggles of identity and belonging, linkage of religious and cultural traditions, preservation and adaptation of faith practices, development of new ways of life, relationship and faith, evolving attitudes and ties to ancestral homeland and host nation, diasporic moral dilemmas as well as biblical reflections of South Asian Christians in diaspora.

The idea for this project was first conceived when I co-edited a volume titled *Malayali Diaspora* (George and Thomas 2013) which was launched at the *Pravasi Bharatiya Divas*, the official annual gathering of non-resident Indians from around the world. My own journey across India and all nations of South Asia exposed me to Christians of different stripes, shades, and creeds. In recent years, I had the distinct privilege of traveling to far-flung ends of the world only to run into South Asians engaged in Christian ministry in their places of habitation. The global missionary activities of the South Asians lie far beyond the institutionalized structures or organized assemblies, and often includes free floating itinerant evangelists and those who work in foreign Christian agencies and churches without any link to South Asia. Some have gone to study or work abroad and end up catching a vision for ministry, while others have married foreigners and minister to people across racial and ethnic lines. Just in the last year or so, I have met or talked with many interesting South Asians in the frontiers of Christian mission work in the world – a church planter in Panama City ministering among Spanish and Mandarin speakers, tentmaker professor in a leading university in China, evangelists and underground church pastors in closed countries in Central Asia and the Middle East, refugee workers in Turkey and Kenya, children and youth worker in Guyana and eastern Europe, software engineer cum pastor in Latin America and South Africa, English teacher in a communist Southeast Asian country etc.

Diaspora: People on the Move

Throughout this book, we prefer to use the term diaspora broadly to include all dispersed people, who find themselves in a place other than where they were born or belong to and their progenies. Some scholars debate about the use of the term 'diaspora' in academic circles to refer to recent migrant communities worldwide as they favor its usage it as in its original concept exclusively for Jewish dispersion. However, as this term has come to be used increasingly to include all forms of human dislocation, contributors of this volume employs a plethora of terms and descriptions to capture the essence of the experience arising out of displacement and practice of Christian faith in widely dispersed locales. Most contributors use the terminology of the diaspora to study the Christian faith of the scattered people originating from Southern Asia.

The word diaspora has a Greek origin (διασπορά) and means scattering or dispersion. It has many references in the Septuagint and a handful of references in the New Testament. It was used originally in referring to the scattering of Israelites or Judean heritage because of forced exile, but now it is broadly applied to all displaced people like migrants, international students, guest workers, expatriates, refugees, and the like. Following the destruction of the First Temple and Jerusalem in the sixth century BCE, the Jewish experience of loss and dispersion from the ancestral home and forced exile to Babylon of a large elite population constitute a central site to situate the concept of diaspora (Charles 2014, 5; Barclay 1996). However, usage of diaspora expanded as more Jews were living outside of the regions of Jerusalem than in it by the fourth century BCE and did not see the condition of being away from ancestral homeland as divine punishment but were comfortable "at home" while living abroad by choice in their diasporic locations (Collins 2000; Rajak 2002).

Though some use the term diaspora synonymously with migration, they are different in usage, meanings and nuanced in its understandings. Migration is primarily used in social sciences and by demographers to refer to the geographical movement of people, whether it be domestic or international. However, diaspora refers to a broader sociocultural, psychological and spiritual condition of living in foreign places because of migration and has an origin in Biblical and Jewish history. Migration is also often used to refer to non-human movements such as bird migration and software or technology migrations. The diasporic reality always includes future generation of migrants, while migration literature is only one generation deep. Moreover, the term migration is exclusively used to represent the foreign-born population and not their descendants who constitute an ethnic minority group in a foreign country or those who have mixed heritage one of which traces back to foreign stock. Diaspora usage generally denotes the context of overseas relocation for long term possible settlement and excludes domestic migration within a political nation-state for a shorter duration as in the case of tourists.

Tölölyan dates the concept of *diaspora* back to the period around 250 BCE when the Jews of Alexandria adopted the term to signify "their own scattering away from the homeland into *galut* or collective exile" (1991a, 3-7). By the early 1930s, scholars had applied the term diaspora to the Jewish, Armenian, and Greek dispersions, what is commonly described as the classical diasporas. Safran argued that scholarly studies have paid "little if any attention… to diasporas" and includes "expatriates, expellees, emigrants, refugees, slaves, indentured workers, alien residents, ethnic and racial minorities" in the category of diaspora (1991, 83-99). According to Vertovec, the term diaspora can be applied to "describe any population that is considered 'de-territorialized' or 'transnational'" (2001, 278). Jacobsen also took a similar approach in his recent study of South Asian religions (2004, xiv) and the establishment of the Center for the Study of Indian Diaspora in Hyderabad, India in 1996 resulted in several researches publications and gave an impetus to the widespread adoption of the term diaspora (Sahoo and Narayan 2008).

The substantial research that tilted the conversation in favor of diaspora came with the publication of the journal *Diaspora: A Journal of Transnational Studies* where he introduces diaspora as "term that once described Jewish, Greek, and Armenian dispersion now shares meaning with the larger semantic domain that includes words like immigrants, expatriate, refugee, guest worker, exile community, overseas community, ethnic community" (Tölölyan 1991b, 4)." Another seminal volume that used the diaspora as its primary term is by Robin Cohen and argues that the usage of the term diaspora has evolved repeatedly to imply a positive and ongoing relationship between migrants' homelands and their places of work and settlements (Cohen 1997).

Many Indian scholars of migration and related fields like Ajay Kumar Sahoo, Brij V. Lal, Laxmi Narayan Kadekar, Rajesh Rai, Prema Kurien etc. have also embraced the concept of the diaspora in their writings. Over the last decade or so, in the field of social sciences, culture studies/Anthropology, and religious studies, the diaspora focus has become quite pronounced and unequivocal. This interest coincided with issues of post-colonialism, identity, multiculturalism, globalization, hybridity, alienation, transnationalism and so on. Diaspora usage is gaining greater momentum and seems to better-suited address complexities of modern human displacement to a myriad of places and cultures.

South Asians are very religious people and in diasporic settings, they exhibit a heightened religious consciousness. For South Asian diasporas religion seems to play a critical role, not only to establish social capital, cultural currency and a much needed cohesive force in foreign lands, but it is resulting in the transformation of religious traditions itself. The diversity of beliefs and practices of South Asian faiths are not replicated precisely in diasporic settings, but they seem to evolve into new forms as result of adaptations and accommodating host cultural elements across generational and geographical spectrums.

The diasporic living is marked by a series of gains and losses in every sphere of life including socially, economically, culturally, politically and religiously for the migrant, their ancestral land, and the immigrant nation. The motivations to move and factors causing displacement fluctuates considerably, depending on people, time of migration and socio-economic conditions in both countries or marriage alliance and family sponsorship. Some are forced to flee when their lives or livelihood are threatened, while others pursue to improve their academic credentials and subsequently economic opportunities. Some are attracted by the possibility of freedom and better living conditions while others are desperately forced to seek refuge in foreign countries because of growing political, religious or social oppression.

The diasporic space is a fertile and potent space for creative energy, adaptations, and creolization not only in music, food and literature but also in matters of faith experiences. The human mobility arising out of the latest transportation methods that are affordable, aided by new communication technologies, are causing intermingling of people and cultures like never seen before in human history. While such cultural diffusion and amalgamation lie at the heart of the development of diasporic consciousness, it also produces much confusion, pain, and conflicts. The new diaspora realities lead to the hybridization of identity, blending of cultures, the transformation of practices and beliefs through imports and exports to and from dominant cultures of settlement. Unlike the migrants of the previous centuries, the modern diaspora communities maintain close ties with their ancestral homelands and sustain a transnational family, social, political and religious networks.

Since "the Bible is a metanarrative of diaspora" (Cuellar 2008, 1), readers of this volume can expect repeated references to biblical narratives of displacement, deportation, and exile as well as Christian theological and missiological dimensions of diasporas. The early Christian expansion occurred upon the Jewish diasporic network who were not only early converts to Christianity but also become a conduit to spread of Christian faith beyond ethnic, cultural and geographical boundaries. Likewise, today's diaspora communities are at the forefront of changes within and advancement of Christianity in surprising ways. The increased human mobility and intercultural interactions in the world at the beginning of the twenty-first century holds profound potential for cultural diffusion of the gospel of Jesus Christ and creating a new era of mission from everywhere to everywhere. As potential missionaries, diaspora Christians play a strategic role in Christian expansion and vitalization through natural cross-cultural interactions and missional involvement of all people everywhere (George 2011).

Diaspora Christianity: A South Asian Version

South Asians speak many languages, over fifteen hundred and more than fifteen official languages. In diasporic settings, the language centric churches hold a powerful attraction to immigrants and most South Asian first-generation diaspora churches are developed along the lines of language and cultural particularities. Such church services momentarily transport people to their ancestral homelands and congregations of their childhood which provide them with a deep sense of security and comfort amidst immigrant wanderings in foreign lands. It creates a strong sense of community and solidarity with their ancestors while meeting the yearning of belonging. For converts from other religious backgrounds, introduces them to alternative worship format and simultaneous immersion into a new culture and community.

It was German, English and other European missionaries who played a decisive role in the translation of the Bible into South Asian languages in the eighteenth and nineteenth centuries which generated great missionary momentum and mobility to the South Asian Christianity. Then in the middle of the twentieth when almost all South Asian countries gained independence from their colonial masters, language specific church, and missionary work thrived across the region. Later, when people began to migrate out of this region, they carried with them vernacular Bibles and their respective culturalized Christianity to far shores of the world. Many scholars have attributed the creation and vibrancy of immigrant churches in the West to the power of vernacular as well as memories and culture specific aspects of Christian faith practices brought from ancestral homelands (Williams; Warner; Kurien; Ebaugh & Chafetz; Leonard).

However, as foreign-born children of the immigrants come of age and lose some of the linguistic and cultural skills, these churches are forced to adapt to minister effectively to the next generations. What defined and established immigrant congregations are getting undone within a generation and by their own children. Most of the subsequent generations of South Asians in Western Europe, North America, Australia, Southeast Asia, and even Africa are abandoning South Asian churches that their own parents began in favor of local churches in their respective nations while maintaining close ethnic links with one's own communities. At the same time, immigrant churches of one era are sustained by subsequent waves of immigrants with the same language, cultural and denominational affiliations. Any changes in immigration policies and the inability of some congregations in incorporating succeeding immigrants are resulting in a decline of those immigrant churches.

The tendency of pervasive politicking and church splits are all too common among South Asian Christian diaspora. Though it produces greater penetration and spread, it comes with deep wounds and mistrust within the community. If you have been involved with any South Asian diaspora congregations, it is inevitable that you have experienced church breakups and may still bear the scars of severing in the body of believers. It may mobilize more into ministry leadership but risks heretical teaching without proper training of leaders and weaken our collective witness to those outside of the walls of our churches. Not all church divisions are always unwarranted, as there are times and circumstances where division may be more faithful option like sinful behaviors of church leaders, heretical teachings or other moral and doctrinal lapses.

Another common trait of the South Asian Christians abroad is the entrepreneurial spirit and starting of new fellowship groups wherever life takes them. Some who did not have any church involvement growing up in South Asia, after migrating overseas get very involved in church activities or becomes a pastor of an independent church, especially in case where his wife easily finds employment with her medical training while her husband is unable to find careers matching their education and prior work experience and end up hosting a prayer meeting at home which gradually grows into a church. There are cases of Indian software engineers having started multiple churches in Europe and North America by starting home-based Bible studies. The conceptual framework of 'migrant as a potential missionary' could help us explain the massive proliferation of South Asian Christian groups in diaspora and resurgence of religious sentiments in lands far from home.

One of the other key issues faced by South Asians in diasporic settings is the challenge of maintaining their unique identity in foreign cultural contexts. Several essays in this volume explore issues of identity, assimilation, community, hybridity and transnational linkages. It exposes the struggle of dealing with the otherness in host societies, fear of being stereotyped, and ambivalence in their sense of belongings. It examines the function of immigrant congregations for the reproduction of ethnicity and conflicts as well as contradictions these congregations create as they seek to pass on their culturalized faith to an Americanized second and third generation – who are more alienated than attracted by the features that met their parent's needs.

An Interdisciplinary Approach: Blending Realities

This book takes a distinctive interdisciplinary approach to investigate a lived religious community by inviting scholars and practitioners from diverse disciplines and geographies. All of them are of South Asian origin and their writings are drawn from their respective domain expertise. These chapters are presented from distinct vantage points of geographical locations (from every continent) and varied vocational backgrounds such as professors, missionaries, pastors, psychologists, journalist and others. They are seasoned and accomplished academicians as well as practitioners from multiple disciplinary expertise like history, Bible, theology, sociology, anthropology, ethics, literature and economics. It raises many profound questions of life such as who we are, where we come from, where we are going, who are around us, how to relate to others, why are we here, where is God in all this etc. It attempts to answer some of these questions and courageously broaches interrogations about life and faith in the context of human displacement. It presents the great diversity and complexity of Christian faith expressions in far flung geographical spaces, whose ancestral root can be traced back to the Indian subcontinent.

Almost all South Asian Christian denominations can be identified in the diaspora and this volume includes major denominations such as Anglican, Baptists, Brethren, Evangelicals, Reformed, Protestant, Pentecostals, and Independents. In a sense, the essays in this volume are community history and have an emic insider perspective. The ethnic backgrounds of essayists are as wide as Keralite, Tamil, Telugu, Bengali, Sindhi, Mizo, Pakistani, and Sinhalese. They make their homes in Africa, Australia, Caribbeans, Europe, Middleast and North America. The subject of diversity is pervasive in this volume in the great assortment of eclectic voices and their characteristic faith practices are evident throughout this volume. As a result of this great diversity of backgrounds, insights and inferences required us to adopt an interdisciplinary approach to study the South Asian Diaspora Christianity.

Scope and Gaps: Boundaries

This volume makes a bold attempt to capture a more global perspective of a religious diaspora group, namely South Asians. Instead of making it exclusively about Indian diaspora, this volume is inclusive of nations in the region. It explores archetypal features of the diasporic Christian faith of South Asians along with some of the promises this frontier offers to the world Christianity as well as some of the predicaments facing scattered religious group in different parts of the world. Although, no one really identifies themselves as South Asian Christian anywhere in the world, we use this theoretical category to include all who hail from South Asia but now have migrated and settled in far-away places.

First, this volume focuses on Christians and does not include other religious groups in South Asian Diaspora, though it includes a few conversion accounts from other religions. It aims to highlight how Christians from this region constitute higher proportions and migratory nature of Christianity. It does include interfaith dimension and explores migratory tendency to established networks, global nature of Christianity, professions that scattered people from South Asia, colonial links and hurdles of religious beliefs that are deterrent to migration.

Secondly, South Asian Christians are not a homogenous entity and come in diverse shades, stripes and shapes. The South Asian region can boast of continual Christian presence for nearly two millenniums and a rich tapestry of religious practices and long convoluted history add to the complexity of writing projects like this. Sincere attempts have been made to be inclusive by adding voices from Sinhalese Christians, Tamil Christians from India and Sri Lanka as well as Kerala Christians of diverse traditions at far-flung destinations. It is unfortunate that the chapter on Nepali diaspora Christians failed to meet the timeline of this publication. Also, this volume does not include voices of Punjabi, Goan or Naga Christians and chapters on diaspora Christians from Bangladesh, Bhutan or Mauritius.

Thirdly, in this volume you may sense the complex task of interweaving disparate voices of Christians from many regions of the world and complicated migration history to paint a portrait of Christianity of the South Asian diaspora. The Syrian Christians of Kerala may trace their roots to the first century, while others are recent converts who embraced Christianity after migrating to foreign lands. The multiplicity of languages and socioeconomic class further confound this study as English is not the primary language of most authors in this volume.

Fourthly, this is a scholarly account of South Asian Diaspora Christianity as most contributors have advanced learning and some are attached to academia doing research and teaching. These papers are well researched and substantiated by author's ongoing community involvement and interest in studying them. This volume is neither comprehensive nor exhaustive but only intended as broad-brush stroke of a particular diasporic community. It fails to be fully representative of all South Asian Christians and does not cover every country or region where South Asian Christians have settled like the continental Europe, East Africa and Latin America.

Fifthly, a book on diaspora cannot be neatly delineated within fixed boundaries and you will find authors transgressing borders of South Asia to be inclusive of the origin and diasporic destinations of the people. E.g. Sindhis origin in Pakistan but after Partition migrated to India (where they are stateless) and then scattered all over the world. Contrarily, Zomis are spread over Burma, India (North eastern states) and Bangladesh. Also, the chapter on South Asian remittances include Afghanistan in South Asia because the World Bank data that was used for the analysis does so.

Finally, this volume is not expected to be the final word on the matter. It has numerous lacunae and we hope it will only inspire more students and scholars to undertake research and publication of Diaspora Christianity. I hope more migration scholars will pay greater attention to religious dimensions of different migrant groups and theologians take note of growing interest in diaspora literatures. The role of digital media, the internet and social media in knitting diasporic consciousness and development of new spirituality is not adequately addressed here. We need more missiological reflections on the flow, hybridity, diversity, interculturality and virtuality. More theological reflections on displacement and diasporic living by South Asians are always welcome. A comparative study between different regions of the world will make an interesting read and with immediate relevance for immigrant churches everywhere.

Outline of the Book: What to Expect?

This volume is divided into four major categories: *first*, biblical reflections by two South Asian Bible scholars, one each from Sri Lanka and India; *second*, five chapters of historical analysis of the Old Diaspora covering East Africa, Burma, South Africa, Caribbean and Singapore; *third*, mapping of the New Diaspora of seven South Asian Christians in diaspora covering regions such as North America, Europe, Persian Gulf and Australia as well people groups/ nationality such as Telugus, Sindhis, Zomis and Pakistanis; *fourth*, four chapters about specific issues facing South Asian Christians in diaspora such as morality, remittances, hybridity, and death. I conclude this vastly diverse narratives by arguing for plural usage of diaspora Christianities in the title and the challenge of unity before the widely scattered South Asian faith communities. An appendix at the end features the latest demographic and infographic of South Asian diaspora population.

References

Barclay, John M.G. 1996. *Jews in the Mediterranean Diaspora*. Berkeley: University of California Press.

Charles, Ronald. 2014. *Paul and the Politics of Diaspora*. Minneapolis: Fortress Press.

Cohen, Robin. 1997. *Global Diaspora: An Introduction*, Seattle: University of Washington Press.

Collins, John. 2000. *Between Athens and Jerusalem: Jewish Identity in the Hellenistic Diaspora*, 2nd Ed. Grand Rapids: Eerdmans.

Cuellar, Gregory Lee. 2008. *Voices of Marginality: Exile and Return in Second Isaiah 40-55 and the Mexican Immigrant Experience*. American University Studies Series 7; Theology and Religion 271; New York: Lang. 1.

Ebaugh, Helen and Janet Chafetz. 2000. *Religions and the New Immigrants: Continuities and Adaptations in Immigrant Congregations*, Walnut Creek: Alta Mira Press.

George, Sam and T.V. Thomas. 2013. *Malayali Diaspora: From Kerala to the Ends of the Earth*. New Delhi Serials Publications.

Im, Chandler and Amos Yong. 2014. *Global Diasporas and Mission*, Eugene: Wipf & Stock.

Jacobsen, Knut and Pratap Kumar. 2004. *South Asians in the Diaspora: Histories and Religious Traditions*, Leiden: Brill. Pp xiv.

Jacobsen, Knut and Selva J. Raj. 2014. *South Asian Christian Diaspora: Invisible Diaspora in Europe and North America*. Surrey, UK: Ashgate.

Kadekar, Laxmi Narayan, Ajay Kumar Sahoo and Gauri Bhattacharya. 2009. *The Indian Diaspora: Historical and Contemporary Context*. New Delhi: Rawat Publications.

Kurien, Prema. 2007. *A Place at the Multicultural Table: The Development of an American Hinduism*, New Brunswick: Rutgers University Press.

_____, 2017. *Ethnic Church Meets Megachurch: Indian American Christianity in Motion*. New York: New York University Press.

Lal, Brij V. 2007. *The Encyclopedia of the Indian Diaspora*, Honolulu: University of Hawaii Press.

Leonard, Karen, Alex Stepick, Manuel A Vasquez, and Jennifer Holdaway. 2006. *Immigrant Faiths: Transforming Religious Life in America*. New York: Alta Mira Press.

Rai, Rajesh and Peter Reeves. 2010. *South Asian Diaspora: Transnational Networks and Changing Identities*, New York: Routledge.

Rajak, Tessa. 2002. *The Jewish Dialogue with Greece and Rome: Studies in Cultural and Social Interaction.* Boston, Leiden: Brill.

Safran, William. 2009. *Transnational Migrations: The Indian Diaspora,* New York: Routledge.

_____, 1991. "Diasporas in Modern Societies: Myths of Homeland and Return" *Diaspora* 1(1), 1991.

Sahoo, Ajay Kumar and K. Laxmi Narayan. 2008. *Indian Diaspora: Trends and Issues,* New Delhi: Serials Publications. Other tiles from the publisher include, *Tracing Indian Diaspora* and *The Indian Diaspora.*

Tölölyan, Khachig 1991b "The Nation States and its Others" in *Diaspora: A Journal of Transnational Studies.* Spring, Issue 1.

_____, 1991a. Preface. *Diaspora: A Journal of Transnational Studies* 1(1).

Vertovec, Steven 2000. *The Hindu Diaspora: Comparative Patterns.* London: Routledge.

_____, 1997. "Three Meaning of Diaspora Exemplified among South Asian Religions. *Diaspora* 6(3): 277-99.

Warner, Stephen and Judith Wittner. 1998. *Gatherings in Diaspora: Religious Communities and the New Immigration,* Philadelphia: Temple University Press.

Williams, Raymond. 1996. *Christian Pluralism in the United States: The Indian Immigrant Experience.* New York: Cambridge University Press.

A Biblical Reflection on Diaspora - Acts 17

Danny Moses

Looking at the Mission of God in relation to issues such as diasporas, globalisation, urbanisation and pluralism has produced a whole lot of literature and interest in recent years (Tira and Yamamori 2016; Im and Yong 2014; Wan 2011, Walls 2010; Brueggemann 2005; Groody 2010; Carroll 2013; Smith-Christopher 2002). The contemporary global migration and diasporic living resulting from modern pull and push factors are not unfamiliar to the Old and New Testament writings. Although direct reference to the term diaspora are only a few, migration and displacement are a key motif in the Bible. The Old Testament pages are filled with narratives of displacement such as expulsion of Adam and Eve out of the Garden of Eden, journey of Abram from Ur of Chaldeans, Israel's sojourn in Egypt, desert wanderings, exile to Babylon, etc. In fact, a major portion of Genesis (12-50) depicts the three Patriarchs being on the move constantly from Syria through Canaan to Egypt without any permanent settlement in spite of the assurance of the land and entire the Exodus is a movement from Egypt to the Promised Land.

Migration and diaspora theme continues through the pages of the New Testament – Jesus's own ministry travels, birth of the church at Pentecost, Paul's missionary travels etc. Most of the first Christians and missionaries were diaspora Jews. Moreover, the scattering of the Jews to "every region of the habitable world" (Philo 1962) prior to the coming of Christ and the *Pax Romana* had prepared the world for Christian mission. Chang points out that, "The birth and expansion of the church would not have been possible without the Jewish diaspora." (2016, 118). Much of the writing of the New Testament and core beliefs of Christian faith were formed in diasporic settings.

In this paper I wish to offer my short reflection on some key texts related to migration, diaspora theology and missiology. I do so as a Bible scholar from the Global South, particularly as a director of a Bible college in South Asia, namely Lanka Bible College near Colombo, Sri Lanka. My reflections emerge in the context of migration of people because of ethnic conflict, full-fledged war, economic unrest, political instability, natural catastrophes and the like that dispersed a large number of Sri Lankans to India, Europe, Canada, Australia and other parts of the world.

Viewing diaspora through Pauline Anthropology: Acts 17.26 following.

God is the ruler of the nations and Adam is the single progenitor of humans, i.e. of every person of the diaspora and all humankind. It is

> From one man [Adam] he made every nation of men, that they should inhabit the whole earth; and he determined the times set for them and the exact places where they should live. God did this so that men would seek him and perhaps reach out for him and find him, though he is not far from each one of us. 'For in him we live and move and have our being'.

This is particularly relevant to God's concern for every person (1 Tim 2.3-7), including those of the diaspora. Paul's reference to the 'every nation' 'times' and 'places' refer to "*the epochs of their history and the limits of their territory*" (NEB). Consequently, as Stott puts it, "although God cannot be held responsible for the tyranny or aggression of individual nations [e.g. consider the Middle East and the refugee crisis of today], yet both the history and the geography of each nation are ultimately under his control." (Stott 1990, 286) Ultimately, it is "*heaven that rules*"

(Dan 2.44; 4.17b, 25, 26, 32; 5.21; 7.13). God designed a variety of human cultures and set people in defined territories and hence, the diaspora of peoples so prevalent today is ultimately under God's control. God's purpose in the diaspora of peoples, all of whom who originate from Adam and are created in God's image (Gen 1.26, 27) is that they might *"seek him"* and *"reach out for him"* (or "feel after him" RSV) *and find him"*. For according to Paul all *"live and move and have [their] being* – in God (citing the 6th century BC poet Epimenides).

Viewing Paul's Last Adam Christology and its Implications to Diaspora Missions

Since Adam is the progenitor of all humankind, phrases such as *"from one [man]"* (Adam, cf. 17.26) complemented by the reference to Jesus as the *"man"* i.e. *"by a man whom he has appointed"* (17.31b) and Paul's association of these terms to *"all men"* (17.31a *"commands all men everywhere to repent"*, 31b *"hath given assurance to all men"*) and his stress on Jesus's resurrection (*"by raising him from the dead"* cf. 17.31d) displays crucial elements in Paul's Adam Christology which he develops in some of his letters. This 'first man' [Adam] 'second man' [Jesus] comparison is illustrated in passages like 1 Cor 15.45-50 and the 'one man' [Adam] and the 'one man' [Jesus] comparisons are seen in Rom 5.12-21. Paul's 'Last Adam' Christology delineates that man created in the image of God, marred by Adam, the 'first man's' sin, could now be regained – and perhaps enhanced (Rom 8.28-30). All of this is due to the "free gift in the grace of that one-man Jesus Christ" which has "abounded for many" (Rom 5.15). I am not here unpacking the whole gamut of Paul's Adam Christology, for even as death "reigned" through Adam's trespass (Rom 5.17a, cf. 1 Cor 15.21-22), "much more will those who receive the abundance of grace and the free gift of righteousness reign in life through the one man Jesus Christ" (5.11b). What is spelled out in his epistles is what is encapsulated in Acts 17.

In our passage in Acts, that idea that God governs diaspora mission in view of his salvific purposes and the idea that it is God who implanted his image in the "one man/Adam" (Acts 17.26) is further advanced by the Paul's argument from creation theology. It is this God who is the Father of all human beings, and quoting from the 3rd century Stoic Aratus, Paul adds *"As some of your own poets have said, "We are his offspring* (28b). *Therefore, since we are God's offspring, we should not think that the divine being is like gold or silver or stone – an image made by man's design and skill"* (v.29). The God of creation is also the God of redemption. On the other hand, even though Paul's quotes from two pagan poets suggests that insights from general revelation may be found in non-Christian authors (Stott, 28), Idolatry localizes, limits and domesticates God and dehumanises man made in the image and likeness of God (v.29, cf. Rom. 1.18). The purpose of Paul's Diaspora mission and all mission, for that matter is to open people's eyes, make them turn from darkness to light, and from the power of Satan to God, that they may receive forgiveness of sins and a place among those who are sanctified by faith in Jesus (Acts 26.17-18). In Acts 17.30 Paul opens the Athenian's eyes of "ignorance" and preaches for a verdict, for the God of creation and redemption is also a God who "judges the world".

God as Judge Intrinsic to Diaspora Missions

Paul's mission to all communities including his own Jewish diaspora and other communities is that ultimately God is supreme judge: *"In the past God overlooked such ignorance* (i.e. the ignorance of idolatry), *but now he commands all people everywhere to repent* (30). *For he has set a day when he will judge the world with justice by the man he has appointed. He has given proof of this to all men by raising him from the dead"* (31). By paying homage 'to the unknown God' the Athenians acknowledge that there is something deficient in their religious system. God, however, has never left himself without a testimony (Acts 14.17) but has revealed himself via 'general revelation' (Rom. 1.19), and is 'the God who made the world and everything in it, being Lord of heaven and earth' (Acts 17.27-28). He is revealed through the natural order albeit now suppressed by human wickedness (Rom. 1.18-23). It is due to his "forbearing mercy that he passed over former sins" (Rom. 3.25) "but now he commands all people to repent" (Acts 17.30) – and this because there is a coming universal judgment, for God 'will judge the world'. His judgment will be 'just' and for this 'he has set a day'. In Acts 10.42 Peter speaks similarly, i.e. *"he is the one ordained by God to judge the living and the dead. To him all the prophets bear witness that everyone who believes in him receives forgiveness of sins through his name"* – a theme which echoes the words of Jesus in John 5.17 *"and has given him authority to execute judgment because he is the Son of Man"*. Diaspora missions in Acts and mission in general was partly fuelled by this realisation.

The Resurrection and Diaspora Missions

According to Paul, God has committed judgment to his Son, and that Day of Judgment is certain and is given proof by God *"raising him [Jesus] from the dead"* (Acts 17.31). Jesus' s resurrection-vindication enables him to become one through whom man could regain *"the image of [his] creator"* (Col. 3.10). And through belief in Jesus and his resurrection one will not be judged (John 5.24). The resurrection of Christ has set the future in motion, for he is the "first fruit" with many fruit to come (1 Cor. 15.20-28), his resurrection points to the resurrection of the believer and the restoration of the world (Rom. 8.18-30). Paul's restoration eschatology has similarity with that of Christ (Matt. 19.28-30). Christ is "the first fruit" and the believer via the indwelling Spirit *"has the first fruits of the Spirit"* i.e. the Spirit himself (Rom. 8.23), and this is a guarantee of his future resurrection (Rom. 8.11; 2 Cor. 5.2). So "the man" Jesus will not only "judge the world" (Acts 17.31) but is the hope of the world, precisely due to his resurrection and the subsequent 'revealing of the sons of God' (Rom. 8.19), in this sense he is *"the first born from the dead"* (Col 1.18). He is a forerunner of those who will be raised, and the indwelling Spirit in a believer is the eschatological Spirit, i.e. the *"Spirit of him who raised Jesus from the dead* [who] *dwells in you"*. And *"he who raised Christ Jesus from the dead will give life to your mortal bodies also through his Spirit which dwells in you"* (Rom. 8.11). It is this restoration eschatology, and the participation of which is open to all – Jews and Gentile – is what fuels Paul's theological convictions for diaspora missions. His commission had come from the risen Lord who was manifested in "blinding light" (Acts 9.3; 22.6; 26.13), it is Jesus who had called him to be a *"light for the Gentiles"* so that he may fulfil the Scripture (Is 49.6 in Acts 13.47) and *"bring salvation to the uttermost parts of the world"*.

Paul's Diaspora Mission Strategy and Methodology in Acts

It is well documented that Paul, although an apostle to the Gentiles, quite often first preached and taught (argued, explained, proved and expounded the Scriptures cf. Acts 17.2) in synagogues of the Jewish diaspora. This seems to have been his missionary strategy. Paul's the Jew first and then the Gentile (Rom. 1.16; 2.9-10) policy is in keeping with Jesus's method (Matt. 10.5-6) and that of God (Gen. 12.1-3). It was something that Paul adopted as his missionary strategy. This is elucidated by the following texts in Acts:

1.   In Acts 13.46 *"it was necessary"* that the word of God should be declared *"to you* [i.e. you Jews] *first"* and this is something that Peter too stressed *"God having raised up his servant, sent him to you first, to bless you in turning every one of you from your wickedness"*.

2.   In 14.1 "as usual", *"as it used to happen"* Paul addressed those in the Jewish synagogue at Iconium (the town of Konya in today's Turkey), "and so spoke that a great company believed, both of Jews and of Greeks".

3.   In Acts 16.13 Paul evangelises at a Jewish prayer group at a riverside at Philippi, initiating the first entrance of the gospel to the West.

4.   In Thessalonica, *"as his custom was"* (Acts 17.2) he commences his ministry in a synagogue, where he *"argued from the scriptures, explaining and proving that it was necessary for the Christ to suffer and to rise from the dead..."*

5.   In 17.10 it is the synagogue at Berea where he first commences his ministry.

6.   At Corinth *"he argued in the synagogue every Sabbath, and persuaded Jews and Greeks"* (Acts 18.4).

7. In Ephesus (Acts 18.19) Paul follows the same pattern, i.e. *"he himself went into the synagogue and argued with the Jews"* and during his third missionary journey (Acts 19.8) he returns to the synagogue in Ephesus *"and for three months spoke boldly arguing and pleading about the kingdom of God"*. It is true that from the synagogue he goes to the 'Hall of Tyrannus' where he continues for two years (19.9-10), but his initial point of contact was the synagogue.

8. During his house arrest in Rome *"he called together the local leaders of the Jews"* and presents the gospel to them (28.17), and in 28.23 the Jews came to *"his lodging in great numbers. And he expounded the matter to them from morning till evening, testifying to the kingdom of God and trying to convince them about Jesus both from the law of Moses and from the prophets"*.

So, diaspora mission was very much part of Paul's missionary methodology and strategy. Whilst the martyrdom of Stephen led to the scattering of the 'Jewish' church (8.4), followed by the mission among the Samaritans (8.5-25), Philip's hand in the conversion of the Ethiopian eunuch (8.20-39), and his mission at Azotus (8.40) seems to have been among diaspora Jewish communities: *"But Philip was found at Azotus and passing on he preached the gospel to all the towns till he came to Caesarea"*. It is not until Acts 11.20, in Antioch, do we see the scattered (Jewish) church engaging in true cross-cultural ministry amid 'the Gentiles': *"But there were some of them, men of Cyprus and Cyrene, who on coming to Antioch spoke to the Greeks also, preaching the Lord Jesus"*. Peter too engages in diaspora missions in 9.32, for he *"went here and there among them all"* which - barring the Samaritans in 8.14-25; 9.31 - refers to diaspora Jewish communities. In 8.32 *"he came down also to the saints that lived in Lydda"* and then went on to Joppa (8.36-43). The conversion of Cornelius and his household in 10.1-48 is that of a God-fearer. So, Peter's too was primarily a diaspora mission among the dispersed Jewish communities. As noted, true Gentile mission takes place in Antioch (11.19-26). It was, as in 8.4, a result of a scattering due to persecution where "some daring spirits among them, men of

Cyprus and Cyrene, took a momentous step forward" (Bruce, *The Book of Acts*, 225) and spoke the word *"to the Greeks also"* (11.20). Diaspora mission was certainly part of God's plan for the world.

Paul a Diaspora Jew Well Suited for Diaspora Missions

It is well documented that Paul of Tarsus a product of the diaspora was naturally suited for diaspora and cross-cultural missions. Paul born and bred in "Tarsus in Cilicia" and having studied under Gamaliel in Jerusalem (*"brought up in this city"* cf. Acts 22.3; Gal. 1.13-14; Phil. 3.5-6) was well suited for diaspora and cross-cultural evangelism. Even though his commission by the risen Christ on the way to Damascus and subsequent occasions predominantly referred to 'Gentile mission' (Acts 26.17; 22.21; 9.15) it also included *"the sons of Israel"* (9.15), this is because, for Paul, both Jews and Gentiles believers together form the "Israel of God" (Gal. 6.16; Rom. 9-11). This Gentile mission, as hinted in passages such as (Matt. 4.12-17 cf. Is 9.1-2; Matt. 8.11; 15.21-28; 32-39; 21.42-43; 28.18-20) was in keeping with fulfilment of Scripture: *"To this day I have had the help that comes from God, and so I stand here testifying both to small and great, saying nothing but what the prophets and Moses said would come to pass: that the Christ must suffer, and that, by being the first to rise from the dead, he would proclaim light both to the people and to the Gentiles"* (Acts 26.22-23).

Jesus and the Diaspora

Matthew in his infancy narrative shows that Jesus himself experienced diaspora of sorts in his exile in Egypt (Matt. 2.13-15) where he was a "refugee". His return to Nazareth fulfilled (Hos. 11.1 cf. Matt. 2.15) with its exodus motifs. Hence the geographical movements of Christ signified new exodus motifs and the gathering of the people of God as prophesied by the prophets.

As Christopher Wright points out "people being on the move permeates the biblical narrative from the day Adam and Eve were driven from the garden in Eden to the scattering of believers in the book of Acts, and it is when people move around (for whatever reason) that seems to be when God is at work in many significant ways" (2016, xii). The 'tower of Babel' episode (Gen. 11), for example, indicates how God initiated the dispersion i.e. a diaspora through the scattering of humankind *"abroad from there over the face of all the earth"*. And as it has been argued, only through the event of the Pentecost (Acts 2) is there a God initiated "gathering" and uniting of peoples – prophetically suggested by the gathering of diaspora Jews *"from every nation under heaven"* – into one body (Acts 2.5-42). Moreover, Paul redefined what it is to be a true Jew (Rom. 2.29) – one is so *"inwardly, and real circumcision is a matter of the heart, Spiritual and not literal"* (Rom. 2.29; Deut. 30.6; Jer. 31.31-34; Ezek. 36.25-27). And one becomes such by becoming *"sons of God through faith"* in Christ (Gal. 3.27-29) and becoming *"Abraham's offspring, heirs according to promise"* (3.27; 4-31). *"Now that faith has come"* (3.25 cf. Rom. 4.1-25; 5.1) 'Abraham's offspring' includes both Jews and Gentiles who believe in Christ (3.28; Eph. 2.13-22; Col 3.10-11). Diaspora and cross-cultural mission facilitates, indeed enforces Jesus's aims and predictions (Matt. 8.10-12; 21.43). It makes experiential God's plan of redemption and incorporation into the one body (Gen. 12.1-3; Joel 2.28-32 cf. Acts 2.16-21).

Paul's Damascus road experience, commission and subsequent missional theology and practice resulted in the creation of the 'people of God' which significantly included diaspora communities: In Acts 26.17-18 the risen Christ sends Paul to *"open their eyes, that they may turn from darkness to light and from the power of Satan to God, that they may receive forgiveness of sins and a place among those who are sanctified by faith in me"*. Moreover, people find *"a place"* amid the people of God by being *"sanctified by faith in me"* (v.18), which according to Rom. 15.16 includes Gentiles being *"sanctified by the Holy Spirit"*. And according to 1 Cor. 6.11 *"you were washed, you were sanctified, you were justified in the name of the Lord Jesus Christ and in the Spirit of our God"*. The role of Christ and the Spirit is also seen in 2 Thess. 2.13 *"God chose you from the beginning to be saved, through sanctification by the Spirit and belief in the truth"*. They appear earlier in Gal. 3.14, where Paul alluding to the Abrahamic covenant in Gen. 12.1-4 states *"that in Christ Jesus the blessing of Abraham might come upon the Gentiles, that we might receive the promise of the Spirit through faith"*.

This remarkable passage links Christ *and* the Spirit with the promise of Abraham in Gen. 12.1-3. Peter links the gift of the Spirit to the fulfilment of Joel 2, but Paul goes to a prior passage in Gen. 12.1-3. Furthermore, in 2 Cor. 3.3, 6 he links one's conversion experience to the fulfilment of Jer. 31.31-34: *"written not with ink but with the Spirit of the living God, not on tablets of stone but on tablets of human hearts"* (cf. Ezek. 36.25-26). In this setting Paul likens himself to a 'new covenant minister in the Spirit', i.e. a *"competent minister of a new covenant, not in a written code but in the Spirit, for the written code kills, but the Spirit gives life"*. Perhaps the question Paul poses to the disciples of John at Ephesus in Acts 19.2 *"Did you receive the Holy Spirit when you believed"* and them subsequently experiencing of the Spirit in 19.6 needs to be taken in such light. In conversion both Christ and the Spirit (in keeping with the Father's purpose) are involved. This is evident in Peter's ministry at the house of Cornelius (Acts 10.14-48 "the gift of the Holy Spirit had been poured out even on the Gentiles" [v.45]; 11.15-17 "if then God gave the same gift to them as he gave to us when we believed in the Lord Jesus Christ, who was I that I could withstand God?" v.17) and his explanation of God's acceptance of Gentiles at the Jerusalem council in 15.7-11 "And God who knows the heart bore witness to them, giving them the Holy Spirit just as he did to us; and he made no distinction between us and them, but cleansed their hearts by faith". It is also significant that Peter associates this conversion with 'faith' and 'grace' "But we believe that we shall be saved through the grace of the Lord Jesus, just as they will". So, conversion is associated with "the grace of the Lord Jesus", "cleansing hearts by faith" and "giving them [Gentile believers] the Holy Spirit, just as he did to us [Jewish believers], and he made no distinction between us and them" (cf. Gal. 4.9; Rom. 14.3, 7).

The Role of the Holy Spirit in Diaspora Mission

Joel's "upon all flesh" is being further fulfilled through diaspora missions. It is to be noted that most of the above-mentioned passages (Acts 19.2; 10.14-48; 11.15-17; 15.7-11) refer to people outside of Jerusalem, i.e. in the context of 'diaspora', it is in context that Joel's prophecy is being fulfilled. *"And in the last days it shall be, God declares, that I will pour out my Spirit upon all flesh..."* (Joel 2.28-32; Acts 2.17f.) and "all who call upon the name of the Lord [are being] saved" (Acts 2.21; Joel 2.32). The usage of the latter (Joel 2.23) is not absent in Paul "for everyone who calls upon the name of the Lord will be saved" (Rom. 10.13). Hence, as evidenced in the book of Acts, diaspora missions fulfils and makes experiential Joel's "pouring out of God's Spirit upon all flesh" (2.28). Consequently, "in the last day" of Joel 2.28-32 is now experienced by believers, both Jews and Gentiles, who have received the 'promised' eschatological Spirit (Acts 1.4; Eph. 1.13; 1 Cor. 10.11; 2 Cor. 5.5), and form the one eschatological people, indeed "the one new humanity created in himself [Jesus]" (Eph. 2.15), *"upon whom the end of the age has come"* (1 Cor. 10.11). The Holy Spirit is the eschatological Spirit (Rom. 8.11, 23; 2 Cor. 5.5), the experiential linchpin who enables the experience of Christ and helps create a community which *"lacks no Spiritual gifts"* as it waits the *"revealing of our Lord Jesus Christ"* (1 Cor. 1.7).

Conclusion

Many push and pull factors have contributed towards Sri Lankan Diaspora and other regions. Migration ranges from voluntary diaspora during the British period to countries like Singapore and Malaysia, to economic migration, and most importantly the 30-year ethnic war has contributed to the largest dispersion from this island republic. It has been estimated that the Sri-Lanka diaspora amounts to around three million all over the world. A notable fact though is that many Sri-Lankans have found the Lord in the countries of their exile. Jeremiah exhorted his exile community: *"Seek the welfare of the city where I have sent you into exile, and pray to the Lord on its behalf, for in its welfare you will find your welfare"* (Jer. 29.7). Given the refugee crisis in the world, Jeremiah's exhortation is something that the Sri Lankan diaspora, and the Christian diaspora communities in the world need to take heed and help missions in their 'Jerusalem' i.e. native country, which undoubtedly some are doing, which is encouraging, but needs to be done more and more. As in the Scriptures God ministers to and through the diaspora communities to fulfil his sovereign plan and purpose.

References

Brueggemann, Walter. 2005 *Cadences of Home: Preaching among Exiles,* Louisville, KY: Westminister John Knox Press.

_____, 1994. *Hopeful Imagination: Prophetic Voices in Exiles,* Minneapolis: Fortress Press.

Carroll, Daniel. 2013. *Christians at the Border: Immigration, the Church and the Bible.* Grand Rapids: Brazos Press.

Groody, Daniel. 2010. *A Promised Land, A Perilous Journey: Theological Perspectives on Migration.* Notre Dame, IN: University of Notre Dame Press.

Im, Chandler and Amos Yong. 2014. *Global Diasporas and Mission.* Oxford: Regnum.

Philo. *On the Embassy to Gaius. General Indexes.* Translated by F. H. Colson. Index by J. W. Earp. Loeb Classical Library 379. Cambridge, MA: Harvard University Press, 1962.

Rad, Gerhard von. 1973. *Old Testament Theology Vol 1: The Theology of Israel's Historical Traditions,* Edinburgh: Oliver & Boyd.

Smith-Christopher, Daniel L. 2002. *Biblical Theology of Exile:* Minneaplois: Fortress Press.

Stott, John. 1990. *The Message of Acts (Bible Speaks Today),* Downers Grove, IL: IVP Academic.

Tira, Sadiri Joy and Tetsunao Yamamori (Eds). 2016. *Scattered & Gathered: A Global Compendium of Diaspora Missiology.* Oxford: Regnum.

Walls. Andrew F. 2010. Theology of Migration

Wan, Enoch. 2014. *Diaspora Missiology: Theory, Methodology and Practice.* Portland, OR: Institute of Diaspora Studies, Western Seminary.

Wright, Christopher. 2016. Foreword in *Scattered & Gathered: A Global Compendium of Diaspora Missiology.* Oxford: Regnum.

'Certain Men' of Cyprus and Cyrene in Acts:

Diaspora Missionaries of the Early Christianity

Simon Samuel

> The initial impetus for a genuine missionary
> outreach among Gentiles came not from Peter (or Paul)
> but from Hellenistic Jewish Christians from Cyprus and Cyrene
> whose names we do not even know. (Schnabel 2002, 672)

Introduction

The Jerusalem-centered Peterine and the Antioch-centered Pauline mission stories appear as a two-part 'mega-story' (Hengel 2003, 2; Baur 2003; Penner 2004) of early Christian mission in the Acts of the Apostles. The Peterine mission focuses primarily on the Palestinian Jewish geo-political, ethno-cultural terrain with occasional, and not so enthusiastic irruptions into the gentile terrains; and the Pauline mission focuses on the gentile regions beyond the Jews, without ignoring the Jewish quarters (Esler 1996, 40f).

In comparison with the Peter-Paul mega-story, the 'acts' of Philip (Acts 8) and the *'tines andres* (certain men) of Cyprus and Cyrene'

(Acts 11.19ff.) in the Samaritan and the Gentile quarters (Antioch) are constructed as a 'mini-story'. But, when we read between the lines and deconstruct the Peter-Paul narrative, we find a decisive remapping of mission initiated by a tiny group of ordinary diaspora Jewish-Christians at the very outset of the early Christian mission. Such a decisive redrawing of early Christian mission receives only an 'abbreviated attention' in Acts. It demands a re-reading of the Lukan story to trace what actually transpired prior to and in-between the Peter-Paul mega-stories in terms of the expansion of the early Christian mission beyond the geo-cultural and ethnic boundaries of Judaism by the diaspora missionaries like Philip and the certain men of Cyprus and Cyrene (Acts 8.1ff; 11.19ff).

When the nameless 'certain men' turned to the gentiles with an apparently 'unacceptable missional vision and practice' were they unconcerned of a potential 'parting of ways' from Judaism? Being Jewish followers of Jesus Messiah were they positioning themselves in a unique space from where they could accommodate and disrupt the Jewish cultural boundaries almost simultaneously? If these questions receive an affirmative answer, then isn't it right to suggest that Philip and certain men of Cyprus and Cyrene were pioneers not only in creating new frontiers of early Christian mission beyond the bounds of Judaism but also in setting a mission trend for Peter and Paul to emulate after Jesus, and perhaps even for others later on in the story of the worldwide expansion of Christianity.

The story of the expansion of the Jesus's movement in Acts 1-5 attests the fact that the earliest followers of Jesus's Messiah were continuously committed to Judaism, especially in the way they involved themselves in the temple cult (Acts 2.46; 3.1). They were accepted by many Jews in the city or elsewhere (2.47; Acts 13.14-15; 14.1) despite some opposition from the Sanhedrin (4.1-21; 5.17-40). In this movement, how and why did certain diverse mission strands (Meyers 1986) emerge – some remaining loyal to the Jewish cultural nationalists who advocate the practice of circumcision, food laws and calendar; others increasingly distancing themselves, by being overtly oriented toward the gentile mission (as a result, severing ties off from Judaism altogether); and yet others posturing a rather ambivalent 'affiliative alterity mode' of relating and distancing themselves from Judaism, who occupied a 'third space', from where they accommodated and disrupted, almost simultaneously, both the native Jewish-Christian cultural nationalistic and the overtly gentile oriented mission discourses.

In this essay, I use the critical tools of postcolonial studies on Lukan account of early Christianity from the book of Acts, particularly the neglected narrative of the certain men of Cyprus and Cyrene and primary text being Acts 11.19-21:

> Now those who were scattered because of the persecution that arose over Stephen traveled as far as Phoenicia and Cyprus and Antioch, speaking the word to none except Jews. But there were some of them, men of Cyprus and Cyrene, who on coming to Antioch spoke to the Greeks also, preaching the Lord Jesus. And the hand of the Lord was with them, and a great number that believed turned to the Lord (NIV).

In my study of the New Testament, I am convinced that the earliest Christian mission was taken beyond the bounds of Judaism and Palestine by the ordinary diaspora Jewish men like Philip and the certain men of Cyprus and Cyrene who with their cultural hybrid experience crossed the geographical and cultural boundaries easily. They initiated the first frontier-crossing mission to the Greeks and the hand of the Lord was with them. They offer inspiring models of missions for contemporary diaspora lay Christians and their future generations who will establish bridges for the cross-cultural diffusion of the gospel to the ends of the earth.

Rereading the 'Acts' of Philip and the 'Certain Men' of Cyprus and Cyrene

Acts of the Apostles 11.19-21 points to one of the most decisive turns of events in the entire (hi)story of the expansion of the earliest followers of Jesus Messiah beyond the geo-political, ethnic and socio-cultural bounds of Judaism. Surprisingly, Luke abbreviates the story of certain persons, whom he calls with an indefinite pronoun *'tines'*, even though his whole purpose of writing the story was to show the expansion of the early Christians beyond the ethno-cultural boundaries of Judaism. One who reads the Lukan story of the early Christian mission would find these men (*tines*) and their deeds to be very decisive in terms of the early Christian mission breaking into new frontiers from its Jewish ethnic and geo-cultural-nationalistic milieu. For some reason, Luke calls them '*tines*' and passes them by without elaborating on their works or mentioning their names. These unnamed men are perhaps part (or associates) of those Stephenite men (Hellenistic Jewish Christians) who are selected to serve in the daily distribution of food, to deal with the issue of poverty and also to mend the cultural divide between the Greek speaking ['Hellenistai'] and the Aramaic speaking ['Hebraioi'] Jewish-Christians (Acts 6.1-7). Their names suggest that they are Greek-speaking Jewish Christians (Hellenistai) from Palestine and elsewhere, and one of them obviously a proselyte from Antioch.

The ensuing story suggests that these ordinary men of Greek speaking Jews engage quite vigorously their fellowmen 'who belonged to the synagogue of the Freedmen (as it was called), and of the Cyrenians, and of the Alexandrians, and of those from Cilicia and Asia' (Acts 6.9) in debate and dialogue, with the Jesus discourse, in Jerusalem which apparently resulted in dispute, disruption and ultimately the dispersion of this segment of the Jewish Christians from Jerusalem (Hengel 2003, 56; Esler 1996, 143). This is evident in the Stephen incident (Acts 6.8ff and ch. 7), facing the wrath of the Jewish cultural nationalists apparently more than the Apostles (Acts 8.1b). In the persecution that ensued, they were targeted and had to flee from Jerusalem. They fled taking the good news of Jesus Messiah along with them to the new frontiers. Both Philip and the '*tines*' went beyond the Judean Jewish boundary, evangelizing as they went. While Philip made inroads into the Samaritan and the African ethno-cultural space (Ethiopian eunuch), the *tines* of Cyprus and Cyrene made inroads into the Asiatic area in Syrian Antioch. These independent, frontier-crossing, Greek-speaking, Jewish-Christian, diaspora missionaries thus became the pioneers of the Syrian church in Antioch which became the center for the eastward and westward expansion of Christianity.

In view of the geographical direction to which they fled it may be assumed that these men are perhaps the ones who preached the gospel at Damascus too during the course of their fearful flight northward to Antioch (Hahn 1965, 59). Then we may conjure that they may be instrumental to preaching Jesus Messiah to men like Ananias (and other Greek speaking Jews) in Damascus (Acts 9.10, 19b) and possibly laying hands on him so that he may be filled with the Holy Spirit. It is this Ananias who later laid hands on Saul/ Paul in order that he may receive 'sight' and the Holy Spirit and that he may continue the frontier crossing mission after the manner of the '*tines*' in the Greco-Roman world. Paul perhaps felt proud of this heritage and lineage as a missionary Apostle. Hence, he says at an opportune moment later in his life, when he was isolated by his rivals (Jewish-Christian cultural nationalists), that he is not inferior to the super-apostles (2 Cor. 11.5).

Despite such radical and far-reaching mission initiative and praxis, in the Lukan mission mapping, the frontier crossing-mission practice of these '*tines*' is subordinated to the Peter-Paul mission stories. In Acts, immediately after the story of Philip in Samaria (8.4-13) Luke seems to be quick in casting a narrative gap between the two new frontier-crossing parallel stories of Philip (in 8.4ff) and the '*tines*' of Cyprus and Cyrene (in Acts 11. 19ff). Luke fills this gap with the stories of Peter's 'supervisory mission' in Samaria (8.14ff), apparently to supplement what, in his sight, is lacking in Philip's Samarian mission. Peter does this by praying for the believers so that they may receive the Holy Spirit (8.14-24). Further, in chapter 9 Luke introduces Paul's call narrative (with minimum details on Ananias and his ministry to Paul), and in chapters 10.1-48 and 11.1-18 he elaborates twice in much detail the story of Peter's ministry in the house of the gentile Cornelius. Luke apparently wants the audience to hear that Paul's call to be the missionary to the gentiles (Acts 9.15) and Peter's mission to the gentiles prelude the gentile mission initiatives of the '*tines andres*' of Cyprus and Cyrene. Though he did not 'suppress' the historical fact concerning the gentile mission of the *tines* Luke seems focused to prepare and frame Peter and Paul as primary players of gentile mission over and above the unnamed '*tines andres*' of Cyprus and Cyrene.

By amplifying the Peter-Paul stories more than the Samarian, African frontier-crossing mission of Philip and the Syrian frontier-crossing mission of the *tines*, Luke wants the readers to hear that the Jerusalem church monitored and perfected the mission in its proper end and order. The visit of Peter and John to Samaria after Philip (8.14ff) and the dispatch of Barnabas and Paul as representatives of the Jerusalem church, after the *tines*, to Antioch (11.22ff) are meant to show that the gentile mission must be supervised by the Jerusalem Apostles, and the gentile churches are connected with the Jerusalem Jewish church. Apparently, Peter played this connecting role by occupying a middle space of mission which later Paul too occupied. It may best be understood as an ambivalent mission strategy that affiliated and distanced the covenant community, almost simultaneously, to the Jewish and the gentile terrains. Luke did it mainly for missional and ecclesial purposes, that is, to place the new covenant community as a united, inclusive community of both Jews and Gentiles.

A Rereading the 'Acts' of 'Tines Andres' of Cyprus and Cyrene

The 'acts' of the *tines* of Cyprus and Cyrene took place simultaneously with that of the 'acts' of Philip as they probably fled together northwards from Jerusalem. But the narrowing in the narration of the overt gentile mission work of the *tines* of Cyprus and Cyrene occurs due to the Lukan tendency in showing Peter and Paul as the pioneer gentile missionaries.

Saul/Paul, a Syrian (Cilician) Jew, was probably a member of the synagogue of the Freedmen or of the Cilician or Asiatic Jews in Jerusalem. His zeal for Jewish cultural traditions must have brought him into a confrontation with the *Hellenistai* Christians and he was probably involved in the conspiracy to kill Stephen (6.9; 8.1a). After the murder of Stephen, he targeted the fleeing Greek speaking Jewish Christian missionaries who went evangelizing the Syrian regions of Damascus on their way north to the Syrian Antioch, the home terrain of Paul. In the 'conversion' of Saul/ Paul, Luke has Ananias, a Damascan *Hellenistai*, coming to Paul and laying hands on him in order that he may receive the Holy Spirit. Thus, Paul is commissioned to preach the gospel to the gentiles (Acts 9.10 following). In this regard, it is worth reiterating that Ananias might have believed in Jesus Messiah through the evangelism work of the fleeing *tines andres* of Cyprus and Cyrene who bestowed the Spirit in him. He, in turn, bestowed that Spirit to Paul.

The anointing and commissioning of Paul to gentile mission thus occurred through this strand of the early Christian mission. Luke is silent on this. But if we read between the lines we may get an impression of a possible link between the missionary work of the *tines andres* of Cyprus and Cyrene and Paul via Ananias of Damascus. After conversion Paul apparently got involved in the missionary work in Arabia, Damascus (Gal. 1. 17; Acts 9. 20-22) and Tarsus (Acts 11.25f), both among the Jews and gentiles as the *'tines andres'* of Cyprus and Cyrene (Kee and Young 1991, 216-219). In this context it is inconceivable that Paul laid the foundation of his mission theology without the influence of the Stephenite *tines andres* of Cyprus and Cyrene.

The laying on of hands and bestowing of the Holy Spirit on Paul are done by Ananias and not by the Jerusalem Apostles (cf. 2 Cor. 11.5). Luke is not keen in elaborating this *tines* – Ananias – Paul nexus and this silence is to present Paul as a pioneer missionary to the gentiles. Peter's distancing from Philip in Samaria and Caesarea and Paul's from the *tines andres* of Cyprus and Cyrene are apparently Lukan attempts to exonerate both Peter (Perkins 2000, 33-38, 88-95) and Paul (Lentz 1993) who independent of each other, pioneered the gentile mission under the guidance of the Holy Spirit. Thus, Luke wants to fuse together the two factions of mission praxis in early Christianity. By fusing them, he 'glossed over' the independent, border-crossing mission initiatives of ordinary men like Philip and the *tines andres* of Cyprus and Cyrene. Hengel thinks Luke 'had one clear aim to which everything else was subordinated: to describe the ideal world mission, that is, Paul's mission'. By doing this he has confined the traditions about the *Hellenistai* like Philip and the *tines* as a 'bridge narrative' between Peter and Paul in his version of the story of the expansion of Christianity. In this narrative construction, all the other characters and their initiatives 'disappeared prematurely' (Hengel 2003, 55).

The Culture and Theology of the Diaspora Stephenite *Hellenistai*

The *Hellenistai* are ethnic Jews who spoke (and are well-versed in) Hellenistic-Greek rather than Aramaic in Jerusalem (Hengel 1989). Due to linguistic (cultural) reasons, perhaps they met separately for prayers, worship and love meals in Jerusalem under the leadership of men like Stephen, and the Seven (Acts 6). Some of them are probably born in the diaspora, and at certain stage came and settled in Jerusalem due to their love for the Temple, the Torah and the land; others are perhaps born and brought up in Jerusalem itself but maintained a cultural connection with the Greeks. A few may be disciples of Jesus who brought Greeks to Jesus (cf. John 12.20ff). The Stephenite *Hellenistai* are the Greek speaking Jews who heard the good news of Jesus in Jerusalem and believed in him as the Messiah. They congregated for worship (in Greek) in Jerusalem and perhaps experienced charismatic experiences. They are apparently men of zeal, wisdom and Spirit with revelatory experiences (Acts 6.10; 7.56) who tried to reach out to their fellow men (Hellenistic Jews) and others with a Moses-Torah-Temple-free gospel of Jesus Messiah (Acts 6.9). This apparently invited trouble from the Jewish and Jewish-Christian cultural nationalists in Jerusalem.

It is probable that persecution too began from the Greek-speaking Jewish cultural nationalists against the Greek-speaking Jewish-Christian group. This group was specifically targeted and as a result, its members had to flee from Jerusalem. They apparently did not receive sympathy or support, from the cultural nationalist Jewish Christian quarters. This selective opposition and lack of support may be due to this group's cultural openness, Christological and eschatological, missiological affirmations and the resultant mission initiatives (i.e., gentile mission without Jewish cultural conditioning). The members of this group probably understood themselves to be bearers of divine wisdom and experienced the freedom of the spirit. According to Hengel, 'this new freedom of the spirit and the wisdom revealed by God is the only explanation for the offence caused by Stephen and his colleagues'.

The Stephen narrative gives us some clues to this wisdom and spirit of the Stephenite *Hellenistai* like that of their Jewish contemporaries who experienced a higher revelatory and experiential understanding of the supernatural beyond the Jewish traditional cultural practices. Stephen in Acts is shown as the paradigmatic bearer of the spirit, power and wisdom (Acts 6.10) and appears to his accusers as an angel. At the end of his speech he sees the heavens open and is filled with the Spirit, sees the glory of God, the heavenly sanctuary and the Son of Man standing at the right hand of God (7.55). Because of such heavenly experiences, he and his group have blurred their national, ethnic and cultural boundaries (such as circumcision, dietary laws, Sabbath observance, calendar etc.). This enabled them to experience the risen Christ, his eschatological Spirit and thus relate with the gentiles much more easily. It distanced them from the tenets and the Temple of Judaism and its salvific rites and observances. They find Jesus as someone greater than the Temple. Hengel claimed, 'We can understand how the Greek speaking synagogue communities in Jerusalem … regarded the new message as an intolerable blasphemy of their most sacred possession, because of which in fact most of their members had come to Jerusalem' (2003, 24). Opposition and expulsion of the *Hellenistai* therefore, became the natural response of the hard-core cultural nationalists against their own compatriots. In turn the Stephenites found their rejection as an opportunity for the Gentiles to enter the salvific grace of God and be the new Israel of God in Christ.

Now we are able to answer our crucial question: why did the *Hellenistai* Christians in Jerusalem take an earnest initiative to gentile mission more than and prior to Peter and the Jerusalem Christian leadership? Obviously, this move is circumstantially motivated, i.e., due to the persecution unleashed against them in particular by the hard-core elements of the Hellenistic Jews. We may also add that the cultural cutting edge that they enjoyed in terms of their ability to communicate in Greek enabled them to relate with the Greeks. In addition to these circumstantial and linguistic reasons, there is an obvious theological reason. When the early Christian (messianic) movement began in Jerusalem, it had members both from the Jewish cultural nationalist background as well as from other Jews with revelatory, visional experiences and with a universalistic ethic and outlook of life. Adherents from the former held on to their zeal in matters relating to the upkeep of the cultural tenets and practices of Judaism along with their faith in Jesus. On the contrary, the others were more open to the Gentiles (Rowland 1985, 201) and their theology and philosophy of life can be seen in Stephen's speech (Acts 7).

Stephen's speech, though a Lucan composition, reveals some distinctive elements of the theology and philosophy of life of the Stephenite segment of Jerusalem's early Christian tradition. This segment believed that the Jewish ethnic descent is not in any way unique. Its descent is from Mesopotamia. Therefore, there is little room for boasting about a separate ethnic identity or specificity. The Jews are ethnically Mesopotamians! Abraham saw the glory of God as a Mesopotamian in Mesopotamia. Before he came and possessed the Promised Land, he believed God because of a revelatory experience. So, ethnicity and land need not be linked with one's belief in God. Similarly, Abraham received God's favor before his circumcision and entry into the land, the two prominent identity markers- one ethnic and the other national. Stephen's speech thus focuses on the fact that the story of the Jews, through Abraham, began from Mesopotamia without the land, ritual, national and ethnic identity.

This Mesopotamian link is maintained by Abraham's descendants through marital means. Isaac and Jacob had their wives from Mesopotamia. Joseph had his wife and progeny from an Egyptian wife. Israel and the twelve tribal heads and their progeny in the earliest phase of their story survived due to the benevolence showed to them by the Egyptian kings. After stressing the Mesopotamian link Stephen thus affirmed the Egyptian link of Israel by elaborating the story of Joseph. The Stephenites in their kerygma perhaps exposed the fathers and mothers and heroes of Israel as ethnic and cultural hybrids whose racial and cultural identity is inalienably interlinked with the Mesopotamians and Egyptians. In the case of Joseph, it was the in-house persecution that paved for his flight to Egypt, which providentially became the lifeline of Israel's survival and formation as the people of God. Though he was persecuted and sold out to Egypt, 'God was with him' (Acts 7.9) and so, he became an intermediary between Israel and Egypt, and thus Israel survived and eventually formed themselves as the people of God.

Stephen relates the climax of the Egyptian connection and Israel's formation as the people of God by referring to the story of Moses. He is specific in affirming the fact that the word 'Moses' is not a Jewish word. It is an Egyptian name given to Moses by his 'Egyptian mother', who in fact saved the great savior of Israel. Later on, when he was rejected by his own people in Egypt, and as a result fled for his life, he was saved by the Midianites. When he was living as a Midianite shepherd along with his Midianite wife and children and father-in-law he experienced the revelation and glory of God. Stephen, by referring and stressing such elements in the Abraham, Jacob, Joseph, Moses stories, appears to stress the ethnic and cultural hybridity of the Israelites even in their foundational (hi)story of forming themselves as the people of God. Stephen tends to be saying that the Israelites owe much to the Mesopotamians, Egyptians and Midianites for their ethnic origin and religion-cultural-national formation as the people of God. Therefore, there is little to boast of their ethnic superiority or cultural, nationalistic identity.

After shedding light on the pluriformity of their ethnic and national origin Stephen refers to the origin of the Torah itself. He focuses on the fact that the Torah was given by God through Moses who was born, bread and named in Egypt. The law was given when Israel was still in a gentile space – Mount Sinai – and not in the Promised Land. The lawgiver Moses and the law itself cannot be detached from their non-Israelite space and agency. Mount Sinai despite its 'gentile-ness' was a holy ground. Moses received the law at a time when the so-called people of God rejected God and turned to become idol worshippers like any other gentiles. Moses brought the law to them at a time when Israel was living like the gentiles, worshipping the golden calf. Ever since this calf worship, the practice of idol worship did not cease in the history of Israel (as seen in the installation of the two golden calves at the ancient cultic centers of Bethel and Dan at the time of Jeroboam I). Hence, the Judges and Prophets preached Israel to repent and return to the God of Israel.

Stephen all through his speech in Acts 7 referred to the fact that Israel was not better than the gentiles. Their root was inalienably interlinked with the gentiles, their upbringing and formation as a people was in the gentile terrain, their great lawgiver's name was a gentile name, and their great law was given when they were in the gentile territory resorting to a gentile life style and worship. God's covenantal *emeth* and *hesed* are expressed to, and experienced by, their ancestors while they were gentiles and living as gentiles. Israel's formation and re-formation have taken place in the gentile terrain and in relation to the gentiles. Stephen then climaxed his message by saying that when Israel entered the Promised Land they localized and confined their God into a Temple like other nations and worshipped him along with other gods like Moloch and Rephan despite their experience of knowing that 'the Most High does not dwell in houses made by human hands' (Acts 7.48). Hence, their expulsion from the Promised Land back to the place from where their first father Abraham began (7.43) so that a new 'calling out' of a new people of God may begin all over again. The Hellenistic Jewish Christian (diaspora) missionaries believed that they are destined by God to do this task. It may commence without any cultural constraints of Judaism just as it all began with God and Abraham in the first place.

Stephen then connects the story of Israel with the story of the Righteous One (Jesus Messiah). As in the case of Joseph, Moses and the Prophets of old, this Righteous One too is rejected by the stiff-necked Jewish people (7.51-52). Stephen then puts himself in the line and says that he too has a crucial role to play in steering the destiny of the people of God in the midst of rejection. Hence, his vision of the glory of God and Jesus as the Son of Man at the right hand of God representing the new humanity of God in the heaven. Stephen's vision of the Son of Man and his sudden, violent rejection and martyrdom exemplifies a distinctive early Christian theology for the formation of a new humanity of God, inclusive of both Jews and gentiles, in Christ (Rowland 1985, 201). The *tines andres* of Cyprus and Cyrene after Stephen continued this tradition, vision and mission of Stephen, which these Stephenites received from Jesus himself.

Jesus and the Origin of the Gentile Mission

Gentile mission of the early Christians apparently has its root in the mission of Jesus. The topic 'gentile mission of Jesus' is a complex one due to the historical, kerygmatic, ecclesial, redactional, and theological nature of the Gospels. All four Gospels attest that Jesus's mission was primarily in Galilee, which according to the biblical and historical sources, had a considerable gentile population before and during the time of Jesus. Because of this Galilee was popularly known as 'Galilee of the gentiles' (Is. 9.1-2; Matt. 4.15ff; I Macc. 5). Ethnically and culturally Galilee from the Assyrian conquest onward had an ethnic and cultural plurality. Jesus probably was exposed to this plurality. The Jesus movement thus originated within this ethnic and cultural, particularly linguistic plurality. The rabbinic sources attest that Galilee was the seed-bed of rabbinic Judaism which composed the Mishnah and later the Jerusalem Talmud.

The four Gospels attest that Jesus during his life came into contact with gentile individuals and communities in Galilee and elsewhere. If informal and individually motivated mission to the gentiles was in vogue during the second temple period, there is no reason for us to doubt that Jesus too came into missional contact with people like the Syrophoenician woman (Mark 7.24ff), the gentile centurion (Matt. 8.15ff.; Luke 7.1-10; John 4.46ff), the Samaritan woman (John 4) and the Greeks (John 12), just as he came into missional contact with the so-called 'lost sheep of Israel'. As the Servant of Yahweh he believed that he came to proclaim justice and hope to both Jews and Gentiles

(Matt. 12.15ff.; Luke 13.28-30// Matt. 8.11-12; Matt 4.24-25; Mark 3.7-8; Luke 4.16ff; 6.17-18). The *tines andres* of Cyprus and Cyrene believed in this Servant of Yahweh and presented him to both Jews and Gentiles as their eschatological savior.

Conclusion

As the church began after the resurrection of Jesus and with the explicit pneumatic manifestation of tongues, signs, wonders and the kerygma of the Galilean disciples of Jesus in Jerusalem (Acts 2-3; 4.30; 5.12-16) it probably drew an increasing number of adherents even from the conservative Jewish cultural nationalist segments (Acts 2.41, 47; 4.4; 6.7), who gradually gained an upper hand in the Jerusalem church. As it was a practice within the sectarian Judaism(s) of the time, James, the brother and head of the family of Jesus in Galilee, was perhaps invited to Jerusalem and recognized as the head of the Jesus movement there. Peter and the other disciples of Jesus too were incorporated in this circle, more than their 'sincerity' and 'straightforwardness about the truth of the gospel' (cf. Gal. 2.14). We know from Paul's letters that Peter was not willing to challenge openly the Jewish-Christian cultural nationalist wing of the Jerusalem church and as a result he gradually fell under their spell (Gal. 2.11ff). Paul and Barnabas too at the outset of their work acted as agents of this wing of the Jerusalem church and participated in the supervisory mission trips to Antioch (Acts 11.22ff).

But later on, Paul, despite the desertion of Barnabas and many other Jewish Christian friends and co-workers (Gal. 2.13; Col. 4.10-11), got increasingly drawn towards the theology and missional practice of the Stephenites and became a missionary to the uncircumcised and assumed an ambivalent stance in his relation to the Jerusalem church (2 Cor. 11.5; Gal. 1.11-2.10; Rom. 15.25-27). Luke in his account of Acts apparently wants to salvage both Peter and Paul from this mire of politics of culture in which they were entangled. He does this by presenting them as pioneers of gentile mission in their own rights because of their respective heavenly revelations (Paul's in Acts 9 and Peter's in Acts 10). While doing this Luke postponed (to Acts 11.19ff) and to a large extent abbreviated the pioneering and radical gentile mission initiatives of the Cypriot and Cyrenian missionaries - initiatives that radically and irreversibly redrew the map of the expansion of the early Christian movement prior to Peter and Paul, and beyond the geo-cultural and ethno-political terrains of Judaism.

References

Bauckham, Richard (ed.), *The Book of Acts in its first Century Setting* (vol. 4): *Palestinian Setting*, Grand Rapids: Eerdmans, 1995.

Baur, FC. *Paul the Apostle of Jesus Christ, His Life and Works, His Epistles and Teachings*, 2 vols. (ed.) E. Zeller; 2nd ed., London: Williams & Norgate 1873-75 repr. in one vol., Peabody, MA: Hendrickson, 2003.

Chilton, Bruce and Craig Evans (eds.) *The Missions of James, Peter, and Paul: Tensions in Early Christianity*, Leiden: Brill, 2005.

Esler, F. E., *Community and Gospel in Luke-Acts: The Social and Political Motivations of Lucan Theology*, Cambridge: CUP, 1987.

_____, *The First Christians in Their Social Worlds: Social-scientific approaches to New Testament interpretation*, London: Routledge, 1994.

Hengel, Martin, *Between Jesus and Paul: Studies in the Earliest History of Christianity*, Eugene, Oregon: Wipf and Stock Publishers, 2003 (1983).

_____, *The 'Hellenization' of Judaea in the First Century after Christ*, trans., John Bowden, London: SCM Press, 1989.

Kee, H.C. and F. W. Young, *The Living World of the New Testament*, London: Darton, Longman & Todd, 1991 (1960),

Meyer, Ben. F., *The Early Christians: Their World Mission and Self-Discovery*, Wilmington, Delaware: Michael Glazier Inc., 1986.

Penner, Todd, *In Praise of Christian Origins: Stephen and the Hellenists in Lukan Apologetic Historiography*, New York: T & T Clark International, 2004.

Rowland, Christopher, *Christian Origins: An Account of the Setting and Character of the most Important Messianic Sect of Judaism*, London: SPCK, 1985.

Samuel, Simon, *A Postcolonial Reading of Mark's Story of Jesus*, Edinburgh: T & T Clark, 2007.

Schnabel, Eckhard, J., *Early Christian Mission: Jesus and the Twelve* (Vol. I), *Paul and the Early Church* (Vol. II), Illinois: IVP, 2004 (German 2002).

Spencer, Scott. F., *The Portrait of Philip in Acts: A Study of Roles and Relations*, Sheffield: SAP, 1992.

William, Larkin, J. Jr. and Joel F. Williams (eds.), *Mission in the New Testament: An Evangelical Approach*, Maryknoll: Orbis, 1998.

Tamil Missionaries in East Africa and Burma in the 19th Century[1]

Daniel Jeyaraj

In January 1893 the editor of the Evangelisch-Lutherisches Missionsblatt (ELMB), the official organ of the Leipzig Evangelical Lutheran Mission in Leipzig, Germany (LELM), informed his readers that Indian Christians had already gone overseas to serve the Protestant missions. He stated that Christians from Tiruvelvêli had already gone to the Telugu speaking Indians in Central India, to Sri Lanka and to other places. Two Tamil pastors were sent to Natal in South Africa. A Hindi speaking pastor sailed to Fiji Islands. Tamil Christian pastors and catechists went to Rangoon in Myanmar and were willing to go to East Africa. The editor assumed that this spreading was a natural event following the model of businessmen and other emigrants. He lays emphasis on the willingness of a few Tamil Lutheran Christians who offered themselves to go as missionaries to East Africa. This is an interesting account to demonstrate the South-South Mission Movement of Indian Christians during the 19th century. This essay,

---

[1] This chapter has been edited and revised from a previously published article: Daniel Jeyaraj. 'Missionary Attempts of Protestant Christians in East and West During the 19th Century' in *Transcontinental Links in the History of Non-Western Christianity*. Klaus Koschorke (Editor). Harrassowitz; Bilingual edition. 2002. Reprinted with permission.

which is not exhaustive, but understood as a 'work in progress', is an attempt to trace the missionary involvement of Tamil Christians from South India to Tanzania and to Myanmar.

I

Tamil Protestant Christianity in South India has an unbroken history of almost three hundred years. However, they were not the first Christians in India: A vast number of St. Thomas Christians in Kerala, the South West Indian State, trace their origin to St. Thomas, one of the apostles of Jesus Christ. According to them St. Thomas was said to have arrived in Calicut in 52 AD. and was martyred in Chennai (Madras) in 72 AD. It is possible that the designation of the Orthodox Christians in Kerala as Thomas Christians and as Syrian Christians goes back to a Thomas of Cana who had led about 300 Syrian Christian families to present day Kerala. Soon they got accustomed to Indian realities and ensured their legitimate continuity. When Portuguese traders and colonizers met them under the Padroado agreement between the King of Portugal and the Pope they wanted to claim their absolute religious supremacy all over India. Very soon they got into conflict with St. Thomas Christians. The Synod of Diamper held in June 1599 attempted to subdue all St. Thomas Christians to Roman Catholic faith. However, in the Coonan Cross Rebellion of 1653 some chose to remain as Romo-Syrian Catholics and other regained their earlier identity. The tension between Roman Catholic missionaries and Roman Catholic Indians became more acute when the Pope appointed the Propaganda Fide in 1662 to supervise all Roman Catholic missionary activities overseas. This internal rivalry between the Padroado and Propaganda Fide was to occupy the Roman Catholics for a very long time. In this context, English, Dutch, French and Danish East India companies began to establish their colonies in different parts of India. Some of their company chaplains (e.g. Abraham Roger and Philip Baldaeus of Netherlands in Tamil speaking South India), made some attempts to introduce their understanding of Christian faith to Indians. However, their efforts remained largely fruitless till the arrival of the Royal Danish Missionaries in 1706.

With the arrival of two young German pietistic students of theology from Halle, Bartholomäus Ziegenbalg and Henry Plutschau, sent by the Danish King Fredrick IV, in the small South Indian Danish colony known as Tranquebar (in Tamil: Tarangambadi, 'village of singing/ dancing waves') on July 9, 1706, a new Protestant missionary era began in India. Their pioneer works in preaching the Gospel of Jesus Christ in Tamil language, their scientific research of belief systems and social behavior patterns of the Tamils, their efforts to establish indigenous churches in and around Tranquebar, especially in many strategic centers of South India (in cities like Madras, Tanjore, Tiruchirappali and Palayamkottai), their contribution to education of school children along with the training of pastors had far reaching effects. The Tranquebar missionary luminary, Christian F. Schwartz (1726–1798), played an important role making South Indian politics stable, when the authorities of Madras Presidency tried to usurp the authority of local Tamil princes. Changed Protestant religious attitude in Great Britain by the end of 18th century, the exemplary works of missionaries Schwartz in South India and William Carey in North West India made the English East India Company in 1833 to grant permission to European Protestant mission agencies to carry out their missionary work in India. LELM was one of the mission agencies to enter India. This essay is an attempt to trace how some Tamil Christians belonging to LELM tried to be missionaries in East (in Tanzania) and in West (in Myanmar, earlier known as Burma).

II

LELM was/ is a missionary organization with a long pre-history. In 1819, a Society for Mission Help (in German: 'Missionshilfsverein') was founded in Dresden, Germany. From 1839 it was known as Evangelical Lutheran Mission Society (ELMS) with a desire to be one single mission agency for all Lutheran Churches all over the world. When the Royal Danish Mission was unable to carry out its work after the death of its last missionary A.F. Cammerer in 1837, the ELMS sent Henry Cordes as their first missionary to India in 1840.

Cordes revived the Protestant missionary work among the Tamils in South India and upheld the missionary heritage of the Royal Danish Mission. Karl Graul, the first director of the ELMS from 1844, travelled through South India during 1849 to 1853. He realized the importance of missionary work among the Tamils. In 1856 the ELMS was transferred from Dresden to Leipzig and came to be known as the Leipzig Evangelical Lutheran Mission (LELM). After the mission work in South India was consolidated some mission friends in Leipzig desired to have a second place for missionary work. Much deliberation followed. It was decided to begin the work in Kilimanjaro in East Africa, which was then under the German colonial rule. Paul Fleisch, the historian of LELM narrates the beginning of the Lutheran mission in East Africa (1936, 265-269). In 1893, four missionaries – Gerhard Althaus, Emil Muller, Albin Bohme and Robert Fassmann – left Tanga and arrived in Madschame, Kilimanjaro to work under the leadership of a LELM missionary, Traugott Pasler († 22.4.1898), who was previously missionary among the Tamils in South India, was asked by LELM to find the Dschagga Mission in Kilimanjaro (Pasler 1894). It was a difficult task for the Lutheran missionaries, not to collaborate with the German military rule in Kilimanjaro and yet to be faithful to their German 'nation'. The tension between the loyalty to one's nation and independence of the mission was always felt. Moreover, Kilimanjaro had experienced some English influence because Rindi († 1891), the native leader of Moschi, had invited missionaries of Church Missionary Society (CMS) in London to work in his place; Hence Anglican missionaries such as Fitch, Wray and Steggal, began their work. The Anglican Bishop Tucker baptized two natives of Moschi in 1892. However, Rindi changed his mind and had invited the German troops to expel the English from his area. In an army encounter on June 10, 1892 the two English missionaries were killed. CMS gave its mission field to the LELM and left the place. The natives were very angry and destroyed the CMS mission houses in Moschi. At this time, the Roman Catholic missionaries established new mission stations in Kiboscho which was between Madschame and Moschi. In the fear that the Roman Catholic missionaries would occupy all the territory, the

Lutheran missionaries were quick to establish their mission centers in other areas. Pasler bought a place in Mamba on June 26, 1894 and made Althaus responsible for it. Johannes, the German military commander in Kilimanjaro, helped Pasler and his activities greatly.

Probably the native Africans seem to have refused to collaborate with the German missionaries in their early days. The refusal of the native workers and their apparent unwillingness to collaborate with those who had the assistance of colonial rulers (Muller 1895, 144) might have been the reason why Pasler was ready to accept the services of the Tamil Lutherans. Previously, Pasler had requested Karl von Schwartz, director of LELM 1891–1911, to allow a group of Tamil Lutherans to join him so that they could build houses with stones and bricks. In the Annual Reports of 1893 von Schwartz mentioned that he had permitted 12 Tamil masons and carpenters to travel from Madras through Bombay to Pasler in Madschame with the hope that they "would transplant a Tamil Church there" and enable the missionaries from the Church building activities to learn Schwaheli language (von Schwartz, 1983, 15). Von Schwartz may have thought that the Tamils would have been better equipped to erect a Church building in the first mission station of the LELM in Africa because the Lutherans in India, by this time, had a long tradition of their own.

The Protestant Christians in Yêrkâdu were known for their masonry works. Missionary O.R. Handmann narrated the history of the Protestant Church in Yêrkâdu in 1907: When missionary Lechler of London Missionary Society, who was working in the city of Salem, desired to have a house on a hill for his summer vacation, he employed Christian masons. After his sudden death in 1860, his widow sold her house Carton Cottage, two years later, to LELM for Rupees 3500. Missionary Herre who was deserted by the Basil Mission looked after the Church in Yêrkâdu and joined the LELM in 1865. In 1876 this house was sold, and a new large property called Lutherpet ('Place of Luther') was bought for LELM. On the western side, a small Church and a school were constructed. Most of the Church members were masons and workers in coffee plantations (Handmann 1907, 450–452). Most of them were Pariah immigrants. In 1888 the Yêrkâdu congregation was annexed to the Lutheran congregation in Erode. Missionary Karl Pamperrien reported in 1890 that the Pariah Christians in Yêrkâdu could read and write; they wanted to buy books and send their children to school; they conducted family devotions regularly (Pamperrien 1891, 311). It is also possible that these Tamil Christians who were invited to Tanzania were also involved in the building of the Lutheran Church in Yêrkâdu as they were professional builders.

In January 1895, missionary Muller justified the need for a stone house for them with the argument that the natives used to build only small insecure huts with bamboo and banana leaves which failed miserably to give protection. Muller explained further as to how a tiger and a leopard killed the cattle reared on the mission compound near the big forest kept in weak stables (Muller 1895, 146). It shows that the missionaries did not pay attention to how the natives lived or built their houses and kept their cattle safe. Pasler reported yet another reason: The German military had employed all the people in Moschi to build a fort (Pasler 1894). So, there was a shortage of work force to build houses for missionaries who were also busy in finding a second center for their missionary activities in Mamba. As a result, they expected that Tamil Christians could help them solve their problems.

III

It is interesting that the Lutheran masons and carpenters who know the art of building houses with stones on hills offered themselves to go to Moschi. According to an annual report the twelve Tamil Christians reached Moschi on June 21, 1894 under the leadership of Catechist Zacharias, who had left his wife in Yêrkâdu. The three masons were brothers of the same family: Sinnappen was married to Thanam and Joseph to Marial. Rajappen was single . The children of the married couple, the nephew Isaiah of the three brothers and their cook Jesudasan accompanied them. The long travel and cold African hill climate affected their health so much that they were mostly sick (Pasler 1894). Six days later they began their work in Mkika so that

Pasler could settle down there. After a few days they left this place and returned to Moschi. With the help of about 150 Swahelis they dug a canal to bring water to the mission station. The Swahelis were quick in building huts while the Tamils were unable. After July 19, 1894, the missionaries showed them the place to erect a stone house and a shed. On July 25, 1894, they began to build a house; within nine days they laid the foundation. Zacharias was willing not only to supervise the entire project with co-operation, but also to learn Swaheli language. Pasler conducted Sunday Services for the Tamils in July and August and so they were very happy. What the Tamils have built is said to have been the first stone house in Moschi. On November 11, 1894 Pasler left Mamba Ashira along with Isaiah and cook Jesudasan. While Pasler proceeded to Germany, Isaiah and Jesudasan sailed back to India.

After their work was over in Moschi, the Tamils proceeded further. Muller reported that six Tamil Christians and their families had arrived in Madschame on January 18, 1895 in order to build large, strong stone houses. The German missionaries were unable to converse with them because the Tamil Christians did not understand either English or German. However, Catechist Zacharias knew some English and became the mediator. As a gesture of welcoming the Tamils the missionaries slaughtered a goat. The very presence of Tamil Christians influenced the native Africans so much that they came forward to assist them in their building projects. Even the village chief who was hesitant to support the missionaries earlier became friendly, offered spontaneous assistance and ensured that no one disturbed them (Muller 1895, 145). It seems that despite the language barrier, the Tamils and Swahelis understood each other and worked together as partners.

It was reported that Isaiah and Marial were suffering from tuberculosis. With the help of a German medical doctor Kretschmer there was improvement for Isaiah. On the other hand, Marial's condition deteriorated so much that the young lady born around 1869 died on October 5, 1895, that too on the first anniversary of the beginning of mission station in Madschame. The Tamils prepared the coffin while the Swahelis carried it to the grave. Though the Tamils were weak they made the first 'sacrifice' to find the Lutheran Church in Madschame. Althaus noted that this event meant a "notable coincidence: The first Tamil Christian woman from the high Servarayan Hills became the first 'seed' that the missionaries 'deposited' on the height of Kilimanjaro in the hope of glorious resurrection." (Althaus 1795, 15). Kiesel, the archivist of the Northern Diocese of the Evangelical Lutheran Church in Tanzania based in Moschi, explains the importance of Marial to the Lutheran Church in Africa: "Marial died from TB in Mama-Ashira on October 10,1894 and was buried the day after by Rev. Althaus. This is the first Christian burial and the first Christian grave and the beginning of the cemetery in the Lutheran Church of North Tanzania."

IV

After the completion of their three-year contract, the Tamils wanted to return home. LELM director von Schwartz had already given them permission to depart. They packed their things on June 27, 1897 and left Moschi on the next day to Tanga, and from there to Madras via Bombay. The editor of the ELMB summarized his opinion of the Tamil mission in Africa:

> It was a pleasant coincidence that with the founding of Dschagga-Mission the elder sister, namely the Tamil Mission, rendered a helpful hand. After the arrival of Tamil Christians in Mamba on June 21, 1894 they built mission houses on three hill stations, namely Mamba, Madschame and Moschi and helped to erect other smaller buildings. This work was not easy for them in the beginning because they were mostly sick; and they had complained of it in their letters. Sometimes the masons troubled the missionaries with their desire for strife and misconduct. However, they remained three years; with their Tamil way of Church service and Church customs they were examples to the non-Christians there [in Tanzania] and with their manual work they helped to find the Church on those high hills. We are grateful to them (Fassmann, 1897, 352).

For the new Lutheran mission in Africa the Tamil Lutheran Christians gave an example: Christian life consisted not only of mere faith, but also of practical work that was done for the welfare of others. What

happened to the Tamil Christians from Tanzania is not known. It is
informed of Zacharias that he had built a chapel in the new mission
station of LELM in Pandur near Madras (Dachselt, 1898, 318). However,
their influence was not forgotten: In 1913 August Schreitmuller, an
artist in Dresden, sculptured a wooden crucifix for the small chapel
in the mission house of LELM in Paul-List-Straße 19 in Leipzig. The
Government of Saxony presented it to LELM on March 16, 1915. On
the left it depicts a Tamil woman carrying a baby in her arms as she
is standing and turning her head to look at the face of the crucified
Jesus Christ. On the right it portrays a standing *Dschagga* warrior with
his very long spear. Both pay their homage to Jesus Christ in their
own way-following the relationship that was started in 1894. Every
visitor to the chapel in LELM can witness this monument beckoning
not only the North-South mission relationship, but also South-South
mission partnership.

V

Tamil Christians made their missionary presence in Rangoon, the
capital of Myanmar. When about 70 Tamil Lutherans from Madras
emigrated to Rangoon in 1878, missionary A. Mayr followed them and
tended them spiritually. In 1886 there were 131 Tamil Christians in
the Tamil Lutheran Church in Rangoon. After their first Tamil pastors
Devasirwadam and Devasirvatham (†1890) and Mayr had returned
to Germany another Tamil Pastor David of Mayavaram (ordained in
1884) took charge of Rangoon mission station in 1890 and worked
there until 1904. Under the leadership of David, the number of Tamil
Christians grew rapidly. In 1895, there were 259 members. For David
it was not an easy task to sustain a self-financing Church in a foreign
city where there were no European missionaries. During this time the
Government authorities in Rangoon did everything to take over the
mission land close to the railway station, originally acquired by Mayr.
He got this large property to make the Church a self-financing one.
Missionary Johann Kabis rushed to the spot, received the help of
German Consul G. Vetter and solved the problem in April 1892. The

LELM missionaries were determined to safeguard the mission property which was situated in the heart of Rangoon, an emerging 'world city'. Pastor David played an important role to consolidate the mission work in Rangoon. There was no European missionary to help him. Yet he managed the mission affairs well (Kabis 1893, 427–430). In Rangoon he looked after the Church, taught in the school, collected rent from the mission houses built by Mayr as they were rented to Tamils of different castes, and sent accounts to Tranquebar. David informed that he was working among Tamil immigrants who lived there for several decades without any hope of returning to their homes; due to homesickness and loneliness in a faraway country many Church members became alcoholics. To reach Hindus with the Gospel of Jesus Christ, he undertook the superintendence of a Tamil-English school on an island where six Lutherans were living and working with the railways (Pamperrien 1891, 326–332).

David was interested in collecting statistics on the number of Christians belonging to different denominations. In 1891, he provided approximate number of Buddhists, Muslims and Christians (Roman Catholics, Armenians, Greek Orthodox, Baptists, Anglicans, Presbyterians, Methodists, Wesleyans, and Lutherans). His main concern was to know the presence and strength of different Christian denominations, to see his own Lutheran mission as part of the larger Christian mission and to devise plans to increase Lutheran missionary enterprise. In 1893, he visited his Diaspora Lutherans in the place called Malmein. They were unaware of distinctive Lutheran teachings but were willing to collaborate with any Christian institution. David felt that a presence of an European Lutheran missionary would help the Lutherans to begin mission work in unreached areas (David 1891, 109). He built 85 houses and rented them to families of all caste backgrounds. However, he concentrated his efforts on school children. He rebuilt the old school and admitted 110 school children. When the newly renovated school was dedicated on April 8, 1894 Van Someren Pope, the 'Director of Public Schools in Burma', himself was present and spoke of the importance of the school. Pastor David did not forget his Tamil cultural tradition: he garlanded every European who was present on this occasion; but for the Tamils he distributed Betel leaves and Areck nuts, which are considered very important for any festive occasion (David 1894, 317). The church members in Rangoon were well pleased with their pastor and the new school. When missionaries Kabis and Pomperrien visited this school in March-April 1895 they were delighted to be with David and his church. It was told that David was an upright, soft-spoken man with spiritual zeal and knew several languages including German and thus could gain the love, respect and trust of native people. David was acquainted with German and German Lutheran liturgy so well that he could hold divine services in German. The Editor of the ELMB told a story that a mother who was praying for missionary work was amazed to find that her son was converted in another land by the missionary for whom she was praying. Similarly, the Tamil Christian David rendered help to the German Lutherans in Burma by conducting divine services and by baptizing German children. The Editor expressed his wish that all the German Lutherans living overseas should be mindful of their high calling and think of the words of Jesus Christ encouraging his disciples to live like lights of the world.

The Editor of the ELMB was happy to communicate the good news to his readers that it was always the German Lutheran missionaries who were willing to serve non-Germans. When a non-German Christian pastor was ready to serve the German Lutherans living overseas it was a significant development. Should the German Lutherans desire to benefit more from Indian Christians, they will receive more blessing. Thus, the Protestant mission enterprise in India during the 19th century was spreading from one country to another and also benefited those who had been sending missionaries. Mission is and will remain an encounter that will benefit both the sender and the receiver.

References

Althaus, Gerhard: Nachrichten von der Station Mamba (Aus Miss. Althaus' Tagebuch 26. Aug. bis 10. Oktober [1894]). In: ELMB, Nr. 1, January 1895, 10–19.

_____. Neueste Nachrichten von der Station Mamba (Auszug aus dem Tagebuch des Br. Althaus', Januar '95). In: ELMB, Nr. 8, April 1895, 147–149.

Dachselt, E.: Eindrücke von einer Reise durch den Madras-Landbezirk, In: ELMB, Nr. 16, August 1898, 317–319.

Das Kilimandscharo-Gebirge in Ostafrika (mit Bild), In: ELMB, Nr. 1, January 1894, 8–13.

David, D.: Ein Blick in die Missionsarbeit in Barma, In: ELMB, Nr. 6, 15. März 1894, 109–114.

_____. Die Einweihung des neuen Schulgebäudes in Rangun, In: ELMB, Nr. 17, 1. September, 1894, 317–319.

_____. Deutscher Taufgottesdienst durch einen Tamulenpastor, In: ELMB, Nr. 21, 1. November, 1895, 396–397.

Faßmann, Robert: Heimkehr der Tamulen - Bericht von Miss. Faßmann in Moschi, In: ELMB, 1897, 352–354.

Fleisch, Paul D.: *Hundert Jahre lutherischer Mission*, Leipzig, Verlag der Evangelisch-lutherischer Mission, 1936.

Handmann, O. R.: Ein Ferienaufenthalt in Ierkâd (Mit Bildern), In: ELMB, Nr. 19, October 1907, 446–452.

Inder außerhalb Indiens missionierend, In: ELMB, Nr. 1, January 1893, 24.

Kabis, Johann: Gesamtbericht über die evang.-luth. Mission in Indien während des Jahres 1892, In: ELMB, Nr. 22, November 1893, 423–4430.

Kiesel, Klaus Peter: Collection of (unpublished) materials from Mr. Klaus Peter Kiesel [Archivist, KKKT ND Archives of Northern Diocese, Moschi] of Tansania. File No. 25 Bundle No. 1. Lutheran Heritage Archives in Gurukul Lutheran Theological College & Research Institute in Chennai (Madras).

Moritzen, Niels-Peter: *Werkzeug Gottes in der Welt — Leipziger Mission 1836 – 1936 – 1986*, Erlangen, Verlag der Ev.-luth. Mission, 1986.

Müller, Emil: Neueste Nachrichten von Madschame, In: ELMB, Nr. 8, April 1895, 144–147.

Pamperrien, K.: Gesamtbericht über die evangelisch-lutherische Mission in Indien während des Jahres 1890, In: ELMB, Nr. 20, October 1891, 305–312 und Nr. 21, 1. November 1891, 321–332.

Päsler, Traugott und Robert Faßmann: Neueste Nachrichten vom Kilimandscharo, In: ELMB, Nr. 2, January 1894, 21–27.

_____. und Gerhard Althaus: Die Anlegung einer zweiten Station auf dem Kilimandscharo, In: ELMB, Nr. 20, October 1894, 381–384 und Nr. 22, November 1894, 422–425.

Sargant, N.C.: *The Dispersion of the Tamil Church*, Revised and enlarged Edition (First published in 1940), Delhi, Indian Society for Promoting Christian Knowledge, 1962.

Taufe deutscher Zwillinge durch einen tamulischen Pastor [David], in: ELMB, Nr. 8, 15. April, 1898, 148–150.

Von Schwartz, Karl: *15. Jahresbericht der Leipziger Mission über das Jahr 1893*, Leipzig, Ev.-luth. Missionsverlag, 1893.

From Cane Cutters to Church Planters:

The Story of the Indian Church in South Africa

Godfrey Harold

Too often there is a misconception that Indians only arrived in South Africa around the 1860s. However, research by Frank R Bradlow and Margaret Cairns (1978) indicated that almost 70 percent of the slaves at the Cape (from the time of Jan van Reibeek in 1652 to British occupation of the Cape) came from Asia and more than a third from India (including what is Bangladesh today). The majority of the Indian slaves originated in Bengal, the Malabar Coast (Mumbai and Goa) and the Coromandel Coast. Over a period of almost 150 years, thousands of Indian slaves were brought to the Cape of Good Hope.

After the abolishment of slavery in 1833 by the British Parliament, there was a dearth of labour to develop the British Empire's rapidly expanding colonies. To fill this demand, indentured labourers from India were transported to British overseas colonies under five and ten-year indenture contracts, with the option to return to India or exchange their free passage for a piece of land. Due to harsh taxation policies, famine, industrialisation and a repressive administration, India was in the midst of a socio-economic crisis (Tharoor 2017) and many Indians were brought to the British colony of Natal in 1860 as indentured labourers and *coolies* on five-year contracts. Indians came to work mainly on sugar plantations where they lived under very harsh and cruel conditions, often referred to as 'new system of slavery' (Tinker 1974).

The first ship to arrive on the shores of Natal was the Turo on 16 November 1860 and the last ship Umlazi was Natal on 11 July 1911. The embarkation ports in India where the most indenture laborers came were Madras and Calcutta. All together, 152,184 indentures Indians were brought in 384 trips in various shipping vessels over a period of over fifty years to primarily work on the sugar cane plantations of KwaZulu-Natal. After five years, they were given the options of renewing their contracts, returning to India or becoming independent workers. To induce the *coolies* into a second term of indenture, the colonial government of Natal promised grants of land on expiry of contracts. However, the colony did not honour this agreement, and only about fifty people received plots. Nevertheless, many opted for freedom and became small holders, market gardeners, fishermen, domestic servants, waiters or coal miners. Some left the colony and went elsewhere. By the 1870s, free Indians were exploring opportunities in the Cape Colony, the Orange Free State and the South African Republic (Transvaal). Those who sought to make their fortunes in the diamond and gold fields were not allowed digging rights and became traders, hawkers and workers.

The continued importation of indentured labour until 1911, though sporadic, encouraged opportunistic traders and merchants from India and Mauritius to emigrate to South Africa. These independent immigrants, known as "passenger" Indians, began arriving in the country from about 1875. Many of them quickly acquired land and set up businesses and trading posts. When their enterprises began to encroach on white settlements, laws and regulations were passed to limit their expansion and acquisition of land. Immigrants living in the Republics, unlike those in the British colony of Natal, were not enfranchised and were not welcome in the Republics and laws were passed to contain their growth and development.

Among the indentured labourers that came to South Africa from 1860-1911, almost 6000 were Christians (nearly 4 percent). Out of the 342 passengers on the first shipment of indenture laborers to Natal on board the ship SS Turo, 60 adults and 30 children were classified as Christians under the category of caste in the passenger records. In fact, the first two families on the list were Christians and believed to be first ones to step out from the ship to Natal. Their names were Davarum (30 years) with wife Nagium (18 years) and two children aged 4 and 2, along with Abraham (38 years) and Sarah (30 years) with four children aged 10, 8, 5 and 2 years old (SAHO). They were from Madras (now Chennai) and legend has it that when most Indian passengers were fearful of stepping into, what was then believed as a land of savages, Davaram took his Tamil Bible and bravely stepped on to the African soil.

The next section will reflect on the growth of the Indian Christian community in South Africa, focusing on two pionerring works namely the Indian Baptist Mission (now divided into Baptist Association of South Africa and the Baptist Mission in South Africa), and the South African General Mission (now called the Evangelical Church in South Africa). Bethesda is now incorporated into the Full Gospel Church in South Africa which was the fastest-growing branch of the Indian Church in the late 1970s and 80s in South Africa. These two denominations are chosen because of their pioneering enterprise among the Indians but, these two denominations still maintain its historical genesis. As per the official census community survey of 2016, nearly 1.4 million people are identified as Indian/Asian (2.5 percent of the total population) and over 873 thousand of them live in KwaZulu-Natal alone (8 percent). Nearly one-quarter percent of the Indian population in South Africa are deemed to be Christians, while Hindus are less than half and Muslims make nearly a quarter with 3 percent belonging to other religious groups (StatSA).

Indian Christians in South Africa

Many consider that European missionary efforts gave birth to the Christian faith among the indentured Indians in South Africa. One only must study the movement of Christianity in India to understand that this is not true. Traditionally it is believed that Apostle Thomas brought Christian message to Kodungalloor, Kerala in 52 CE and was killed in Mylapore, near Chennai in 72 CE. This Christian community survived over centuries but remained as favored minority group amidst other religious and political conditions in Southern India. When European colonies were established in India, renewed missionary efforts were made to reach native people with the Gospel of Jesus Christ. By the 1800s there were many Protestant movements in India (Hough 1860). Many of the Indian Christians who were brought from the port of Chennai to port Natal were already Christians and had a strong understanding of their Christian faith.

Most Indian Protestant Christians who worked on tea or sugar cane plantations would have been ministered by the church that the estate owner attended as in the case with Sir Hullets in Stanger who was a Methodist, however a need to be ministered in their own vernacular language gave rise to two pioneering works amongst the Indians which is discussed below.

The Evangelical Church in South Africa

The first missional attempt to penetrate the greater Indian community with the gospel was in 1882 when Dr. Andrew Murray of South Africa speaking at a Keswick, UK invited Willian Spencer Walton to come to South Africa. In 1882 Dr. Andrew Murray and Mr. Spencer Walton gave rise to the Cape General Mission, with Mr. Walton becoming its first director and Dr. Andrew its first President. During this time another Mission was organized in Natal called the Southeast Africa Evangelistic Mission, with its headquarter in Durban. In 1884 The Cape General Mission and the Southeast Evangelistic Mission amalgamated forming the South African General Mission (SAGM). In 1896, Spencer Walton took up residence in Durban to work among the Indians. Mahatma Gandhi spoke affectionately of Spencer Walton "When I was in Durban, Mr. Walton the head of the SAGM found me out, I almost became a member of his family...this friendship kept alive my interest in religion" (McLewin and McLewin 1970).

Two ladies also offered themselves – Miss M. Day and Miss E. Hargreaves who commenced studying the Tamil language in Durban. On Sunday mornings they would hold meetings in the barracks where Indian people lived. Initially, much of their sharing the Gospel was done through interpretation (Engles and McLewin 1970). In 1898 these ladies found an opening to share the Gospel on a sugar estate near Phoenix. A house and a chapel were made available to them where they formed the Hope Mission Station. They soon commenced a school and had over 50 pupils.

In 1901, the SAGM began its work among the Telugu speaking Baptist. The meetings were in the barracks of the Africa Boating Company, Point Road, Durban. The same year a young man of about 24 years walked into the office of the mission in Durban with a letter addressed to Dr. Andrew Murray. He was Nelson Tomlinson from Australia. Upon interviewing him, Spencer Walton found out that Tomlinson was born in India and could speak the Telugu language well and that he seemed to be the perfect answer to prayer for a missionary to work amongst the Indians. However, Nelson Tomlinson felt called to work amongst the Africans, so for a short time, he took a secular job. In the meantime, Mr. J. S. Young, a SAGM missionary who worked mainly among the soldiers and sailors in Durban invited Nelson Tomlinson to go with him to the Telugu quarters of the Point Barracks and interpret for him. The reception which they received from the Indian people was very heartening, especially when the Indians realised that a white man could speak their language so well. In 1902, Nelson Tomlinson married his fiancée also from Australia in Durban and in 1904, they became missionaries to the Indians until their retirement in 1949. Initially, they were stationed in Phoenix to start a school for Indian children. On seeing opportunities to witness to Indians in Durban, the Tomlinsons returned to Durban and while working there, he saw that many indentured laborers were reallocated to sugarcane plantations in the South Coast of KwaZulu-Natal.

While attending a conference in Port Shepstone, Tomlinson discovered that some Indians have been in South Africa for over forty years and never heard the Gospel. Tomlinson had a vision of Indian churches like lighthouses along the South coast of KwaZulu-Natal. In 1910 Tomlinson moved to Umzinto 50 km South of Durban and the first Indian church of the South African General Mission was planted in 1910 and another church at Beneva was planted in 1913. The same year, a group of Christians in Illovo were praying for someone to come and help them and in 1915 a church was built at Illovo as well. The Indian ministry under the Tomlinson grew, with other churches being planted along the coast like Port Shepstone, Park Rynie and Sezela. Alongside these churches, mission schools were also brought into existence to educate the children of the community from both Christian and Hindu families (Engles and McLewin 1970).

Within 11 years of planting the first church, in 1921 the Indian church of SAGM held its first conference and by 1924 churches became financially independent, thus choosing T. Stephen to be its first treasurer and H. Samuel to be its secretary. Due to the work of evangelists like M. Timothy, P. Daniel, T.P Stephen, P. David and V. Peter despite the persecution that came their way, these men were resilient in spreading the Gospel of Jesus Christ. At the 1924 conference with a total of six churches in attendance, the conference decided: 1) To travel third class in order to save money, 2) At their own expense to build two rooms at the Port Shepstone church for missionary visitors, 3) To build a house at the Sezela church for evangelists, 4) They agreed to pay half the salary for every new evangelist, and 5) They undertook to financially support an evangelist working with the Muslims.

It did not take long for the Indian congregations to take financial accountability for each of its own churches. In 1951, the missionaries ceased to serve as officers of the denomination and in May 1966 gave complete autonomy to the Indian Church, thus constituting the Evangelical Church in South Africa (ECSA) with Andrew Kodi as its first president. Today, there are 30 self-administrated churches within the ECSA most with full time trained theological practitioners.

Indian Baptist Mission

In 1903, the Home Mission Society in India responding to a call from 150 Telugu speaking Baptist members led by Benjamin working in the tea plantation of Kearsney sent John Rangiah a qualified teacher and trained theologian from India to serve as their missionary (Nathaniel 1953, 12). Arriving on the shores of South Africa on 13 June with his wife and daughter, the Rangiah was greeted by Rev. Tomlinson of the SAGM. Nelson Tomlinson offered John Rangiah a home and an opportunity to work with SAGM. However, Rangiah understanding his call to work with the Indian Baptist in Kearsney arrived in Kearsney a few months later. The joy of Benjamin and others was indescribable because they did not know whether their correspondence reached the Home Mission, as they did not receive any letter alluding to the arrival of John Rangiah (Israel 2004).

Sir Hulett, the estate owner of the tea plantation, was impressed by John Rangiah that he offered the missionary family a ten- roomed bungalow set in an orchard of ten acres. Rangiah named the property Gospel Hill, appropriately, as for many years to come it sent the light of the gospel out to many. Hulett provided regular provisions and a stipend. The company and the home, in turn, provided shelter and care for the next three generations of missionaries (Israel 2004). The first Telugu Baptist Church was established on December 27,1903 with 64 members (Rangiah 1905, 2). From 1903 to 1906 eight churches were planted by John Rangiah, placing within these churches a leader to which its membership can look to for guidance (Paul 1991).

Church	Date Established	Pastor	Membership
Kearsney	December 27, 1903	John Rangiah	64
Verulam	May 2, 1904	K.Daniel	32
Darnall	June 12, 1904	B. Ellamanda	30
Durban	October 30, 1904	A. Reuben	30
Stanger	December 25, 1904	L.R. Frank	15
Tinley Manor	May 10, 1908	K.. David	12
Dundee	June 5, 1908	T.C.Tyler	21
Amatikulu	January 11, 1909	P.Reddy	12

Except for the pastor in Stanger, all the other workers were supported by their local churches. Combining his role as a minister and development worker, John Rangiah understood the need for education and with his experience of being a school principal in Nellore, John Rangiah began schools in the following areas Kearsney, Stanger, Tinley Manor and Amatikulu. These schools became state-aided school and government institution of primary education today (Rangiah 1964, 9). Due to the growth of the ministry in South Africa among Indians in the North Coast of KZN when Dr. David Downie from India visited Natal in 1909 Rangiah impressed on him the need for a second missionary. Rev. V.C. Jacob arrived in 1912, who led the Durban sector of the ministry. However, due to illness Rev. V.C. Jacob had to return to India.

The Spilt of 1914

There are number of reasons that have been alluded as to what gave rise to the spilt in 1914, some of which were the preaching against sin (which was misinterpreted as excommunication), the caste system, cost and the time spent in Scotland and that Rangiah lived a lavish life. On receiving a letter from a group of members led Y.A. Lazarus and A. Reuben, the Home Mission Society sent Dr. W.B. Bogges to investigate and resolve the dispute. A very lengthy meeting chaired by Dr. Bogges to discuss the allegations began at 19:30h on May 30, 1914 and ended at 20:00h the following day led to no resolution between the parties. Bogges ruled in favour of the dissenting group (Paul 1991). Further attempts at solving the problems did not succeed. Rangiah's resignation as a missionary from HMS was accepted on the September 29, 1914 from its membership. A split was inevitable. During December 26 and 27, 1914 of the eleven churches, eight remained with John Rangiah thus forming the Natal Indian Telegu Baptist Association (NITBA) now the Baptist Association of South Africa. And the other three maintaing its relatioship with HMS as the Indian Baptist Mission.

Today, it is is known as the South African Baptist mission with 10 churches in its jurisdiction. In 1915, Rangiah's health gradually detiorated and his good friend Nelson Tomilison took over his preaching appointments. John Rangiah died on December 23,1915. The same Rev. V.C Jacob that retuned to India due to ill health, on the request of Y.A Lazurus, J.H. Batts and Ruben Eliza requested that Rev. V.C. Jocob return to South Africa to continue the work of the Indian Baptist Mission. On December 13, 1915, Jacob arrived in Kwazulu Natal (Jacob and Cornelius 1964, 13). These two Baptist ministries namely, The Baptist Association of South Africa and Baptist Mission of South Africa still have a very strong presense within the Indian community in South Africa, predominately in the province of KwaZulu-Natal.

Many other missionaries from India came to work with the Baptist Association in South Africa namely: T. M Rangiah, the son of the late John Rangiah, (who at the tender age of 10 was sent back to India to get a better basic and tertiary education) returned to Durban on March 5, 1921, and like his father was met by Rev. Thomilson and a delegation from NITBA (Nathaniel 1953, 36). After the death of T. M. Rangiah in 1947, Rev. David Newton Nathaniel and his family arrived in Durban in 1951. The unique aspects of the Indian Baptist work in South Africa is that the ministry from its onset was led by Indians from India who were supported by local churches. Thus each church planted were self supporting churches which are still gathering today.

These poineer works among the indentured Indian namely the Evangelical Church of South Africa and the Indian Baptist Mission, became the umbilical chord through which other works among the Indian community flourished. The Apostolic Faith Mission amongst the Indians had its genesis from members of Darnal Baptist Church in the early 1930s (Reddy 1992, 63-53) and Bethesda under the leadership of J.F. Rowland began his work among the Indians in Durban with familes from Somseau Road Baptist Church in Durban. The Pentecostal churches became so active that between 1925 and 1980 the Indian membership of the Pentecostal churches grew larger than all the other Christian denominations put together (Pillay 1997). In the early 1990s Bethesda merged with the Full Gospel Church in

South Africa, this still has the largest membership of church goers within the Indian community and the Indian division of the AFM became part of AFM South Africa.

The two pioneering denominations, ECSA and IBM without any help from the government of the day built mission schools to uplift its communities through evangelism and social engagement and set the tone of what it is to be on mission with God. The impact of the Christians on the Hindu faith was noticably observerd by P. Kumar "Hindu leaders in South Africa saw conversion as a threat to their faith. At its 1918 council meeting, the Hindu Maha Sabha, a council established by various Hindu organizations, urged all Hindu parents to protest the religious instruction given at the Christian mission schools" (2016). Apart from other Indepedent churches within the Indian community, the two pioneering work still maintans its independendence and are still led soley by South Africans of Indian descent.

Conclusion

From humble beginnings as indentured laborers on sugar cane farms and tea plantations, the Christian witness impacted every sphere of the South African community up to this very day. Some of the largest churches in South Africa are within the Indian community. Indian churches did not only receive missionaries but now are the ones sending missionaries to India, China Malaysia, Philippines, other countries in the continent of Africa are reciepnts of Christian workers soley from Indian supported churches. Indian Christians impacted South Africa politicalty through the Natal Indian Congress, that Mahatma Ghandhi founded, as a forum to engage social justice issues in South Africa. Christians in South Africa today impact every sphere of the South African land scape e.g. Business, Economy, Health, Education, Law and Politics just to name a few. From a meager 4 percent of Christians among Indians in South Africa between 1860-1911 to current 24 percent of Indians are Christians in South Africa. Indeed, from cane cutters to church planters and social transformers is the story of the Indian Christians in South Africa.

References

Brain, J.B., 1983, *Christian Indians in Natal 1860–1911. An Historical and Statistical Study*, Cape Town: Oxford University Press.

Engles, W. and Mc Lewin HR. 1970, *The Evangelical Church in South Africa (formerly SAGM) A Short History*. Durban: Mercantile Printers

Hough, TGP (ed) 1860, *The History of Christianity in India*. Edinburgh: John Greg and Sons.

Frank R Bradlow and Margaret Cairns 1978. *The Early Cape Muslims. Cape Town:AA Balkema.*

Israel NM 2004, "John Rangiah and a Century of Indian Baptist Work" A paper presented at the Baptist `World Alliance, Seoul Korea, July 2004.

Jacob A and Conelius JP, 1964. *Indian Baptist Mission, Golden Jubilee*. Durban: Coastal Printers.

Kumar, P. Pratap. 2016, "Behind God Swoping in the South African Indian Community". https://theconversation.com/behind-the-god-swapping-in-the-south-african-indian-community-part-1-60954 Viewed Febrauary 10, 2017.

Nathaniel David 1953, NIBA News: Founder's Golden Jubilee Vol. ¼ 1903-1953. Durban: Mercantile Printers.

Paul, Timothy. 1991, *From Telugu Baptist Church to Open Church: A Stydy of the Indian Baptist Missionary Enterprise in South Africa (1903-1989)*. University of Durban Westville: Unpublished PhD Thesis.

Pillay, Gerald. 1997. *Christianity in South Africa: A Political, Social and Cultural History*. Cape Town: David Philips.

Ragwan, Rodney. 2010, *The Narrative of The Baptist Association of South Africa and its Significance for Indian Baptist Church in KwaZulu Natal*. University of Pretoria: Unpublished PhD Thesis.

Reddy Dean. 1992. *The Apostolic Faith Mission of South Africa with special reference to itsa rise and development in the "Indian "Community*. University of Durban, Westville: Unpublished PhD Thesis.

Rangiah, John. 1905, The First Annual Report of the Telugu Baptist Mission, South Africa. Madras: Madras ME Press.

SAHO – South African History Online. Indian Indentured Labour in Natal 1860-1911. www.sahistory.org.za/article/list-passenger-truro-16-november-1860 Viewed August 1, 2017.

Statistics South Africa Community Survey 2016. http://www.statssa.gov.za/publications/03-01-06/03-01-062016.pdf Viewed August 1,2017.

Tharoor, Shashi. 2017, *Inglorious Empire* United Kingdom: C. Hurst and Co.

Tinker, Hugh. 1974. *A New System of Slavery: The Export of Indian Labour Overseas 1830-1920*. London: Oxford University Press.

The People of South Africa: Indian South Africans https://reprobate.co.za/the-people-of-south-africa-indian-south. Viewed 15 January 2017. Viewed 20 February 2017.

Crossing *Kala Pani:*
Overcoming Religious Barriers to Migration

Sam George

Introduction

I was born in the Andaman and Nicobar Islands, an archipelago in the Bay of Bengal south-east of India. It is well-known for its scenic beaches, tropical rainforest and coral reefs. It is a popular tourist destination and often called as the Hawaii of India. It is nearer to other countries such as Thailand, Myanmar and Indonesia than India itself. It was a British and Japanese colony before its eventual independence to become a Union Territory of India.

In the early 1950s, when there were very little job prospects in Central Kerala, my dad left his hometown for the nearest big city of Madras (now called Chennai) looking for a gainful employment. After living there for a few months, he heard about employment opportunities in the Indian government service in the Andaman Islands. Surprisingly, he found that most people did not risk sailing across the seas for a job as the Islands were considered as a death sentence during the colonial era.

The Andaman Islands were a penal settlement during the British Raj for Indian convicts, political enemies and worst of the Indian freedom fighters, and were sent to the infamous jail in the Islands. Its location, being far from mainland along with the strong currents and shark infested waters surrounding it, made it as a high-security prison and impossible to escape from. The Andaman Islands were known as *Kala Pani* (meaning black waters in Hindi) and made famous through an award winning Indian movie.[1]

The concept of *Kala Pani* emerges from Hindu religious restrain on crossing any seas, caste demotion resulting from religious pollution, and social ostracization people experienced upon crossing large bodies of water. In this paper, I explore various civilizational concepts that kept people of South Asia rooted in place and resistant to migration. It begins with a brief migratory history and identifies select religious ideas that prevented large scale long distance long term migration of people of the Indian subcontinent. Then, it analyzes how such a migrant resistant people overcame these conventional notions to become one of the largest and most dispersed diasporic people in the world today.

History of South Asian Migration

Although human migration is as ancient as human beings themselves, migration out of the Indian subcontinent was sparse and far in between as compared to its population until recent times . Historians have claimed that from the ancient times people of the Indian subcontinent had maintained clear lines of communication with West Asia, Mediterranean region, Central Asia, China, Tibet and Southeast Asia (Lal 2006; Sowell 1992; Basham 1952; Cohen 1997 and Kadekar 2009). Stephen Neill claimed that factors of geography kept the subcontinent isolated over long periods of time from the rest of the world (1970, 11). The mountain ranges in the north and oceans in the south were natural barriers to human migration to and out of this region. It has

---

1 *Kaalapani* is regarded as one of the classics in Malayalam cinema and written and directed by Priyadarshan (1996). It was later dubbed in Hindi as *Saza-E-Kala Pani*, Tamil as *Siraichalai*, and in Telugu as *Kaala Pani*.

been only through the passes of the northwest frontier that most invaders have reached the subcontinent such as Aryans, Alexander the Great and Moghul Emperors.

Most early migratory interactions were initiated by foreigners and foreign rulers for trade, conquest, political or other reasons and resulted in taking people out of this region. Most early migration to and out of the subcontinent was land based over the ancient Indus Valley region (modern Pakistan and Northwestern India) and Indo-China region in the East (modern Myanmar and Thailand).

The discovery of monsoon winds boosted the influx of distant merchants to Southern India and Ceylon, without having to undertake circuitous coast hugging voyages along Arabia and Persia. The Jewish presence in India predates Christianity, while Chinese and Arab sailors came to India for spices in the later centuries. The devout pilgrims visited holy places such as Kailash Mansarovar and Haridwar, and scholars came to learning centers like Taxila. The Muslim merchants and conquerors took their converts on Haj pilgrimage to Mecca and European colonist took subjects back to their land as servants, soldiers or trophies. Some were taken as slaves or as indentured laborers to work in plantations and factories after the abolition of slavery. The artisans were hired for their skills and merchants ventured to trade centers to buy and sell for profit.

Since the ancient times, the South Asians did not venture too far out of the habitations over land or sea. They were not enterprising enough to find ways to fly over mountains in the north or sail far beyond its long coastlines. The South Asian region comprised of hundreds of small kingdoms who kept fighting between themselves and never dreamt of conquering or ruling lands far away. They were easy victims to foreign invaders, who took advantage of their great diversity and exploited its rich natural resources and people. The limited modes of transportations were a major constraint to distances people could travel as most people lived in villages and depended upon local agriculture. Some exceptions were the coastal communities of Malabar and Coromandel who were involved in limited maritime activities and caravan cotton textile trade links to the Silk Road, the Middle East and East Africa. Furthermore, the people of South Asian region lacked the technological advances in automotive, ship building, aeronautics and communications as compared to the Arabs, Chinese or the Western European counterparts. They might not have lacked in courage but did not possess any imperial aspirations or had the means to undertake overseas voyages. At the heart of this resistance to migration lies people's captivity to certain civilizational beliefs and worldviews as they were imprisoned to religious ideas and feared religio-social consequence of nonconformity.

Of course, there are several exceptions among South Asians who have ventured abroad. Buddhism originated in India and spread to Ceylon, Southeast Asia, China and elsewhere through the travel of its adherents. After his conversion, Emperor Ashoka is believed to have sent out Buddhist missionary monks to many parts of Asia and Buddhist traders were found even as far as Alexandria in Egypt back in the first century (Rawilson 1952). Also, *Jatakas* makes references to Buddhist merchants and their adventures on voyages to distant countries. *The Periplus of the Erytherian Sea* by Alexandrian sea captain at the time of Emperor Nero mentions about his travel to India in the first century. Another major imperial kingdom was the Chola Empire in southern India who had ruled the Sumatra, Malaysia and many parts of Southeast Asia by conquering the Indian Ocean. I would argue that reason behind their adventurous explorations overseas is breaking out of Hindu religious constraints of crossing seas.

Other exceptions of smaller migrant communities in India are Malayalam speaking Mappilas and Tamil speaking Chulias, who were descendants of early Arabs and Persians who had intermarried locally and were traders or sailors by profession. They were Islamic in faith and did not have constraints of sailing across seas. The Hindu communities who went abroad were often despised by higher caste and orthodox Hindus for transgressing rules of *Kala Pani*. They include: Chettiars from Tamil Nadu whose main activities were trade and moneylending and firmly established their presence in Burma and Southeast Asia;

and Gujaratis were another major trader along the western coast of India and was disrupted by the arrival of Portuguese in the Indian Ocean in 1498, and the attempts of Dutch and British to dominate India's textile export. The earliest arrival of Indians in the US dates back to December 29, 1790 and is an unnamed dark complexioned "a native of Indies from Madras" who sailed with Captain John Gibaut from the Malabar Coast in the Southern India (Bentley 1905, 228).

Religious Baggage: *Kala Pani, Punya Bhoomi,* Caste and Cremation

According to the Hindu beliefs (*Samudrolanghana*), traversing large expanses of water is often associated with contamination, defilement and loss of a "purified" Hindu essence. In Indian culture, this taboo of seas causes loss of varna or caste status and orthodox Hindus were forbidden to go across seas. The rationale behind is the inability to carry out the daily rituals and the sin of touch or contact with 'impure' foreigners. The sense of religious purity is compromised by crossing seas and such travels meant breaking family and communal ties. It was commonly related with expatriation of convicts, "low" castes, social pariahs, and other "undesirable" elements in society. This cultural and religious taboo kept South Asians from developing navigational technologies or shipbuilding industries and eventual failure to rise as a maritime power in the world.

The fear of crossing seas also derives from the notion that it entailed the end of the reincarnation cycle, as the traveler was cut off from the regenerating waters of the Ganges. British Governor General Lord Cornwallis advised his commanding officers 'to lessen and if possible to remove prejudice which Hindus of every description entertain against going to sea.' (Rai 2004, 12). When the British East India Company recruited high caste Hindu soldiers they had to adapt its military practices to religious requirements and the Bengal Army preferred to march to Chittagong by land than go by sea. The British found Sikhs better suited for military operations as sepoys in its vast empire and as foot soldiers in their various wars, primarily because they were less hesitant to cross[ing] seas than Hindus. The Colonial masters found it difficult to recruit indentured laborers because of these fears and developed a clever strategy of placing water from the Ganges in large cauldrons on the ships to ensure the continuity of reincarnation beyond the *Kala Pani*, making seas voyages less fearsome (Khan 2004, 123 and Lal 2006, 120).

According to Hindu mythology, the oceans are resting places for gods and they should not be disturbed. Those who venture out into oceans incur the wrath of gods and may face fierce demons and monsters. Both *Manusmriti* and *Dharma Sutra Baudhavana* specifically dissuades Brahmins from sea travels and if one did so, penance was very severe (Pathickal 2012, 1). *Manusmriti* (written circa 200 BCE) in chapter 3, verse 158 and *Baudhavana* in book two chapter 2 and verse 2 prohibit sea voyages. The loss of caste, denial of *shraddha* (annual appeasement of spirits and various rituals performed to pay homage to one's ancestors), social exclusion (sea travelers grouped with prisoners and prostitutes) and expenses incurred in penance on return were sufficient enough to keep Hindus landlocked for centuries.

Those who returned after polluting voyages were required to go through ritual purification before they could be accepted back into their communities. As a result, a disproportionately smaller number of Hindus as compared to other communities made such sacrilegious journeys and returned to India. When Swami Vivekananda returned after his first US tour after speaking about Hinduism at the 1892 World Parliament of Religions, he was considered impure by Hindu religious leaders in India for sailing across the Pacific Ocean. Similarly, Mahatma Gandhi's mother feared to let him go to London to study law and made him vow in the presence of a Jain monk that he will not touch meat, alcohol and a foreign woman. Upon his return to India from England in 1891, Gandhi had to go through ritual purifications to shed the pollution of foreign travel and readmission into his caste (Walpert 2004, 28). Similar accounts of return are recorded about Tagore and Ramanujan. Even today, Tirupati temple does not allow priests who have crossed seas to enter its sanctuary.

Kala Pani theme features prominently in Indo-Caribbean history and literature in English (Naipal 1969; Khan 1961; Selyon 1952 and others). These voices arising out of transatlantic voyages and indenture experience of the old diaspora vividly portrays scenes of departure from India, longing for home, arduous journeys and fears of no return. Similar discourse and psyche are embedded in some French writings as well (Banerjee 2010). The new diaspora writers of South Asian origin are many and varied in style and substance, and continue to bring out many of the diasporic realities of purity, displacement, intermingling, hybridity, pollution, identity, belonging, memory and longings of home, hopes of return etc. (Rushdie, Mukherjee and Lahiri).

The pollution from sea crossings also occurred because of inability to maintain dietary restrictions for Hindus. They could not eat fish or meat or anything containing blood but only vegetables and food prepared by non-Brahmins was a taboo as well. The early sea migrants were dependent on the cooked meagre rations given to them on-board of which salt fish was an important part. The long voyages over oceans over extended periods of time were problematic for strict vegetarians and meal times were a particularly traumatic experience daily. Sea sickness and vomiting only confirmed their fears and uneasiness over sea travels. After reaching their destinations, dietary restrictions and regional preferences underwent profound alterations on account of survival instincts and adaptation pressures in foreign lands.

Ensuing the African slave emancipation, the labor shortage in the west Indian sugar fields forced the 19th century European planters and British colonial government to transport indentured laborers from the Indian subcontinent to plantations as far as Surinam and Trinidad. Despite the fears of crossing the black waters, they wanted to escape from the abject poverty, severe famine, caste discrimination and colonial inflicted anguish to embrace the harsh realities of three months long ship journey across the Indian and Atlantic Ocean. During their voyages to distant destinations, the unknown co-passengers become *Jahaji Bhai* (ship brother), a form of brotherhood created by dehumanizing common experiences and alienation from home that continues even among their progenies (Balbir Singh 1988).

Enduring the hardship of voyage across *Kala Pani* bonded the uprooted people with a new sense of camaraderie and solidarity across caste lines, besides it was a worthwhile risk to take as it offered new possibility to renegotiate identity beyond structural dissolutions of caste, class, gender and religious boundaries that occurred during long oceanic voyages. These exilic experiences, haunted by loss and uncertainty of what lay ahead, hoping to survive the arduous passage with no hopes of ever returning what was once their homeland, profoundly transformed the *jahaji bhais* permanently. The voyage itself was meant to dissolve social boundaries and dispel some of the religious taboos of the old world.

Moreover, Hindus also believed people must live and die near to where they were born. Hence, they abstained from wandering or drifting too far away that they could return to their place of birth and origin. They were also limited by modes of transportation and went to places where their feet could carry them. Being agrarian, they were dependent on water and tended to stay close to sources of water or travelled only along the waterways. As per Indian family and communal codes, particularly the joint family system, patriarchal obligations, gender structure and dowry kept generations bound together to each other and wealth confined within the larger family.

Most people of the Indian subcontinent believe land of their birth as *Punya Bhoomi* (holy or sacred land) and it is closely linked to the notions of *Janma Bhoomi* (land of birth), *Karma Bhoomi* (land of duty) and *Moksha Bhoomi* (land of salvation or deliverance). Migration out of the sacred land was believed to disrupt caste hierarchies and pollute the soul. Such relocations ended personal devotion to local deities and gods were perceived to have territorial limits. Because of many such religious myths and legends, Hindus venerate their own land while keeping the devotees rooted and landlocked in a geographical confine. Acquiring property in foreign nations remains a high value for Indian diaspora and decisively cuts them from ancestral homeland allegiances, while some own properties in both places for investment sake. The practice of pilgrimage to holy sites further accentuates the importance and holiness ascribed to ancestral homelands. A related concept is *Pitru* and *Matru Bhoomi* (father and mother land), where the land of birth demands fidelity of emigrants. *Bharatmata* (Mother India) is considered as the mother of all Hindus as well as Indians. In Hindu scriptures, Lord Rama tells Laxman after their victory over Ravanna, "Mother and motherland is greater than heaven itself." These ideas have been used to stoke nationalistic and patriotic feelings while the notion of Hindu Rashtra is being used by radical Hindu groups to oppress religious minorities in India.

Another major deterrent was the possibility of dying overseas and the potential conflict due to Hindu tradition of cremation of the dead (*Antyesti* or *Antima Sanskar*) (Pandey 2003, 411-413). According to Hindu traditions and its sacred texts, only a male family member like a husband, father or son, can perform the last rites and cremation must be done within a day of death. In the past, due to the absence of proper means of preservation and transportation of a dead body back to the native land, there was always the fear of dying in foreign lands in the mind of Hindus. There were incidents of public cremation ceremonies that caused friction with local communities and discriminatory laws against such funeral practices in Central Asia, Fiji Islands and Trinidad in the eighteenth and nineteenth century (Lal 2006, 39). Furthermore, the requirement of the eldest son lighting the funeral pyre of parents, bound the future generations from going too far from their ancestors. The eternal destiny of the departed soul depended on proper funeral rites and some journeyed back to India to immerse the ashes of the dead in the Ganges or visit many pilgrimage sites to seek blessings for the departed soul.

Conquering Fears: Crossing the *Kala Pani*

Hinduism is a rooted religion and land locked in its beliefs and practices. Most Hindus in the world still live in India and Nepal. However, the neo-Hindu who are forward-looking, western educated, technologically savvy young and upwardly mobile, after dispersing to

major economic centers of the world, are attempting to universalize
its tenets and are sensing increasing pressure to modernize, especially
from its new adherents in the Western countries who are drawn to
its mystical aspects as well as practices such as meditation and yoga.
Hindu gurus and the New Age proponents have been a major force
for reform within modern Hinduism and have criticized the age-old
customs associated with seas. Today, learned Hindus argue that Rama
and Hanuman crossed oceans to kill Ravana and bring back Sita, thus
justifying migration and nullifying the taboo against crossing seas.

Moreover, the religious rules against crossing seas were applicable
only to the highest caste and lower ones readily broke the rules
for personal advancement and economic advantages. For example,
Nambuthris in Kerala instilled similar rules on Nairs and restricted their
movement even out of their districts. Rules were harsher on women
who were not allowed to leave their general dwelling places. Because
of these strictures in place, most noblemen and higher caste people
lived well away from water. From the ancient past, it was the Jews,
Christians, Muslims *Mukkuvas* and other foreigners who were located
along the coastlines of Malabar. In tracing the history of Malayali
migration, Indian historian Oommen noted that Malayalis were migrant
resistant people until the mid-19th century and explores how it became
the largest per capita migrant state in India (2013, 4). He found that
lower caste Dalits were pioneers of mass migration in the state and
high literacy forced people to pursue employment in other cities of
India and eventually go abroad.

The overseas Hindus erected many temples in their adopted
homelands as per strictest orders of various religious sects to claim their
religious adherence, devotion and purity (Rukmani 2001, 387). They
helped to facilitate migration of Brahmin priests through sponsorship
and employment as well as the export of various religious symbols
to their overseas location. Priests and religious leaders from India are
brought to several foreign locations on a regular basis for special *pujas*
(worship ritual) and to give discourses on Hinduism. Their presence
through religious television programs and Internet can be felt all

over the globe today. Hindu business and political leaders are well connected to their scatter global family and quick to leverage their wealth, knowhow and clout for their own advancement.

In the recent decades, when migrants returned home intermittently, they flounder their success and wealth accumulated from overseas. They build luxurious homes and give generous gifts to family and friends, often resulting in status escalation than demotion through required ritual cleansing for religious violations. They refused to submit to caste relegation and claim to have preserved purity while living abroad. Instead, they contend to reform Hinduism itself from its archaic beliefs and practices. Some of these tendencies further diluted the traditional cultural notions of Hindus toward crossing seas and encouraged many to undertake polluting voyages.

These days, all Hindu emigrants out of South Asia use transcontinental flights to migrate to foreign destinations, without having to sail across black waters or the guilt of crossing them. Journey time lasts only few hours or at the most a day. Unlike the old diaspora, emigrants from the subcontinent now maintain regular contacts with their ancestral homelands and the surety of return when needed has eroded the superstition linked to *Kala Pani*. Migrants do not perceive themselves as permanent exiles any longer and there is a great sense of freedom and empowerment knowing they could fly back 'home' at short notice. Latest mobile communication tools, the Internet and affordable flights have abolished feelings of estrangement or alienation from ancestral homelands. Some airlines offer special provision to transport dead bodies back to *Punya Bhoomi* and new options of cremation in foreign lands have dissipated fear of dying abroad.

Furthermore, there is no more fear to break dietary rules over long voyages. Most flights to and out of India now offer vegetarian food and growing vegetarianism in the West has lowered their prohibition to foreign travel. The global presence of Indian grocery stores and export of caste appropriate food conscious Indians have significantly overcome the resistance to migrate. Even *shudh* (pure) water from the

Ganges is packaged and marketed as Ganga Jal and can be ordered online for door delivery worldwide. Indian diaspora has cleansing power of Ganges at their fingertips and fear of pollution is eliminated.

In contemporary India, particularly in urban centers, there are greater incidences of inter-caste, inter-regional and inter-religious marriages among the younger populace. They favor places that do not curtail their freedom to break social prejudices and tend to live in relative anonymity in other cities with hopes of relocating to foreign lands to break the hegemony of caste sensibilities. The prospect of getting married to overseas bride or groom remains a preferred option for parents in Punjab, Gujarat, and the southern four states of India. In diasporic settings, family life becomes nuclear and many drop their caste names to adopt other naming conventions. Several studies in recent decades have shown that caste identities have eroded significantly in the New Indian diaspora globally (Pillai 2017, 29; Kurien 2007; Rangasamy 2008).

Another interrelated reason for the low rate of migration in the past was the decline of Buddhism in South Asia, which had played a critical role in major people's movement across South Asia, Asia and beyond. It resulted in a loss of linkages with major trade centers of the world and prevented the migration of future generations of people from South Asia. The South Asian Christians population may be very small, but they were more migration prone than other religious groups. They leveraged Christian connections and colonial establishments to migrate as teachers and to Commonwealth nations in Africa and elsewhere. Many embraced Christianity after going abroad as it reclaimed social status with the colonizers and ability to provide better economic and educational prospects for their future generations. Some low caste Hindus and *dalits* in India have become Christians to go abroad and more importantly escape from the religious oppression of higher caste and to gain social and economic upward mobility.

After the economic liberalization of the 1990s and political aspiration to be a major world power, new India is breaking out of cultural and religious shackles of the past. With nearly half the population of India below the age of 30 it is quickly spreading beyond its geographical boundaries with a new global outlook, technological prowess and eager to shed her past bondages. Its ambition for maritime trade and dominance of the Indian Oceans is well captured by the last President of India, "after nearly a millennia of inward and landward focus, we are once again turning our gaze outwards and seawards, which is the natural direction of view for a nation seeking to re-establish itself, not simply as a continental power, but even more so as a maritime power, and consequently as one that is of significance on the world stage." (Mukerjee 2007). This line of thinking in geopolitical circles has drawn from American naval strategist Admiral Alfred T. Mahan, "Whoever controls the Indian Ocean dominates Asia. This Ocean is key to seven seas in the 21st century. The destiny of the world will be decided on these waters." (Brewster 2014). For this to happen, Indians and Hindus have to quickly break out of religious imprisonment of *Kala Pani.*

Conclusion

Hindus were seldom seafarers in India and most sailors came from and seaports were established in Malabar, Coromandel, Gujarat and Bengal regions among non-Hindus or lower caste people. All of which clearly shows the inherent bias against crossing seas in the mind of people of South Asia and it can be traced back to religious notions and prohibition of *Kala Pani.* The proximity to waters has helped certain communities to overcome age-old beliefs and geography seems to determine the destiny of people with a large coastline . The exceptional success of global Indian diaspora today has eroded the resistance of many Hindus to migration. However, we must not forget that some 40 million people abroad remain a very miniscule part of the large population of nations of South Asia.

A few months before my father expired, as I was working on my doctoral research in the field of migration and global Indian diaspora, I had the opportunity to glean a few insights from his first ever sea journey to the Andaman Islands. I inquired about his motivations, concerns, fears and details of going to the *Kala Pani.* He replied,

"Waters did not look all that black! It was beautiful blue and lands beyond the seas was beckoning me to come." Then he reasoned, "Didn't Jesus tell us to go to the ends of the Earth?" The Andaman Islands might have seemed like the edge of the world back then to a recently arrived 20-something young man from central Travancore but he was courageous enough to break out of prevailing cultural confines of his times. From the beaches of Madras, as the world expanded in his mind beyond the village he had grown up in, he was willing to go further along than his ancestors, driven by both push and pull factors of migration. Above all, I saw a biblical worldview has helped him overcome his dominant religious prohibition of his times to cross black waters to *Kala Pani*.

References

Baham, Arthur L. 1952. *Cultural History of India,* New Delhi: Oxford India.

Birbalsingh, Frank. 1988. *Jahaji Bhai: An Anthology of Indo-Caribbean Literature,* Toronto: Tsar Publications.

Banerjee, Rohini. 2010. The *Kala Pani* Connection: Francophone Migration Narratives in the Caribbean Writing of Raphaël Confiant and the Mauritian Writing of Ananda Devi, *Anthurium: A Caribbean Studies Journal,* Vol 7, Issue 1, April.

Bharati Mukerjee, *Jasmine* (1989), New York: Grove Press.

Bentley, William. 1905-1914. *The Diary of Rev. William Bentley DD (1759-1819)* Vol 1. Salem, MA: Essex Institute. Online - https://archive.org/details/diaryofwilliambe01bent (Accessed Mar 31, 2017)

Brewster, David. 2014. *India's Oceans: The Story of India's Bid for Regional Leadership,* Oxon: Routledge, 2014. The original quote is attributed to A.T. Mahan's book *The Influence of Sea Power upon History* (1890).

Cohen, Robin. 1997. *Global Diasporas: An Introduction,* New York: Routledge.

Kadekar Laxmi N. 2009. *The Indian Diaspora: Historical and Contemporary Context,* Jaipur, Rawat Publications.

Khan, Aisha. 2004. *Callaloo Nation: Metaphors of Race and Religious Identity among South Asians,* Durham, NC: Duke University Press.

Khan, Ismith. 1961. *The Jumbie Bird.* London: Macgibbon & Kee.

Kurien, Prema. 2007. *A Place at the Multicultural Table: The Development of an American Hinduism,* Rutgers University Press.

Lal, Brij V. 2006. *The Encyclopedia of the Indian Diaspora*, Honolulu: University of Hawaii Press.

Mukherjee, Bharati. 1989. *Jasmine*. New York: Fawcett Crest.

Mukherjee, Pranab. 2007. Admiral A. K. Chatterjee Memorial Lecture. Kolkata. 30 June.

Naipal, V.S. 1969. *A House for Mr. Biswas*. New York: Penguin Books.

Neill, Stephen. 1970. *The Story of the Christian Church in India and Pakistan*, Grand Rapids: W. B. Eerdmans.

Oommen, George. 2013. "Re-imagining a Migratory Self: History of Malayali Migration" in *Malayali Diaspora: From Kerala to the Ends of the Earth*, Eds. Sam George and T.V. Thomas, New Delhi: Serials Publishers.

Pandey, R.B. 2003. *The Hindu Sacraments (Saṁskāra)* in S. Radhakrishnan (Ed.) *The Cultural Heritage of India*. Calcutta: Ramkrishna Mission Institute of Culture.

Panikkar, K.M. 1951. *India and Indian Oceans* London: Allen & Unwin, 1951.

Pathickal, Paul. 2012. *Christ and the Hindu Diaspora*. Bloomington, IN: WestBow Press.

Pillai, Anita Devi and Puva Armuguam. 2017. *From Kerala to Singapore: Voices from the Singapore Malayalee Community*, Singapore: Marshall Cavendish.

Rai, Rajesh. 2004. "Sepoys, Convicts and the Bazar Contingent: The Emergence and Exclusion of Hindustani Pioneers at the Singapore Frontiers," in *Journal of Southeast Asian Studies* 35(1).

Radhakrishnan, S. Editor. 2003. *The Cultural Heritage of India*, Vol. II, Kolkata: The Ramakrishna Mission Institute of Culture.

Rangaswamy, Padma. 2008. *Namaste America: Indian Immigrants in an American Metropolis*, Philadelphia: University of Pennsylvania Press.

Rawilson, H.G. 1952. "Early Contacts between India and Europe" in *Cultural History of India* by Arthur L. Basham. New Delhi: Oxford India.

Rukmani, T.S. 2001. *Hindu Diaspora: Global Perspective*, New Delhi: Manoharlal Publishers.

Rushdie, Salman. *East, West* (1994) and *The Satanic Verses* (1988).

Sowell, Thomas. 1992. *Migration and Cultures: A Word View*, New York: Basic Books.

Selvon, Samuel. 1952. *A Brighter Sun*. London: A. Wingate.

Wolpert, Stanley. 2003. *Gandhi's Passion: Life and Legacy of Mahatma Gandhi*, New York: Oxford University Press.

Indo-Caribbean Christian Diaspora

John Lewis

Introduction

I was born in St. Vincent and the Grenadines. My grandparents came from India to the Caribbean as indentured laborers. The East Indians were known for their large families and between both sides of grandparents, I had over 30 uncles and aunts and scores of cousins. In the village where I grew up almost the entire village were our family. My parents were influenced by the Methodist but later as a family we grew up in the Brethren Church. We enjoyed a strong Christian heritage where daily devotions were held, and we participated as a family in church activities on a weekly basis.

I became a believer when I was eleven years and was baptized at twelve. I attended a Christian high school and was actively involved in the Inter-School Christian Fellowship movement. I served as a volunteer with the local chapter of Youth For Christ (YFC) and later became its National Director. I met my wife Denise in YFC and were married in 1982. We both graduated from the Jamaica Theological Seminary (Jamaica) and the Columbia International University (USA). We developed training centers for theological education in St. Vincent and the Grenadines as well as in Grenada in conjunction with Miami International Seminary over the past fourteen years. I have worked with several Christian organizations including the Alliance of Evangelical

Churches both in St. Vincent and the Grenadines and Grenada as its President. I was privileged to attend and make presentations at regional and international conferences in 1986 and 2000, Lausanne 2010, The Global Proclamation Conference in Thailand and Youth For Christ International Conferences in Kenya, Hong Kong, the Philippines, and England. These along with other significant conferences gave me a global perspective on ministry.

Indo-Caribbeans

Indo-Caribbean's are Caribbean people with roots in the Indian subcontinent and are mostly descendants of the original indentured workers brought to the West Indies by the British, the Dutch and the French during the colonial era. Because of the ancestry in India and not to be confused with the Native Indians in the Americas, they were often called as East Indians. They are alternatively called Hindustani, *Girmitya*, *Bharatiya*, *Desi*, *Kantraki*, *Jahaji* or *Indiawale* in various literature and common usage. *Coolie* is another term often used as derogatory racial slur and referring to indenture laborer.

Indo Caribbean or Indians in the West Indies belong to over twenty-five sovereign states such as Trinidad and Tobago, Jamaica, Guadeloupe, Martinique, French Guiana, Barbados, St. Vincent and the Grenadines, Grenada, Haiti, Puerto Rico, Belize, St. Kittis and St. Martin. Other noticeable settlement of people of Indian origin in the region include St. Lucia, Aruba, Belize, Dominica, Anguilla, Antigua and Barbuda, Bahamas, Cayman Islands, Montserrat and others. Indian diasporic presence can be in South American nations such as Guyana and Surinam arising out of indenture labor system as well as subsequent migration of Indo-Caribbean's to Columbia, Argentina, Peru, Brazil and Chile.

As per current estimates, there are over one million people of Indian origin in the Caribbean and the largest share being in Trinidad and Tobago (nearly half a million) while, Guyana (320,000), Surinam (150,000), Jamaica (74,000) and St. Vincent and the Granadines (22,000). In recent years, migrants from India have landed in the Caribbean Island nations, mostly Sindhi merchants, Indian doctors, Gujarati businessmen as well as migrants of Indian origin from Kenya and Uganda. Also, many Indo-Caribbean's have migrated to the United States, Canada, Netherlands, Spain, France, United Kingdom, Panama, Argentina, Peru, Venezuela, and other parts of the Caribbean. Since 1990s, each year May 30 is celebrated in Trinidad and Tobago as Indian Arrival Day to mark the arrival of Indians way back in 1845. Now other countries of the old Indian diaspora countries with the history of indentured laborers are commemorating the arrival of their ancestors such as Jamaica (May 10), Martinque, St. Lucia, Guyana (May 5), St. Vincent (June 1) and Surinam (June 5).

Most Indo-Caribbeans are Hindus, preserving faith of their ancestors from India, but its beliefs and expressions have evolved significantly. According to the Operation World 2010, the Hindu population in the Caribbeans is estimated as 0.81 percent with a significant share in Trinidad and Tobago (22 percent), Guyana (30 percent), Surinam (23 percent), and in St. Vincent only 3.8 percent are Hindus (Mandryk 2010, 45). Over many generations and complex socialization process, many are ethnically blended with natives and other migrants from other parts of the world resulting in a unique syncretic culture. Through conversion and intermarriage, many also switched religious allegiance, while Hindu temples have established in many places in the West Indies and cultural as well as religious bodies created to preserve religious adherence among settlers. Many Hindu temples can be located in the Island nations of Caribbeans as well as northern Latin American nation with sizable India diaspora population.

Historical Perspective

After slavery was abolished in 1834, the British colonial government began to look for cheap labor. They persuaded the British government of Delhi to answer their persistent call. As a result, many Indians responded to the temptation of a better life in a foreign country who were suffering from famine and oppression during the colonial rule. Many repeated attempts to bring Portuguese, Chinese and others to

Central Americas as indentured laborers had failed. Finally, the British succeeded in taking over a million Indians from the Indian subcontinent between the periods of 1838 and 1917 to thirteen mainlands and island nations in the Caribbeans to address the labor shortage in sugarcane plantations.

Indians came to the Caribbean for variety of different reasons: to escape economic distress, losing their land to British colonial powers, famine in the land, hopes of earning higher wages, to breakout out of social and caste discrimination etc. They were brought on five-year indenture contracts, but also inherited harsh treatment of the era of slavery. Many were tricked by recruiters, endured protracted arduous journey across major oceans, inhumanly deemed by colonial masters, exploited by supervisors and suffered from new diseases without any medical help (Sowell, 1996). Most of these indentured laborers remained in the region beyond the contractual terms of five or ten years by acquiring land to create livelihood as peasant farmers and their subsequent generations produced the contemporary robust Indo-Caribbean populace.

The Indo Caribbean background vary widely. In the early years of indentured migration to Trinidad and Guyana, and throughout the period of immigration to the French territories of Guadelupe and Martinique, indentured workers were drawn from Tamil and Telugu-speaking regions of South India. Yet by far the bulk of immigrants who came to the British and Dutch West Indies originated in the Gangetic plains in northeastern India, especially Bihar and what is now eastern Uttar Pradesh. There are considerable linguistic, economic and ecological, cultural, and religious differences among indentured recruits. These differences were compounded by caste, social class and religious affiliations. Devastating famines, the restructuring of revenue and land tenure systems, the collapse of the textile industry, mass unemployment, and other economic crises which plagued northeastern India during the latter half of the nineteenth century provided significant push factors affecting the decisions of Indians of all backgrounds to enter upon contracts of indentured labor abroad (Vertovec 2010).

However, these laborers were in for a shock. They were ill-treated and exploited and regarded as uncivilized. They were for the most part ripped from their families. They found no replacement for their extended family network which they left at home. Their life in the barracks mitigated against any family life. There were few single women among the indentured laborers therefore little hope of starting a new family. Their Indian rituals were stifled as their new landlords insisted that they fit in to the existing practice. They also faced language barrier thus failing to communicate their true feelings.

Most of the documented research of the arrival of the East Indians are focused on Guyana, Suriname and Trinidad and Tobago. According to the *Encyclopedia of the Indian Diaspora*, between 1845 and 1917, a total of 143,939 Indians were taken to Trinidad under the system of indenture to work in sugar plantations (Lal 2006, 278). The earlier emigration involved wooden sailing vessel of teak and journey around the Cape of Good Hope in the southern tip of Africa took over 90 days to reach the destination. However, following the advent of steamships and the opening of the Suez Canal in 1869, the voyage was shortened to 50 days. Between 1838 and 1917, there were 238,909 Indian laborers were taken to British Guyana. (Lal 2006, 287), while Surinam brought in 34, 304 laborers between 1873 and 1916 and Jamaica 36, 412 between 1845 and 1913 (Lal 2006, 46).

The nature of the indentured system is vigorously debated. It is seen by some as highly experimental in nature which lacked organization. However, according to the Immigration Ordinance of 1854 to 1917 in Trinidad the system has some semblance of stability. For example, there was the granting of crown lands in exchange of a free return passage to India between 1869-1880. Generally, it was a very harsh system of labor and punishment. Guyanese historian Water Rodney underscored the "harshness of indentureship system" and its "neo-slave nature." Another Guyanese scholar Basdeo Mangru argues that "slavery and indenture showed remarkable similarities in terms of exploitation, cruelty and degradation." Hugh Tinker called the new arrangement of labor immigration as "A New System of Slavery" (1974).

The Indians, however, proved to be hardworking and reliable workers and developed the sugar industry and later became the owners of the estates in the islands. They pursued social, educational and economic upward mobility, excelling in politics, education, medicine, cricket and many other fields. Indo-Caribbeans have made significant contributions to their adopted homelands and particularly to the diasporic writings and politics. Notable figures include Indo-Trinidadian Noble Laureate V.S. Naipaul, former Prime Minister of Guyana Cheddi Jagan, former Prime Minister of Trinidad and Tobagao Kamala Persad and Shridath Ramphal distinguished himself as two term Commonwealth Secretary General. Others include cricketers, Hollywood actress, educators, politics, singers, musicians and activists.

A feature of the Indo-Caribbean culture that we cannot ignore is the 3 C's- cricket, calypso and carnival. The East Indian descendants adapted the 3 C's quickly. They have written poems like "Kuli man has come to stay" what called attention to their legitimacy and permanence. In music their 'chutney-soca' was a combination of their folk dance and song. They made their mark on cricket. In 1950, Sonny Ramadhin of Trinidad became a right-hand spin bowler in test Cricket. Others like Joe Solomon and Alvin Kallicharan proved their excellence in cricket.

Early immigrants and their children were kept out of the educational main stream. They were hindered from any educational opportunity unless they learnt English. Their Hindi language was seen as backward and affiliated with foreign beliefs and traditions. However, the ensuing generations were able to learn English language and gained economic and political mobility for the entire community. Currently the East Indians in Caribbeans are well integrated. They are for the most part seen as middle and upper class in these countries. Many still have an agricultural background however, they are also very active in other sectors and professionals such as doctors, lawyers, teachers and interestingly, many civil servants.

Indo-Caribbean Religions

Most emigrants to the shores of Caribbean were Hindus with a strong sense of regional and ethnolinguistic affiliations and constitute as much as 84 percent of the indentured laborers. Other religious expressions include Islam and Jainism. The indenture system involved long oceanic journey that came to be called *Chalan*, which was intended to break down barriers of caste, language and place of origin. The transoceanic voyage, plantation life and severing family ties of the ancestral homelands brought about decisive socio-religious change in the form of demise of caste sensibilities. A wide range of festivals mark religio-cultural fervor of the Caribbean Hindus in the form of *Diwali, Dussehra, Holi, Kali Puja, Pongal, Tai Pucam* and others. The reformist and renewal efforts in the form of sending Arya Samaj missionaries from India to Surinam occurred as early as 1912. Other major religious group that came to the Caribbean from India were Muslims from northern India. Their literature and ritual language were Urdu and most celebrated festivity of Muslims in Surinam was Muharram and *Eid-al-Fitr* . The Indo Caribbean festivals acquired a secular character because of creolizations and broader participation.

A Hindu remnant can be seen even today in the Caribbean: over one-third of the total population in Guyana and nearly quarter of the population in Trinidad and Surinam are Hindus. The epic tale of Ramayana and themes of exile and banishment continue to be recounted by subsequent generations of Indians with the hope of eventual triumph of good over evil. According to the Operation World, 0.81 percent of whole Caribbean are Hindus while nearly 83 percent are considered as Christians (60 percent Catholic and 18 percent Protestant). In St. Vincent and the Grenadines, 90 percent of the population are considered Christians, 4 percent Hindus and 2 percent Muslims. In Trinidad and Tobago, 65 percent of population are Christians, 22 percent Hindus and 6 percent Muslims. In Jamaica, 83 percent are Christians and Hindus as well as Muslims make up less than 1 percent each. In Guyana, 53 percent are Christians, Hindus are 30 percent and Muslims 10 percent. In

Surinam, 50 percent are Christians while Hindus make up 23 percent and Muslims 17 percent (2010).

Both Indian Hindus and Muslims were reached out to by Christian missionaries in the Caribbeans through evangelistic activities and education. The indentured laborers sent their children to schools run by missionaries with hopes of getting employment and socioeconomic upward mobility. In the initial stages, they were classified as pagans mainly due to the ignorance and insensitivity of missionaries. The Wesleyn Methodist Missionary Society of 1852 made the first attempt to preach Christianity to the Indians. The Anglicans and Roman Catholic Church had very little success.

The Canadian Presbyterian Church established the Canadian East Indian Mission in Guyana in 1860. Their chief missionary of the Canadian mission was Reverend James B. Cropper who provided educational opportunities for Indians and successfully used education as a bridge to evangelize. The Lutheran Church started its work in Guyana in 1919 and built a primary and secondary school at Skelden and Corentyne (East Berbice) respectively. The Canadian Mission encouraged wearing of the *dhoti* and *sari*, the use of Hindi, and singing of *bhajans*. They trained Indian catechist to narrate the *Yisu Katha* in Hindi in homes.

In spite of the evangelical works, the conversion rate was minimal in comparison to the population of Hindus and Muslims. For example, in 1931, there were 124,000 Indians in Guyana out of which approximately a 1000 were Lutherans. There were 1958 Roman Catholic and 3465 Anglicans among the Indian population. One notable exception is the dramatic change in the religious affiliation of the Jamaica diaspora which was once home to nearly 25,000 Hindus until the middle of the twentieth century but by 1970s, only 5000 were identified as Hindus while 2011 Census reported only 1836 Hindus.

Most have converted to Christianity, the major religion of the Island. The migration to western nations have also facilitated conversion of Indo Caribbeans to Christianity. On the contrary, in Trinidad nearly

88 percent of immigrants in the indenture system practiced various facets of Hinduism. Upon completion of their five-year contractual term, over 90 percent chose to stay back and make Trinidad as their permanent home. Although Hindus practices can be traced to early settlement, various elements of the religion were modified, diluted and expunged continually. In the early years, Indian religious expressions were met with lots of contempt and disinterest by others. But over many decades, they have been well integrated into Trinidadian multicultural sensibilities. During this time the Canadian Presbyterian Church, the Anglicans and the Roman Catholic Church were influential in attracting the East Indian population. In 1891, out of a total of 2432 Indians in Grenada 1501 were Anglicans, 165 were Presbyterians and 185 were Roman Catholic.

Ron Sookram claimed that the Indian community is the largest minority group in Grenada. In respect to religion in Grenada it must be noted that a Creole culture which came with the African slavery and European hegemony existed before the coming of the Indian immigrants to Grenada. The colonial government of Grenada intended to assimilate the Indians into its culture. The following is a statement from a colonial official cited in St. George Chronicle dated 5 April 1862:

> What are we to do with these people? Leave them to grow up from year to year in worse than brutal ignorance? This would be wrong: we bring them hither, and we thus become responsible for their Christian Instruction; not indeed, by coercion, but by the gentle and insinuating influences of our holy Christianity. Tolerate them not in their Hinduism! Does not our Christianity compel us to seek to benefit those barbarians thus placed within our reach…it is not enough to depend on the docility of the coolies. That docility may co-exist with considerable subtlety and cunning. (cited Sookram, 32)

Grenada's white colonists to impose their own Christian cultural values formed the *Association for the Instruction of Indian Immigrants*. This organization functioned to implement special programs for Indian transformation. It was aimed at converting Indians to Christianity and their goal was clearly expressed as following:

The character of our Association may be understood that our principle of membership is so broad as to embrace all religious denominations. We have no connection with any sect. All may come under our flag...The immigrants finding themselves objects of competition, would stand out for a high price, and would thus be petted and spoiled; whereas, seeing us actuated by a disinterested desire that they should know the truth and they are quick enough to see this, our power over their conscience will be without any drawback ... our object is neither to make the immigrants Roman Catholic nor Protestants, but to bring their souls in the contact with the word of God... to make them Christians. (Sookram 33).

Challenges Facing Indo Caribbean Christians

Identity is a major issue in postcolonial societies and particularly complicated in diasporic setting where majority of Indians in some West Indian nations are Hindu and majority religions in those nations are Christians. Conversion is often seen as abandonment of ethnic community or adoption of the religion of the colonial masters who mistreated and exploited our progenitors. The notion of selfhood is further complicated and entrenched because of strong racial consciousness with people of African descent who form the majority of the population in many of the nations in the Caribbean. A healthy self-concept of being a person of Indian origin, born and raised in the Caribbean, being a follower of Jesus Christ and belonging to multiracial faith community and neighborhood is needed to gain liberation from historical, cultural and religious bondages.

A related challenge to the issue of identity is the issue of creolization. Throughout its history, various group of people from different parts of the world arrived in the Caribbeans who brought their distinct cultures with them. The contemporary Caribbean culture is a multifaceted blend of cultures that occurred over a long period of time. However, Caribbean theology and church is struggling to meaningfully engage vernacular and songs of the current generation in its liturgy. Much immediate attention needs to be given by Indo Caribbean Christians to being relevant in its practices and ministry to the current social contours of a diaspora community.

Another challenge before the Indo-Caribbean Christian is reality of lived experience of persistent poverty in the region. Although in some nations in the region, people of Indian descent have gained social and economic mobility or have migrated to western nations, many Indo-Caribbeans are economically disenfranchised. The culture of enslavement, colonization and European dominance have infused a sense of inferiority coupled with lack of opportunity, discrimination, life diminishing and distorting realities of daily lived experience of the people of Caribbean. The high rates of homicides, addictive behaviors, violence and family breakdowns are only symptomatic of prevailing economic and social injustice in the land.

According to the latest official census released in 2015 of the St. Vincent and the Grenadines, there are total population of the island stands at 109,557, out of which 55,739 were men and 53,818 were women (Census Report 2015). During the period of three prior years (2011-2013), there was an average of 508 marriages and 30 divorces in the Islands. Over the last ten-year period, the number of divorces has steadily declined from 85 in 2004 to 29 in 2013. An average of 1768 live births was recorded over the three-year period 2011-2013. The gender ratio was even at nearly 103 males to 100 females in 2013. The total number of births to teenage mothers (under age 19) declined between 2011 and 2013 and stood at 17.6 percent in 2013. A definite concern in the demographic data is illegitimate birth in the Islands. Births to unmarried, divorced or widowed women (illegitimate births) accounted for the largest percentage of total births. In 2011, 2012 and 2013, illegitimate births accounted for 83.9 percent, 84.7 percent and 82.8 percent of total births respectively.

Conclusion

Currently, there are limited specific outreach to the East Indian population in the Caribbean. However, there are attempts in Guyana, Trinidad and Suriname to study the Muslim and Hindu faiths to be able to communicate with them. They have assimilated into local cultures for the most part and there is interest in mission works among some

Christian organizations who have been currently led by third or fourth generation East Indian descendants. We have seen this in organizations such as Youth For Christ, Inter-School-Christian-Fellowship, Hospital Christian fellowship, Full Gospel Businessmen Fellowship (FGBMF) and other service organizations. As noted earlier, descendants of the Indian population have emerged as lawyers, psychologists, doctors, businessmen and women, architects, engineers, bankers, civil servants and other professions. Many of these professionals influence their nations because of their Christian witness in the marketplace.

There is a huge task to reach the Hindu and Muslim population in the Caribbean region. Christians need the relevant training and expertise to intelligently present the Christian faith unapologetically. We need to become more deliberate and intentional in learning the beliefs of other faiths among the East Indian population in the Caribbean. We have far too long lumped everyone in the "lost" crowd rather than doing due diligence to unearth the mindset of generations. There must be a wake- up call for the Christian church and to embark on a thorough survey of the Christians among the East Indian population which should lead us to design a strategic plan as how to be a responsible Christian witness and missionary efforts in the region. We may need the help of our brothers and sisters in Christ outside of the region to help with specific training modules. As far as I am aware there are no theological schools in the Caribbean region that offers study of world religions. Perhaps that could be a starting place. The hour is late, and time is short. Let us arise to the challenges.

References

Census Report 2015. Census Report 2015. - http://stats.gov.vc/ (Accessed June 15, 2017)

Lal, Brij V. 2006. *The Encyclopedia of the Indian Diaspora*, Singapore: Didler Miller.

Mandryk, Jason. 2010. *Operation World: The Definitive Prayer Guide to Every Nation*, 7th Edition. Colorado Springs: Biblica.

Sookram, Ron. *Immigrants to Citizens: The Indian Community in Grenada, 1857 to Present.* https://www.brunel.ac.uk/__data/assets/pdf_file/0007/186073/ET63SookramRevsED.pdf (Accessed July 1, 2017)

Singh, Sherry-Ann. 2013.The Experience of Indian Indenture in Trinidad: Arrival and Settlement in Cruse & Rhiney (Eds.), *Caribbean Atlas*. Trinidad and Tobago: University of the West Indies St. Augustine,. http://www.caribbean-atlas.com/en/themes/waves-of-colonization-and-control-in-the-caribbean/waves-of-colonization/the-experience-of-indian-indenture-in-trinidad-arrival-and-settlement.html. (Accessed July 1, 2017)

Sowell, Thomas. 1996. *Migrations and Cultures: A Worldview,* New York: Basic Books.

Tinker, Hugh. 1974. *A New System of Slavery: The Export of Indian Labour Overseas.* London: Oxford University Press.

Vertovec, Steven. 2010. *Migration.* New York, NY: Routledge.

St. Thomas Christians of Singapore

George Joseph

Introduction

In March 2016, the Singapore Mar Thoma Syrian Christian Church celebrated its 80th anniversary and over a century of the community presence in Singapore. This parish is one of the earliest diasporas of the Kerala Christians out of India. To mark this important milestone of a diasporic community, the church undertook an initiative to document its long history and produced a mammoth volume, *The Journey in God's Green Pastures: Mar Thoma Church in Singapore (1936-2016)*. At the beginning of its yearlong celebrations of the church, I had the pleasure of reconnecting with Sam George, who shared about this book project on Indian diaspora Christianity and invited me to contribute a chapter on St. Thomas Christians of Singapore. It is essential to note that St. Thomas or Syrian Christian of Kerala includes many denominations, Mar Thoma Church being one of them and is the primary focus in this paper.

I was born and raised in Singapore and my parents were among the early Malayali Christians settlers in this part of the world. I worked as a journalist for over 30 years with newspapers of the Singapore Press Holdings group, formerly, The *Straits Times Press*. My father, the late Parapuram (P.J.) Joseph, and uncle, Parapuram Joseph John were among the pioneer Indian journalists who joined English newspaper groups owned by the British in Malaya and Singapore. They arrived here just before the outbreak of World War II.

In this chapter, I briefly want to trace the arrival of Indians, Malayalis and St. Thomas Christians to Singapore and sketch the history of the Mar Thoma Church in Singapore. I explore the work and contributions of the St. Thomas Christians in Singapore and conclude by remembering some of the pioneers of the community in Singapore. I have drawn from published, extracts from our centenary book and personal reflection for this paper.

The Syrian Christians of India

Christianity was brought to India in AD 52 by Apostle Thomas, one of the twelve disciples of Jesus Christ of Nazareth. Thomas is believed to have planted seven churches in the Malabar region (modern Kerala) and was martyred in AD 72 in Madras (now known as Chennai) (Mundadan 1989; Neill 2004; Frykenburg 2010). The St. Thomas church continues to thrive in the southwestern state of Kerala in India and is one of the oldest Christian churches in the world. Those Christians, who trace the roots of their faith all the way back to the apostolic church came to be known as St. Thomas Christians.

Another term that was used to describe the Christians of Malabar was *Nasrani* (www.Nasarani.net). It is an equivalent of Nazarene and refers to all followers of Jesus of Nazareth. The early Christians of India kept themselves as a distinct community in terms of culture and religion. Though they followed chants in a foreign language (Syriac) at all their religious gatherings, they remained very Indian in all other matters. They were characterized as, "Nazranis are Indian in culture, Christian in faith and Syrian in liturgy."

By the end of the first century and early second century, these Christians in the Malabar region came under the Patriarch of Antioch in Syria, who was appointed by the First General Council of Nicea in 325 AD. Bishop Johannes, one of the Bishops who attended the Council, represented not only Persia but also India (possibly the church in Malabar). They followed liturgy in the Syrian language and thus came to be known as "Syrian" Christians. Some of them also had Syrian heritage and were treated fairly by the dominant castes and rulers of southwestern India. Among the pioneer Indian immigrants who came to the British Colony in Malaya were a small group of Kerala Christians who began a tide of Christian migration out of Kerala. These Indian Christians preserved their distinct rituals and practices in their places of settlements and kept close institutional ties in ancestral homelands. They preserved the historic Syrian Christian traditions of Kerala and were nourished by it.

Indian Migration to Singapore

The island city-state of Singapore started as a trading post of the British East India Company in 1819 and later ceded to British colonial rule as the Straits Settlement in 1826. During World War II it came under Japanese occupation and after their surrender, continued as a British colony until 1965 when it gained independence to become a sovereign nation. Since then, Singapore under the rule of its own elected government and has emerged as a global hub for trade, transportation, technology and finance, bringing much prominence and prosperity to its people. Just in a lifetime its economy transformed from a third world condition to that of first world affluence and became a city of great significance globally. Indians have been a part of the local population right from the time of the arrival of Sir Stamford Raffles, the founder of the island. Today, people of Indian origin constitute 7.4 per cent of the population, with Tamil being one of the official languages of Singapore, together with English, Mandarin and Malay, reflecting the multi-racial nature of the nation.

From 1826 Singapore (together with Penang and Malacca in Malaya) came under the Eastern Presidency of the British-Indian Government and later under the direct control of the British Colonial Office. For close to half a century, Singapore was effectively a part of India as it came under the Legislative Council in India till 1867. This period left its imprints in this British colony and the permanent presence of an Indian community in Singapore right through the British colonial rule over the prospering island-state to independence in 1965 and local rule (Lal 2006, 177).

The movement of people within the British Raj was unrestricted and considered as an internal matter as the Straits Settlements were administered as a part of British India. Traders, soldiers, and convicts were sent to the Straits Settlement outpost as well as teachers, clerks and English-conversant civil servants. Most of labor migrants were from the then Madras Presidency (now Tamil Nadu), particularly because of widespread famine, population growth and high unemployment in the early twentieth century. Most were from the poor districts closest to authorized ports of departure in Nagapattanam and Madras (now Chennai). The Colonial authorities preferred Tamilian workers as they were deemed "docile, malleable and easy to manage and good for repetitive tasks", as compared to their Malay or Chinese counterparts (Lal 2006, 174).

Indians who migrated to Singapore in the nineteenth century included sepoys of the Bengal Infantry, Sikh policemen, Bihari workers and others such as *dhobis* (washermen), *doodh-wallahs* (milkmen), *chai wallahs* (tea makers) and domestic servants. As the economy grew, Singapore attracted other migrants which diversified the Indian community with small entrepreneurs, merchants, shopkeepers, contractors and financiers. It also drew people from North India like Parsis, Gujaratis, Marwaris and Bengalis. Sikhs and Sindhis established a prominent place as soldiers and textiles traders with links to Hong Kong, Jakarta and Bombay (Rai 2014).

The introduction of English education in schools and colleges by the Travancore rulers was a turning point in the migratory movement of people out of Kerala. Despite centuries of interaction with Jews, Arabs, Chinese and Europeans, people of the southwestern coast of India were migration resistant. But after receiving English education and contacts with British colonial masters, plantation owners and Christian missionaries, the young in Kerala did not aspire anymore to be mere farmers like their ancestors and were ready to venture out of the state to pursue white collar jobs in colonial establishments and private enterprises. Thus, most Keralites who arrived in Singapore in the nineteenth and early twentieth century were Pillays, Menons, Nairs and Syrian Christians from the Central Travancore region (presently, central and south Kerala).

The early migration was mostly a foray for young men and there was a substantial gender imbalance among the immigrant community. It resulted in some marriages among Indians to locals in Malaya and Singapore, while at present there is greater gender equity and families have been nuclearized in Singapore. The Malayali cultural associations, literary clubs, *Onam* festivities, lessons in Malayalam language and dance forms, knitted the community together. However, according to recent publication on Keralites in Singapore, with the rising affluence of the Singaporean Malayali community, the cohesiveness as well as spiritual fervor have eroded steadily and progressively (Pillay and Armugham 2017).

Indians have played a significant role in catapulting Singapore into the global stage and their distinct contributions have been well recognized. They hold prominent places in the political, economic, cultural and social spheres in Singapore today, with two Presidents who were of Indian origin - the late Mr. Devan Nair a Malayali and the late Mr. S R Nathan, a Tamilian. Singapore's transformation into a multi-racial and multi-cultural society with relative peace and security and economic progress made it a desired destination for many aspiring migrants in India as well as in other parts of the world. And this continues till today with "expatriates" from all over the world living and working here on long-term employment passes and taking up permanent residence and even citizenship.

The Singaporean St. Thomas Christians

In early years, all Syrian Christian sub-communities worshipped together and the distinctions that separated them along the lines of tradition, doctrine or practices back in India were not as important then. However, as the numbers swelled, the different strands of Indian Christianity went their own way to form their own church groups.

Christians from Kerala hail from diverse traditions such as Mar Thoma Syrian, Syrian Orthodox, Malankara Catholic, Reformed, Evangelical, Pentecostal and Brethren. The Mar Thoma Syrian Christians were the first to build their own church building in Singapore at Mar Thoma Road, off St. Michael's Road in 1952, while the Orthodox Syrian Christian community built theirs, at Topaz Road, not far from Mar Thoma Road, in 1958. Other Syrian Christian denominations sprung up in the 1960s and 1970s.

There were Indian Christians who were Tamil, Telugu, Hindi, Gujarati, and Punjabi speakers. They mostly belonged to the Anglican, Methodist and Roman Catholic traditions. Some belong to other denominations of India and continue to maintain close links with the ancestral ecclesial institutional structures. In the 21st century, several new independent churches were established by Indian Christians and those who have converted to Christianity after coming to Singapore. A new trend among St. Thomas Christians, especially the second and third generations, who were born and raised in Malaysia or Singapore, is a tendency to seek membership with local, English dominant churches than being part of an immigrant church where Malayalam is largely used in the services.

As a spirit of nationalism pervaded the Indian homeland of the pioneer generation, so did questions arise about their future in Singapore. There was the stark reality of their identity in a foreign land, which posed the question: Should we go back to India or strike roots in Singapore. The 1950s to 1960s was a time of political awakening as a Singaporean identity began to evolve. The political parties were being formed and the independence movement was gaining ground all over the Commonwealth nations. The thought of the British being forced out and the local population attempting to be the masters of their own destiny, was troubling in the minds of the pioneers. They were a minority among minorities in Singapore. Communism was taking root in certain sectors of the population. There was industrial strife and riots, and yet there was potential for this island colony to do well and be more than just a British trading post.

After Singapore gained independence, people faced the issue of citizenship. They were at crossroads - the Malayali St. Thomas Christians of India had to decide if they were going to take up citizenship and put down roots in Singapore or return to India. It was a serious dilemma before with lots of uncertainties no matter what direction they pursued. Their children, the first generation of Singapore-born St. Thomas Christians were becoming more Singaporeans than Indians, immersed in a multi-cultural landscape locally.

There are now some 253,000 people of Indian origin in Singapore. Out of this, about 26,000 are Malayalis, according to a census in 2010. As of 2017, the number of Malayalis is estimated at 30,000. There has been no census of the St. Thomas Christians among this Malayali community. An estimate based on the number attending the main Syrian Christian churches in Singapore is 5,000. The Singapore churches with members who may be the descendants of the original St. Thomas community of India are the St. Thomas Syrian Orthodox Cathedral, the Mar Thoma Syrian Christian Church in Singapore and St. Mary's Jacobite Syrian Cathedral. There are also parishes belonging to the Church of South India following Malayalam, Tamil and Telugu services, several Kerala Pentecostal churches, as well as independent churches with loose links to Christianity in Kerala.

The Singapore Mar Thoma Church

The first known Syrian Christian to arrive in Singapore is believed to be Mr. Isaac Benjamin (Inspector Ninan) in 1911, while Mr. and Mrs. T.G. Thomas, of the Mar Thoma strand, arrived in 1920. The first Mar Thoma worship service was held in Klang, Malaysia in September 1926 and the Very Rev. V. P. Mammen of the Mar Thoma Syrian church in Kerala came to assess the needs of the Syrian Christian community in Malaysia and Singapore in December 1928. The Syrian Christians met in homes to renew their social as well as religious ties on a regular basis without formal worship services.

In April 1932, at a meeting at the Jubilee School in Klang, a formal resolution was passed to request the Mar Thoma Church in Kerala to send a resident priest to minister to the Marthomite community in Malaysia and Singapore. The Church sent Rev. T.N. Koshy who landed in Malaya on April 21, 1936 and came to visit Marthomites in Singapore and celebrated the first Holy Communion at 13, Dhoby Ghaut in September 1936. The first parish management committee of the Singapore Mar Thoma Church met in September 1936 in a class room of then Teo Hoo Lye Institute at Handy Road, where the Cathay cinema stands today. A year later, regular worship service began at the Armenian Apostolic Church of St. Gregory the Illuminator at 60, Hill Street Singapore and continued till 1947. In February of 1947 worship services shifted to a new location at St. Andrews School Hall in Woodsville and continued till 1953. The parish joined the Malayan Christian council (now National Council of Singapore) as its founding member.

In 1950 a land site was identified near St. Michael's Road to construct a church and the building was officially dedicated by the Lord Bishop of Singapore Rt. Rev. H.W. Baines of the Anglican Church in 1953. The community worshipped at this location till 1991. It is no accident that one of the pioneer of Mar Thoma Christians to arrive in Singapore, was a school principal and teacher Mr. T.G. Thomas, in 1929. He was head hunted by the Methodist Church to be a senior teacher at one of Singapore's best schools, the Anglo Chinese School. One of the biggest contributions of the community to a new and emerging independent Singapore was through education. The community produced a group of educationists – teachers and principals for Singapore, far above our composition in the total population.

The Singapore Mar Thoma community started the St. Thomas School in 1954 as a private institution set up to give a second chance to school dropouts and over-aged students. It was later upgraded as a government aided secondary school. In 1954 the Singapore City Council named the road in front of the church and school as Mar Thoma Road. The name remains until today, even after both the church and the school had been re-located to other parts of Singapore. Besides starting of the St. Thomas School in Singapore, several St.

Thomas Christians have served in various capacities as members of the government service. They regularly conducted charity work and provided food aid to locals and all needy people. They offered medical clinics regularly and arranged outreach to foreign workers as well as legal services and various support to recent immigrants.

After gaining independence from the British on September 16, 1963, Singapore became part of Malaysia. Then on August 9, 1965, it became the Republic of Singapore and adopted a parliamentary democratic form of governance. Both the church and community flourished through these political and economic transitions. It brought more educated Syrian Christians with professional skills in science, technology and banking. Since 1990s, many of the Marthomites who were born and raised in Malaya and Singapore have migrated to Australia, the United Kingdom or the USA, but a new wave of St..Thomas Christian migrants from central Kerala and other cities of India have arrived in force and revived the declining and sagging sentiments of the Mar Thoma community in Singapore.

Remembering the Pioneers

The pioneers of St. Thomas Christians in the Straits settlement would deserve special mention for their exceptional courage and deep faith in migrating to a relatively unknown place back then. They arrived in this little known British Colonial port city, seeking a better life for their families when there was little prospect for them in their native lands. Both India and Malacca were under British colonial rule and British East India Company were operating regular ships across its many ports transporting goods and people. Most of these pioneers sailed out from the port city of Madras Presidency (now known as Chennai) and others from Calcutta (now called Kolkata).

To embark on a tumultuous journey to an unknown port in Singapore required courage and was unparalleled in the early 20th century for people in Travancore. This migration may have been due to the close proximity of Malaya and Singapore to India and made easier as parts of this region were also under the same British Colonial rule that India was under until Independence in 1947 and did not have any visa requirements. This made Malaya and Singapore more welcoming of English speaking Indians, giving them opportunities for jobs in British run estates, railways and the administrative services.

The first Syrian Christian believed to have arrived in Singapore was Mr. Isaac Benjamin in 1911. He was the son of a Church Missionary Society (CMS) missionary from Malapally and was an inspector of the Travancore Police. He was known to be an honest, trustworthy, efficient and strict officer of the British colonial administration in India. After coming to Singapore, he worked in Adrian Cane Company and later brought his family along after securing a firm footing in Singapore. As more Syrian Christians started arriving in Singapore in 1920s, Mr. Benjamin formed a "Syrian Christian Association" in 1930 to cater to the social and recreational needs of the community. He died of natural causes during the Japanese occupation in 1942.

The first Mar Thomite to arrive in this region was Mr. K.C. George who landed in Malaya in 1911. His wife and oldest son joined him a couple of years later. They encouraged many friends and relatives to come to Malaya and offered much practical help in finding jobs and looking after them till they became independent. People gathered in their home regularly for fellowship and support. Out of these gatherings sprung a desire to pray and worship God in Malayalam and liturgies they were used to. Along with other early Mar Thomites, he sent numerous requests to the home church in Kerala for a resident Mar Thoma priest and in creation of the first overseas diaspora community of the Mar Thoma Church in Malaya and Singapore.

The first Mar Thomite to arrive in Singapore was Mr. T.G. Thomas, who arrived in 1920 at the young age of 29. He started his career as a teacher at the Syrian Christian (SC) Seminary in Tiruvalla in 1916. A year later, he joined the Hindu School in Jaffna, Ceylon (now known as Sri Lanka) as its headmaster and was the first Christian teacher there. He went on to become the principal of the American Mission School at Manippai in Ceylon. A few years later, he was invited to serve as a senior teacher at the Anglo Chinese Methodist School (ACS) and took up membership at the Singapore Tamil Methodist Church. In 1930, as the number of Syrian Christians in Singapore increased, he formed the Syrian Christian Union. He was also treasurer of the Indian Association and was editor of a magazine 'The Indian'. Their children were sent back to India for medical studies – their oldest child died of typhoid in Madras in 1939; their daughter was the first overseas student to have graduated from Christian Medical College in Vellore; two other children pursued medicine and accountancy in India. Their youngest son John recounts a harrowing incident after the British surrender to the Japanese.

"My parents and I left for India from Singapore harbour in February 1942. I was about 11 years old then. Our ship was part of a convoy and escorted by warships. We headed first to Perth where some more passengers embarked. Then we headed for Palembang in Sumatra. Throughout the voyage, we were tracked by the Japanese reconnaissance planes and there were many attempts to attack the convoy. Some days later, when I was in the Straits of Malacca, near Palembang Port, our ship was bombed and badly damaged. Despite the bilge pump working continuously, the ship started sinking... we reached the port on life boats. All personal belongings were lost. We had to stay in warehouses for two days while the authorities arranged for the journey to Colombo on another ship... Japanese planes tried to bomb our ship. By God's grace we escaped. After two weeks, we reached Colombo... then took a train ... ship to Madras ... then train to Kerala." (Roy et al. 2016, 60).

Things did nott happen inadvertently for the pioneers. They suffered many hardships, loneliness, the ravages of a terrible war, and the years of occupation by the Japanese army. Many fled to Malaya and left their wives and children in the hands of relatives and friends who lived in the plantation estates, which were thought to be safe as the invading Japanese army marched south through the Malay Peninsula to strike at Singapore. But soon, the prayers of mothers and wives, children and parents, were answered. Almost all survived the war and were reunited with their fledgling families both here and in India. Allow me to quote the words of one pioneer lady, the late Mrs. Saramma Zachariah.

"During the Japanese Occupation, we left Singapore to live in Endau, in Malaya because my husband went to work there. When the war was over, we were eager to return to Singapore, but there was no transport available readily. A Chinese man in the neighborhood offered to take us to Singapore in his open lorry. There was no roof or seats. I sat on an overturned drum with our two-and-a-half-month-old son in my arms, while my husband and our three other children sat on the floor of the lorry. We left at 7am and arrived at 7pm. The weather was just perfect throughout. The God, who led the people of Israel with a pillar of cloud and fire, had graciously protected us too and brought us back safely." (Roy et al. 2016, 82).

After the Japanese surrendered on September 12, 1945, the people of Singapore slowly began to pick up the pieces of their shattered lives, dreams and livelihoods. As the post-war years began, the community began to regroup and reorganize themselves. One of the biggest assets of the Malayali community in Singapore then was that most migrants from Kerala were educated and spoke English. With the relative peace and prosperity everyone was determined to seek a better life for themselves. By then there were 30 worshipping centers and some 1400 families as church members in Malaya and Singapore.

Conclusion

The St. Thomas Christian community in Singapore continues to flourish amid new challenges and opportunities. Although it has fragmented into many churches of diverse traditions and liturgies as the population grew, the common cultural heritage and Christian faith binds them together tightly. After many generations living here, people of St. Thomas heritage are well educated, settled and integrated into the Singaporean society. They are readily accepted in the mainstream society and have intermarried or migrated elsewhere to places such as Australia, UK and USA.

In recent years, St. Thomas diaspora in Singapore is being strengthened with the arrival of more Indian professionals and executives, especially in the IT and financial services, as Singapore opens its doors to qualified non-citizens to top up its manpower requirements in its drive for economic growth. The St. Thomas Christians are blessed to live in Singapore, with people of different races and cultures, enjoying the fruits of Singapore's economic success, peace and stability.

References

Frykenburg, Robert Eric. *Christianity in India: From Beginning to Present,* Oxford: Oxford University Press, 2010.

Lal, Brij V., *The Encyclopedia of Indian Diaspora,* University of Hawaii, Honolulu, 2006.

Mundadan, A.M. *History of Christianity in India,* Bangalore: CHAI Publications, 1989.

Neill, Stephen, *A History of Christianity in India,* Cambridge, UK: Cambridge University Press (2004)

Roy, Rachel, Roy Joseph, Sangeetha Mariamma, Alison Joseph, Natasha Ann Zachariah, George Joseph and Rev. John G Mathews (Editors). *The Journey in God's Green Pastures: Mar Thoma Church in Singapore (1936-2016).* Singapore: Singapore Mar Thoma Syrian Church, 2016.

Rai, Rajesh. *Indians in Singapore (1819-1945): Diaspora in the Colonial Port City* Oxford: Oxford University Press, 2014.

Pillai, Anitha Devi and Puva Arumugam, *From Kerala to Singapore: Voices of the Singapore Malayalee Community,* Singapore: Marshall Cavendish, 2017;

Sandhu, K.S. *Indians in Malaya: Aspects of their Immigration and Settlement (1786-1957),* Cambridge University Press, 1969.

South Asian Diaspora Christianity in the Persian Gulf[1]

T. V. Thomas

Introduction

A vibrant church life is not what one thinks about when we deliberate on the Persian Gulf region, which is primarily Muslim (Kapp 2008, 1). Little is known about the state of Christianity in this vast region and there is a colossal degree of ignorance because not many studies are undertaken, and little is published. Whatever is published does not receive the wide circulation it deserves. Some of the reluctance to disperse collected information is caused by self-imposed restrictions to ensure the security of the followers of Jesus and to protect their worship sites.

Although there are South Asians and expressions of South Asian Christianity throughout the Middle East, this study is restricted to five small countries that line the Persian Gulf namely Kuwait, Qatar, Bahrain, Oman and the United Arab Emirates. In undertaking this study, I realize there are very few printed resources and negligible statistical

---

[1] This chapter has been edited and revised from a previously published article by T.V. Thomas "South Asian Diaspora Christianity in the Persian Gulf" in *Global Diasporas and Missions*. Chandler H. Im and Amos Yong (Editors). Wipf and Stock Publishers, Eugene OR, 2014. Reprinted with permission.

records. Only pragmatic approach was to conduct one-on-one interviews with Western and non-Western Christian leaders, lay pastors, and lay people. For this reason, I traveled to Kuwait and the UAE to conduct 51 face-to-face interviews over a two-week period. I also conducted similar interviews with 28 South Asian Christians in the USA and Canada who had recently migrated from the Persian Gulf countries. In addition, I conducted telephone interviews with another 23 South Asian Christians from Bahrain, Qatar, and Oman. For the security of the interviewees and by mutual agreement, the names of some are being withheld while the remainder are pseudonymously identified. This study is an overview of South Asian diaspora Christianity in the Persian Gulf and is far from being exhaustive.

The Coming of Christianity to the Persian Gulf

According to tradition, the gospel was preached in southern Arabia by the Apostle Bartholomew (Holzmann 2001, 17). Christianity began flourishing in the first century and was introduced in the southern part of Arabia, which then spread to the Gulf region. Historical records indicate that Qatar was a Bishopric as early as 225 CE (Koshy 2003, 37) and three churches existed in Yemen by 356 CE. Bishops from Arabia were participants at the Council of Nicea in 325 CE. By the fourth century Nestorian Christianity dominated the southern shores of the Persian Gulf. Tiny ancient Christian communities existed in pre-Islamic times, but they almost disappeared when Islam became a dominant presence. For over 1,200 years Christian influence was virtually absent in the region.

With the arrival of the Portuguese in the Persian Gulf in 1506, the region's inhabitants began to renew their acquaintance with Christianity (Thompson 2011, 25-26). However, the indiscriminate killing of women, children, and the aged, and the destruction of property at Khor Fakkan under the direction of Portuguese sea Captain Alphonso de Alburquerque left a bitter legacy with Portuguese Christians. The Portuguese soon dominated the eastern coast of Arabia and exercised their power over the locals by building forts.

In contrast, Captain Thomas Perronet Thompson of Britain, with deep Christian convictions, was a bridge-builder (Thompson 2011, 27). Upon arrival in Ra'sal-Khaimah in 1819, Thompson learned Arabic. This acquisition proved to be a great asset in relationship building with the local Arabs. In 1820, he crafted the General Treaty of Peace for the Cessation of Plunder and Piracy, which was signed by Britain and the Gulf States (Thompson 2011, 30-31). With this initiative, formal relationships were established which were mutually beneficial.

With the influence of William Carey, the English Baptist Missionary Society was launched in 1792. This was catalytic in the formation of numerous missionary societies, including the London Missionary Society in 1794, the Church Missionary Society in 1799, and the American Board of Commissioners for Foreign Mission (ABCFM) in 1810. The initial effort to spread the gospel in the Persian Gulf was by Henry Martyn, a chaplain of the English East India Company. Martyn translated the New Testament into Arabic and distributed copies of it (Skinner 1992, 46). Then in 1843, John Wilson, a Church of Scotland missionary based in Bombay sent some Bible teachers to the Persian Gulf. In 1848, a new Arabic translation of the Bible was initiated by the ABCFM. Thomas Valpy French, an Englishman and a retired Anglican Bishop from Lahore, Pakistan, arrived in Muscat, Oman, in February 1891 to open a new mission (Skinner 1992, 50).

Samuel M. Zwemer, James Cantine, Philip T. Phelps, and John G. Lansing from the United States organized the Arabian Mission in 1889. They soon set sail for the Persian Gulf region for evangelism, education, and medical care. They set up hospitals, schools, Bible shops, and organized tours. Zwemer, with the help of the Reformed Church in America, co-operated with Bishop French from the Church Missionary Society to expand the Christian witness in the region (Nazir-Ali 2009, 144). The medical ministry of the Gulf-wide work of the American Arabian Mission was what won the favor and gratitude of the local people (Thompson 2011, 31). First Protestant church services were held as early as the 1900s in Kuwait and Bahrain. The construction of church buildings followed only much later. The first resident Roman

Catholic priest only arrived in Kuwait in 1948 (George 2005, 301). The establishment in 1960 of the hospital and church in Al-Ain, a desert oasis in the UAE by The Evangelical Alliance Mission opened doors for Christian witness and outreach home visits (Ebenezer 2011).

The marked Christian presence in the Persian Gulf is a very recent phenomenon related to the large economic migration of people into the region. The rulers of the Gulf region have been very tolerant and have granted freedom for expatriates to gather for Christian worship and have even donated land for the construction of church edifices (Robehmed 2012). Every Friday, thousands of Christians gather to worship the God of the Bible, often at the same time as Muslims have Friday prayers in their mosques.

Most Christians belong to several denominations and nationalities. These include the Anglican Church, Reformed Church, Roman Catholic Church, Coptic Orthodox Church, Greek Orthodox Church, Armenian Orthodox Church, Mar Thoma Church, Syro-Malabar Church, Malankara Orthodox Syrian Church, Syrian Jacobite Church, Church of South India, St. Thomas Evangelical Church of India, Pentecostal Churches, the Brethren Assemblies, and more. In addition, there are hundreds of independent congregations and house groups of various traditions and sizes.

Figure 1: Estimates of Christians in the Persian Gulf (Sources used)

	Total Population	Christian Population	Percentage of Country
United Arab Emirates	8,260,000	980,000	11.9
Kuwait	3,600,000	550,400	15.3
Oman	3,090,000	320,000	10.4
Qatar	1,840,000	340,000	18.5
Bahrain	1,248,000	147,600	11.0
Grand Total	18,038,000	2,338,000	

South Asian Diaspora to the Persian Gulf

The five Persian Gulf countries have great wealth from oil. But with low populations, they face acute labor shortages. These shortages are met not by open migration, but using temporary import workers (Weiner 2007, 127). These transient migrants constitute more than two-thirds of the labor force of these nations and the population numbers of import workers are proportionately larger than the local citizens. The spectrum of migrants' ranges from highly skilled to non-skilled workers. The major growth in immigration to the Gulf followed the oil boom of 1973-74 (Raghuram 2008, 173) and South Asians constitute the biggest expatriate community in the Gulf region with Indian migrants being the largest. The remaining hail from Bangladesh, Pakistan, and Sri Lanka. The Nepalis began appearing in large numbers from the early 1990s (Perry 1997, 173).

The largest single group of South Asian workers in the Gulf are in the construction industry and a sizeable number are employed by the private sector and the Gulf governments. South Asian migrants often come with no baggage of political ideologies and make few demands. Furthermore, temporary migrants are not accorded any political representation (Walton-Roberts 2009, 210). Their wages are often less than their Western or Arab counterparts (Weiner 2007, 127). They are generally paid about half the salary of locals but do twice the amount of work (*INF Diaspora Digest No. 10,* 2012, 4). The number of South Asians who are merchants, shop owners, and traders are also significant considering the law that requires each foreigner to have a local Arab partner to obtain a business license outside the free zones.

Figure 2: Estimates of Indian and Pakistani Populations
in the Persian Gulf (Sources used)

	Total Population	Indians	Percentage of Country	Pakistanis	Percentage of Country
United Arab Emirates	8,260,000	1,900,000	23.0 percent	1,250,000	15.6 percent
Kuwait	3,600,000	650,000	18.1 percent	230,000	6.4 percent
Oman	3,090,000	500,000	16.1 percent	70,000	2.3 percent
Qatar	1,840,000	450,000	24.4 percent	120,000	6.5 percent
Bahrain	1,248,000	240,000	19.2 percent	80,000	6.4 percent
Grand Total	18,038,000	3,740,000		1,750,000	

South Asian Christian Presence in the Persian Gulf

The first South Asian Christian congregation in the Gulf region was believed to be the 'Ahmadi Christian Congregation' in Ahmadi, Kuwait. It was non-denominational and primarily consisted of Malayali Christians from Kerala, India, who worked at the Kuwait Oil Company. More Malayalis arrived in Kuwait City from Kerala and the Kuwait Town Malayalee Christian Congregation was formed in 1953 (Koshy 2003, 39).

With oil exploration and drilling expanding to the other Gulf States beginning in the 1960s and exploding in the 1970s, the need for migrant workers escalated. Waves of migration from various South Asian countries took place to tap into the economic boom. Among the thousands of South Asians were also Christians who brought their languages, cultures, Christian traditions, and worship styles. Multiple congregations were established primarily in larger urban centers or in areas where there were significant enclaves of South Asian Christians. The largest group of Christians in the Gulf States are South Asians, with the predominance being Indian Christians. South Asian congregations can be categorized by language, location, or liturgy. I found seven distinct types of congregations in my fieldwork

Mother-tongue congregations. Most South Asians worship in their own mother-tongue congregations: Malayalam, Tamil, Telugu, Urdu, Hindi, Punjabi, Nepali, etc. These groups are transplanted congregations of denominations in their respective country or state. The established denominations like the Anglican Church, Church of South India, Mar Thoma Church, Malankara Church, Syro-Malabar Church, Malankara Orthodox Syrian Church, Syrian Jacobite Church, St Thomas Evangelical Church of India, Pentecostal churches, and Brethren Assemblies have one or more congregations in each of the five Gulf nations. Using the mother tongue has been crucial to impact unreached peoples globally and to develop disciples and churches (Grimes 2009, 565). To ensure transmittance of cultural values and pride in their heritage and identity, some congregations offer weekly mother-tongue language instructions for Gulf-born children of their families.

English language congregations. South Asians who prefer English medium worship services choose to go to congregations which are often Western-based, Western-led, and trans-denominational. Often, these are multinational, multicultural, and multiethnic in composition. Therefore, diversity is highly valued, passionately pursued, and embraced. In recent years, a few mother-tongue congregations have offered English worship services for their second-generation youth.

Church compound-based congregations. Most of the denominational mother-tongue and English-language congregations are registered with the governments. With diverse worship styles and practices, they gather weekly at the state-designated church compounds in major cities. These huge compounds, like the National Evangelical Church of Kuwait (NECK) compound in Kuwait City, have multiple buildings which facilitate the weekly worship services of 85 congregations of all Christian traditions and languages with a combined attendance of 20,000 (Reeve 2012). The facilities are also used for various gatherings like congregational leadership meetings, discipleship classes, training, membership classes, and baptisms. NECK is a beehive of kingdom activity every day and most evenings. Since the early 1970s, a similar broad scope of ministries has occurred in Dubai at the Holy Trinity

Church compound at Bur Dubai. Likewise, at the Dubai Evangelical Church Centre at Jebel Ali since 2002, and at the Religious Complex in Doha, Qatar, since 2008.

Non-church compound-based congregations. One respondent informed that several Christian groups throughout the region not registered with the governments are mushrooming. They are often independent groups who meet for worship and prayer in large villa-type homes or hotel meeting rooms. Most operate with uncertainty and run the risk of being discovered and shut down by the governments.

Labor camp congregations. Thousands of South Asian male, blue-collar workers live in labor camps some distance from the urban centers. Transporting them to churches in the cities is a major challenge. As they come to Christ, they are organized into small 'house churches' which are male-dominated. Pastors and Christian workers from the cities provide the leadership, co-ordination, and spiritual nurture of these groups.

Liturgical congregations. Most of the South Asian historical churches use prescribed, standardized, and printed liturgy during their worship services. The liturgy could be in English, but often it is in the peoples' mother tongues. Some larger denominations have worship books containing not only their liturgy in the mother tongue, but also a Romanized version to encourage the second generation to participate in corporate worship. Some traditions use icons and incense in their worship ritual and liturgy.

Non-liturgical congregations. The Baptists, Brethren, Pentecostals, and other independent churches are non-liturgical. Therefore, their worship is more informal, extemporaneous, and contemporary. Their singing may range from solemnity to joyous hand clapping and sometimes are accompanied by sacred rhythmic movements.

Leadership in South Asian Christian Congregations

The criteria, structures, and roles of congregational leadership differ widely and depend upon their respective Christian heritage and tradition.

I want to further explore in detail the roles and responsibility of pastors, women, and lay leader in the Persian Gulf context.

Role of Pastors. The congregations of established denominations have duly-appointed priests and pastors who are granted time-sensitive clergy visas to serve the Gulf congregations for three to five years (Kurien 2012). These theologically-trained clergy with proven ministry track records in their homelands are often appointed to specific parishes by the hierarchy of respective ecclesiastical headquarters overseas. Volunteer lay people are elected to serve as officers on church boards or councils under the leadership of the clergy. Together, they fulfill their governance functions according to well-established constitutions and by-laws and agreed-upon policies. Dialogue, discussion, and even debate on issues are welcomed in the decision-making process.

Most of the independent congregations are led by bi-vocational or lay pastors. A clear majority of such leaders have not undergone much formal theological training. Most have had no opportunity. Only a few see the need for extra training because the majority believe that the success in leading and sustaining their group legitimizes their call and effectiveness. This is obviously a subjective evaluation and conclusion. I found a few who are seeking to upgrade and enhance their ministry competence by enrolling in distance learning avenues like theological education by extension courses offered modularly onsite or through the Internet. Seminaries are even offering their courses in Malayalam and Telugu. One frequent observation by interviewees was that there was a greater tendency of pastors of independent and/or charismatic congregations or fellowship groups to be autocratic and dictatorial in their leadership style.

Role of Women. The traditional roles of South Asian men and women are demarcated. These roles are maintained in the Gulf as well, even if a congregation is constituted by a women majority in membership and attendance. Women are seldom in pastoral roles or serve any major leadership role that involves key decision-making for the congregations. In general, the women's role is the traditional one. Women serve in the kitchen, prepare meals for their community fellowships or special functions, and clean up. Women also serve in some lesser leadership roles in ministries related to women, children, and youth. There is generally neither friction between men and women in regard to their roles nor do women voice dissent about lack of authority. South Asian Christian women do not define themselves as being in an inferior and powerless position. Rather, they see their role as different (not necessarily less important) than that of men. Women value their traditional family structure because of the power it gives them over their children.

Emergence of Lay Leaders. The adage 'Necessity is the mother of invention' is a daily reality in Gulf congregations. The dearth of competent clergy to lead congregations and fellowship groups provides the appropriate context for the lay person to step into leading roles. Many of them incrementally learn about the joys and pains of leadership through experimentation with hardly any mentoring. They often polish up their leadership skills through the 'school of hard knocks'.

In the last two decades, lay people in major centers have had access to excellent ministry leadership training. These one- to two-day or multi-evening seminars are often parachuted into the region from the West, but increasing options are originating from South Asia as well. This explains why there are proportionately higher numbers of competent lay leaders in the Gulf congregations than their sister congregations back home or elsewhere. Several lay leaders sensing God's call have entered fulltime or bi-vocational ministry.

South Asian Diaspora Christians in the Persian Gulf and the Great Commission

The Great Commission is Christ's command to 'make disciples of all nations' (Matt. 28:19-20). One of the primary emphases of the late Donald McGavran was: 'The purpose of missiology is to carry out the Great Commission. Anything other than that may be a good thing to do, but it is not missiology' (Hesselgrave 1988). Diaspora missiology is a new strategy for missions and can be defined as the 'Christian

response to the diaspora phenomenon in the twenty-first century'
(Wan 2011, 105). It can be viewed in three ways as one focuses on
South Asian diaspora in the Persian Gulf: missions *to* the South Asian
diaspora, missions *through* the South Asian diaspora, and missions *by*
and beyond the South Asian diaspora (Wan 2011, 115).

Missions to the South Asian Diaspora

South Asian diaspora populations in the Persian Gulf countries
are relatively unreached. There is little evidence of attention being
drawn to highlight the need for a missional emphasis among them or
any orchestrated mobilization being undertaken to reach them. The
estimated total number of South Asians in the Gulf ranges from 6.5
to 7 million (Indians are the largest component of South Asians with
a total of more than 3.79 million followed by 1.75 million Pakistanis.
Statistics about other South Asians are not readily available or accessible).
Many of the South Asians are Hindus, Muslims, Buddhists, and Sikhs.
Despite the lack of a concerted and comprehensive vision or strategy
to reach South Asians, many are turning to the Christian faith. Several
respondents in this study confirmed that among several people groups,
the rate of conversion is significantly higher than among their own
people back in their homeland. The following are various outreach
methods among South Asians in the Gulf.

Relational evangelism. God has used diaspora South Asian Christians
to reach out to their fellow South Asians with the gospel using the
relational paradigm (Wan 2011, 145). Authentic relationships have
proved to be key for much of the spiritual harvest. Since South Asian
society is highly relational, the pain of loneliness is especially intense
for migrants away from family and friends. Such displacement of
people from their familiar surroundings causes them to 'seek God, if
perhaps they might grope for him and find him' (Acts 17:27). This is
an important aspect of diaspora mission. Because of displacement,
unsaved South Asians like the Roman centurion Cornelius (Acts 10:1-
11, 18) are coming into proximity of the gospel and are being saved
(Ott 2011, 84).

Christian television. Christian television plays a major role in pre-evangelism and evangelism. Channels like God TV, Power vision, and Holy God TV offer popular Western Christian television shows sub-titled in South Asian languages. In addition, a plethora of South Asian-produced Christian programs cater to the major South Asian languages. Hundreds of people from other faiths who respond to the Christian message in the privacy of their residences often rely upon these television programs and other messages on DVDs to nurture them spiritually. Frequently, this happens many months before they join any fellowship group or congregation.

Visiting ministers. In the last two decades, there have been an increased number of South Asian itinerant pastors, evangelists, and musicians who have been sponsored by Christians for brief periods of time to do focused ministry in the Gulf States (Khan 2012). Some conduct large-scale evangelistic crusades within the church compound, while others conduct multiple small home meetings or provide leadership training or counseling seminars. The net result is that other faith South Asians are becoming followers of Jesus while nominal and relapsed Christians are revived, and the Kingdom of God is expanding.

Distribution of gospel materials. A ministry volunteer at a labor camp informed about distribution of gospel booklets and JESUS DVDs in various Indian languages has proven fruitful. One respondent stated that the periodic coming of Operation Mobilization ships to Gulf ports with their grand book exhibitions has galvanized evangelism. Curiosity attracts hundreds to go on board to tour the vessel, visit the book displays, purchase books and Bibles, pick up gospel literature, and even hear the gospel preached. The Bible Society and Christian bookstores operating in the region also serve as invaluable sources for appropriate literature and media resources for churches to use in evangelism, discipleship, and spiritual growth.

Labor camp outreach. Labor camps are very fertile for gospel outreach. With high levels of functional illiteracy among labor camp residents, the interactive chronological Bible story evangelism is proving effective.

Furthermore, Christmas and Easter seasons are especially conducive for concentrated evangelistic thrusts which has proven to be very fruitful. A lay pastor informed me that several city congregations and various ministry agencies visits labor camps every week to provide counseling, conduct gospel studies, and even lead worship services.

Youth outreach. Younger South Asians are highly responsive to the gospel. One youth leader informed about many retreats, camps, and Christian groups on university campuses are proving effective in presenting the truth claims of Christ and in discipleship. An analysis of the evangelistic results indicates many South Asians from unreached and unreachable people groups in their home countries are being saved in their host countries.

Missions through the South Asian Diaspora

Most of the first generation of South Asian diaspora Christians and congregations in the Gulf demonstrate little mission interest beyond their own mother-tongue people. On the other hand, there is an encouraging, emerging trend among the second-generation South Asians. A tentmaker Westerner told that second-generation South Asians are in a state of flux because they cannot call the Gulf region their home and feel alienated from ancestral homelands. However, some of these believers are growing in vision and passion to reach out to others cross-culturally with the gospel. Some have taken advantage of small-group training in evangelism and have been exposed to world-class mission events like the Urbana Student Missions Convention.

Missions by and Beyond the South Asian Diaspora

One of the commendable traits of South Asian Christianity in the Gulf is its engagement with missions beyond their immediate region. The Gulf South Asian Christians and churches have become a funding source for many ministries, primarily in South Asia: evangelistic thrusts, church planting, orphanages, church-building projects, etc. Their generosity is widely known. It is not uncommon to find a prayer fellowship committed to raising funds to support an evangelist or a church planter back in his or her home country. A lay respondent informed that several ministry representatives from South Asia regularly visit the Gulf region, sometimes making repeated visits or annually, to secure financial resources. They often chart an itinerary of several weeks in all five Gulf States. Seldom are they disappointed with the gracious and bountiful response to their appeal.

Numerous new South Asian Christians have returned to their homelands and witnessed to their family and friends. As a result, many house-based churches and church-plants have been established (Maharaj 2012). A retired pastor told me how several South Asian diaspora churches in Australia, Canada, the United Kingdom, and the USA have been blessed by leadership of some South Asian Christians who have migrated from the Gulf.

Concerns and Challenges

The following are ten major concerns and challenges South Asian Christianity faces in the Persian Gulf that I identified from my field study:

a) There is an acute lack of theologically equipped leaders who can serve as pastors, teachers, and leaders of congregations and prayer fellowship groups. Many current leaders are untrained and untested. The result is that spiritually-impoverished congregations are surviving without balanced or sound doctrinal teaching.

b) The gospel preached is sometimes watered down and people embrace an 'easy believism.' The result is that believers do not receive solid biblical instruction or pursue serious discipleship or training.

c) Much of the evangelism approaches are less than holistic. The result is that maximum potential gospel impact for the kingdom is not attained.

d) About 30-40 percent of South Asians are functionally illiterate. The result is that evangelizing and discipling them is a challenge which needs to be addressed sensitively and creatively.

e) Frequent splits in congregations occur for non-biblical reasons, including egotism or regionalism. The result is that suspicion and mistrust among leaders and members of various congregations are sustained.

f) Some churches are fiercely independent and tend to be insulated and isolated. The result is that non-collaboration with the rest of the body of Christ robs every believer of corporate witness and partnership.

g) Some visiting ministers manipulate their audiences and raise obscene amounts of money for personal and family use, while others teach spurious doctrine. The result is that there is a loss of credible witness by tarnishing the gospel and confusing believers.

h) Many of the established denominational congregations employ traditional and formal styles of worship. The result is that second generation Christians feel disconnected from the service and neglected in the meeting of their needs or preferences.

i) Most congregations are monocultural and/or monolingual. The result is that an ethnocentric worldview and attitude which discourages intentional cross-cultural evangelism is developed.

j) Most Christians and congregations have neither a burden nor a strategy to reach the local Muslim populations. The result is that there are missed opportunities to communicate the good news of Jesus even within the restrictions imposed by the Islamic rulers.

Conclusion

A few could conclude that South Asian diaspora Christianity in the Persian Gulf is dormant or dull. The spiritual passion and church attendance are commendably high. The congregational life is generally meaningful and vibrant. Many from Hindu, Sikh and Muslim backgrounds have embraced Christianity and actively involved in local churches. With strong, godly, collaborative leadership coupled with kingdom-minded visionary strategy, the region can be a powerhouse for local and global missions in the future.

References

Ebenezer, Vikram 2011 'Roots for the Redemption of the Arab Arabians' PhD Dissertation. Pasadena, CA: Fuller Theological Seminary.

George, K.M. 2005 *Development of Christianity through the Centuries: Tradition and Discovery,* Tiruvalla, India: Christava Sahitya Samithi.

Grimes, Barbara F. 2009 'From Every Language', in Ralph D. Winter and Steven C. Hawthorne (eds), *Perspectives on the World Christian Movement: A Reader,* 4th ed.; Pasadena, CA: William Carey Library.

Hesselgrave, David. 1988 is quoting from a personal letter he received from the late Donald McGavran on 7 April 1988. See also Hesselgrave, *Paradigms in Conflict: 10 Key Questions in Christian Missions Today,* Grand Rapids: Kregel Publications, 2006, 316.

Holzmann, John (ed). 2001. *The Church of the East,* Littleton, CO: Sonlight Curriculum Ltd.

INF Diaspora Digest No. 10. 2012, Kathmandu, Nepal: International Nepal Fellowship, August.

Kapp, Annegret. 2008. 'In Dubai Christians Pray Side by Side but Not Always Together', *Earned Media.* 19 May.

Khan, Gabrial 2012. Interview, Kuwait, March 31 .

Koshy, K.P. 2003. 'Christianity in the Arabian Gulf and Kuwait: The Role of Kuwait Town.

Malayalee Christian Congregation', in *The Kuwait Town Malayalee Christian Congregation Golden Jubilee Souvenir,* Safat, Kuwait: published privately.

Kurien, C.M. 2012, Interview, Kuwait, April 2.

Raghuram, Parvati, Ajaya Sahoo, Brij Maharaj, and Dave Sangha (eds), 2008. *Tracing an Indian Diaspora: Contexts, Memories, Representations,* New Delhi: Sage Publications.

Maharaj, Dinesh 2012 Interview, Kuwait, April 9.

Nazir-Ali, Michael 2009 *From Everywhere to Everywhere: A World View of Christian Mission,* Eugene, OR: Wipf & Stock Publishers.

Ott, Craig. 2011. "Diaspora and Relocation as Divine Impetus for Witness in the Early Church" in *Diaspora Missiology.* Enoch Wan (Editor). Portland, OR: Institute of Diaspora Studies at Western Seminary.

Perry, Cindy L. 1997 *Nepali around the World: Emphasizing Nepali Christians of the Himalayas,* Kathmandu: Etka Books.

Prakash C. Jain (ed). 2007. *Indian Diaspora in West Asia: A Reader,* New Delhi: Manohar Publisher.

Raghuram, Parvati. 2008 'Immigration Dynamics in the Receiving State: Emerging Issues for the Indian Diaspora in the United Kingdom', in Parvati Raghuram, Ajaya Kumar Sahoo, Brij Maharaj and Dave Sangha, Tracing an Indian Diaspora: Contexts, Memories and Representations. New Delhi: Sage Publications. 171-190.

Reeve, Warren 2012, email message to author, September 6.

Robehmed, Sacha 2012 'Christianity in the Gulf', *Open Democracy* 13 August, available at www.opendemocracy.net/sacha-robehmed/christianity-in-gulf (Accessed August 14,12).

Skinner, Raymond F. 1992 'Christians in Oman: Ibadism in Oman and Development in the Field of Christian-Muslim Relationships', unpublished paper.

Sources for Figure 1 to arrive at rounded-off estimates: 1) Foreign and Commonwealth Office, United Kingdom – www.fco.gov.uk/en/, 2) Local Government Agencies –www.dubaifaqs.com/population-of-uae.php; www.qsa.gov.qa/eng/index.htm' and 3) BBC: Information on Christian Population – www.bbc.co.uk/news/worldmiddle-east-15239529 (Accessed June 2014).

Sources for Figure 2 to arrive at rounded-off estimates: 1) CIA, The World Fact book – www.cia.gov/index.html, 2) Foreign and Commonwealth Office, United Kingdom – www.fco.gov.uk/en, 3) The World Bank –www.data.worldbank.org/country/unitedarab-emirates, 4) Indexmundi – www.indexmundi.com, 5) Local Government Agencies – www.dubaifaqs.com/population-of-uae.php and www.qsa.gov.qa/eng/ index.htm.

Thompson, Andrew. 2011. *Christianity in the UAE: Culture and Heritage* (Dubai, UAE: Motivate Publishing).

Walton-Roberts, Margaret. 2009. 'Globalization, National Autonomy and Non-Resident Indians', in Laxmi Narayan Kadeker, Ajaya Kumar Sahoo, and Gauri Bhattacharya (eds), *The Indian Diaspora: Historical and Contemporary Context* Jaipur, India: Rawat Publications.

Wan, Enoch. 2011. 105 *Diaspora Missiology: Theory, Methodology, and Practice* (Portland, OR: Institute of Diaspora Studies at Western Seminary).

Weiner, Myron. 'International Migration and Development: Indians in the Persian Gulf', in *Indians in West Asia: A Reader* Ed. Prakash C.Jain. New Delhi: Manohar Publishers 2007. 121-41.

Intergenerational Differences within Indian Christian Churches in the United States

Prema Kurien

This chapter draws on my new, *Ethnic Church Meets Megachurch: Indian American Christianity in Motion* (2017), on the Mar Thoma church in the United States.[1] The Mar Thoma denomination is part of the Syrian Christian church in Kerala that traces its origin to the legendary arrival of Apostle Thomas on the shores of Kerala in 52 CE. While the denomination is based in Kerala it is now a global church with branches around the world, including the United States. According to 2012 figures from the Pew Research Center, Indian Christians constitute around 18 percent of the Indian American population. Syrian Christians from Kerala constitute the largest group of Indian Christians in the United States, and among Syrian Christian denominations, the Mar Thoma church is considered the best organized and most active. The book is based on a research which I conducted in different parts of the

[1] Research for this project was made possible by funding from the Pew Charitable Trusts, the Louisville Institute, the American Institute for Indian Studies, an Appleby Mosher award, and a summer project assistant award from Syracuse University. I am grateful for the research assistance provided by Laurah Klepinger-Mathew.

United States and in India between 1999 and 2015 and it examines the shift in the understandings of Mar Thoma members regarding their ethnic and Christian identity as a result of their US migration and the coming of age of the American-born generation.

Some Mar Thomites, including Mar Thoma *achens* (pastors), arrived in the United States in the early decades of the twentieth century for higher education, including Christian theological education (assisted by the ecumenical connections between the Mar Thoma leadership and Protestant institutions in the United States), but at that time, due to the immigration laws in place, US settlement was not an option. Consequently, these individuals returned to Kerala after their education and many provided leadership in the Mar Thoma church. The large-scale Mar Thoma American immigration began in the late 1960s after the passage of the 1965 Immigration Act.

Religion and religious institutions generally play an important role in shaping the out-migration and settlement patterns of immigrants. This is true of the Mar Thoma case as well, where church networks have enabled the global migration of Mar Thomites, and helped them to find jobs, and get acclimatized in their new contexts. Mr. Thomas Mathews was a middle-aged migrant from Kerala in the Bethelville church (a pseudonym) who had arrived in the United States in the 1980s and was a friendly and active member of the congregation. When I asked him how he had located the church (which was far away from where he lived), he told me, "the first thing Mar Thoma Christians do even before getting to a new place is to find out where the nearest Mar Thoma church is!" A second-generation member of another Mar Thoma parish, Reeni, talked about how the Mar Thoma church became "a translator" of American society to her parents when they arrived from India. "And like people who had been here for thirty years could explain to them oh . . . that's just how they do it . . . I mean, just the basics of everyday living, they picked up [from people in church]".

But immigrant churches like the Mar Thoma also face several challenges to successfully institutionalize as an "ethnic" church in a context where Christianity is the majority religion. In the post-denominational society of the United States, where Christianity is the majority religion, it becomes difficult for Syrian Christians to use religion as the locus of their ethnicity as they can do in Kerala. They must deal with the US population's lack of familiarity with their ancient Indian Christian community – but more important, they have trouble transmitting the distinct liturgical, ritual, and ecclesiastical practices of the traditional church to their children. An important issue is how to retain the allegiance of the second and later generations to an "ethnic" Christianity in the face of the intense competition from American evangelical churches.

There is a lot of scholarship on how nondenominational evangelicalism and the rise of American mega churches are "remaking" American mainline churches and American religious traditions. But American evangelicalism also has had a profound impact on the 'ethnic' churches of recent immigrants. In the Mar Thoma case, the widespread prevalence and dominance of American evangelicalism created an environment in which the traditional practices of the Mar Thoma church seemed alien to its American-born generation. Evangelical Christianity in the United States is not monolithic. Second-generation (and some first-generation) American Mar Thomites have participated in a variety of evangelical institutions including campus groups, Bible study fellowships, and an array of evangelical churches. Television, internet, and radio ministries, internet websites, music and books provide other sources of influence. In interviews and conversations, however, the type of church that came up most frequently and to which the Mar Thoma church was compared, was the large trans-denominational or non-denominational churches – the US mega churches. Mega churches offer several services over the weekend, and sometimes even during the week, with slick multimedia presentations and contemporary music led by professional bands. They also have programming for a variety of age groups.

Describing the attraction of such churches, Vilja, a 1.5 generation (those born abroad who immigrated as young children) woman in her forties, explained that the youth in her Mar Thoma congregation liked "the short contemporary service, the music, pastors who are fluent in English, and sermons that are well put-together, and have life application." She mentioned that they also liked the fact that many of these pastors provided an outline of their sermon and the key points on a screen while they were speaking. Shobha, a second-generation Mar Thoma American who had left the Mar Thoma church, was enthusiastic about the large non-denominational church she attended along with her husband. "They have an amazing band, and amazing musicians. And we just love worshiping there. It brings a lot of people from the community in because it's like a free concert on Sunday morning – bagels and doughnuts too!"

Shobha's description of the service at the mega church that she attended as a "free concert on Sunday" is very apt. In these churches, the carefully choreographed, emotionally charged productions with dramatic mood lighting, video enhancement, and professional music are designed to create an uplifting atmosphere. This is probably why many of the Mar Thoma youth described such churches as being "on fire for Christ." They contrasted this type of worship experience with the sedate, formal service and the off-key congregational singing in the Mar Thoma churches. Evangelical mega churches are also structured very differently from the Mar Thoma church. While the Mar Thoma churches are small and community-oriented, mega churches are large and impersonal – but many of the second generation that I interviewed thought that the lack of community orientation of these evangelical churches helped to foster spirituality. Although the older, immigrant generation said that it was important for them to know "the person who is sitting next to me in the pew," the younger generation considered the social aspect of the Mar Thoma church a hindrance to being able to focus on God during the service. The services at mega churches are also much shorter than at the Mar Thoma church, which means that people could fit in many other activities during the day. If they went to a Mar Thoma church on the other hand, most of the Sundays were spent on the commute, the service, and church activities. The financial obligations for Mar Thomites attending mega churches were also lower than at a Mar Thoma church. Due to these considerations, in the United States, small, ethnic churches like the Mar Thoma face competition for their youth from the large mega churches that have become a ubiquitous part of the contemporary American Christian landscape.

As a result of absorbing evangelical ideas, second-generation Mar Thoma American understandings of religion diverged greatly from that of their parents. The Mar Thoma church emphasizes the importance of corporate worship and its liturgy, and immigrant members generally interpret being Christian as the outcome of being born and raised in a Christian family, sacralized by infant baptism into the church community. The second-generation Mar Thoma Americans, on the other hand, were imbibing the anti-tradition, anti-liturgical, and individual worship orientation of evangelical Christianity and tended to view a Christian identity as the outcome of achieving a personal relationship with Christ, often beginning with a "born-again" experience. Religion and ethnicity also played different roles in the lives of the two generations and consequently, immigrants and their children had distinct ideas about the role of the church, Christian worship, and evangelism, sometimes leading to misunderstandings and disagreements. My book focuses on these intergenerational differences since the topic of generational cleavages within the church emerged right from the beginning of my fieldwork and continued over the course of the rest of my research.

Immigrant Perspectives

Religious and Ethnic identity are Intertwined

For the immigrant generation, being Christian was inextricably intertwined with being Syrian Christian Malayalis. Except for those women who had become a part of the Mar Thoma denomination by marriage, it also meant being a Mar Thoma Christian. In other words, for most of this group, heritage, faith, and denomination were bound together and were all conferred by birth, as was the case of most other social groups in India. Since the church that Mar Thoma Christians traditionally attended was the one that they were "born into," there was no question about which church to go to when they came to the United States (provided, there was a church of the denomination in the area). Although, as we will see, many of the second-generation members seemed to view the social and cultural function of the church as a distraction from its primary spiritual mission, most of the immigrants I interviewed emphasized that what they valued about the Mar Thoma church, particularly in the United States, was that it was not only their faith community, but also their social and cultural community. As the primary community center for immigrants, diasporic religious institutions take over a variety of functions not performed by religious institutions in the homeland. As Nimmi Verghese told me, "Since our families are around in India, we are not so close to friends or members of the church. The church community here substitutes for the family we had in India." Thus, the social lives of the members of the immigrant generation were closely tied in with the church. Most of them indicated that their close friends were other church members.

Many immigrants said, however, that the main reason that they had decided to join the Mar Thoma church (and drive the long distance there and back every Sunday) was for the sake of the children. "We wanted them to know our culture and to grow up in it." For instance, when I asked Priya Ittycheria, a woman in her late thirties who had immigrated to the United States when she was twelve years old, spoke with an American accent, and was very comfortable with American culture, why she attended the Mar Thoma church instead of a local church, she told me: "I like the traditions, I feel comfortable with my people and with Indian culture. I want my children to grow up with the Indian culture. This is the primary reason I attend the Mar Thoma church instead of a local church."

But the loyalty of the older generation to the church was not just because of the community they were able to form or because it was part of their cultural heritage. Many spoke about how they appreciated the spiritual benefits of the liturgical service and the *qurbana*, which they had been used to from their youth. They found the liturgy comforting, and it also put them in the "mood" to pray their personal prayers. For instance, despite the warmth with which Gracy Mathai described the fellowship and support she had obtained in the Mar Thoma church when her mother died, it was the liturgy that she said she had missed the most. The same was the case with the traditional Malayalam hymns, sung to the accompaniment of the organ. For example, Sosamma Mathew said she went to the English service for the sake of her children but that she did not like it. "It is not religious for me. I just go and come but don't feel spiritual at all." Perhaps because of this, many Mar Thoma churches had a much lower attendance for the English service.

Mathew Alexander, an immigrant in his fifties, probably summed the feelings of many in the immigrant generation when he articulated the reason he continued to attend the Mar Thoma church,

> I grew up in the Mar Thoma church. It was ingrained in me. I feel lost and left out [in the United States] and it is the Mar Thoma church that gives me a sense of proportion. We can go to a white man's church, but our community is in the Mar Thoma. How much can we integrate into the local church? Do they accept us from their heart – for instance if we want to conduct a funeral or baptism our way, will they accept it? I don't think so.

Despite being a highly successfully executive, Mr. Alexander speaks poignantly about his sense of alienation within American society and his need for the Mar Thoma church to provide him with a moral and personal compass, as well as his community.

Second-Generation Perspectives

Intertwining ethnicity and religion compromises spirituality

Although second-generation American Mar Thomites grew up in the church and attended the services regularly in their childhood and teenage years, they had a very different understanding of the relationship between ethnicity and religion from the immigrant generation. Like many other religiously oriented second-generation Asian Americans, almost all of the second-generation members who were regular church goers-whether they currently attended the Mar Thoma church or a nonethnic church-separated their religious identity from their ethnic or sectarian identity and said that their Christian identity was primary. In Sheila's words: "Being a Christian is more important than being a Mar Thomite. Mar Thoma is a secondary part of who I am. Being Christian is first and foremost-to know that Jesus Christ is our Lord and Savior. And only after that am I a Mar Thomite."

This decoupling of religion and ethnicity was partly a consequence of how they had learned about Christianity. All the young people I talked to who said that religion played an important role in their lives indicated that their primary sources of information about Christianity were not their parents or the *achen* (pastor), or even the Sunday school, as had been the case for their parents. Many had attended private Christian schools and so had first learned about Christianity through the classes and speakers at the school. School and college friends and campus Christian groups were an even more important source of knowledge and of support. A few had done a lot of reading on their own. They also mentioned television programs and web sites. Most of the older cohorts of Mar Thoma second-generation members indicated that when they left home for college they "became Christian" through their involvement in evangelical churches and groups.

While my qualitative study cannot provide numbers regarding the proportion of dropouts from the Mar Thoma church, every one of the older, post-college young people that I talked to indicated that large numbers of their cohorts had left. This exodus began when they went away to college, but many did not return to the church even after they had moved back for jobs in the area. Many became unchurched, but those who were religiously oriented attended large, predominantly white or multiracial evangelical churches that were within commuting distance. In the words of Anu, a young woman in her late twenties who had grown up in the Mar Thoma church but now attended a large, multiracial evangelical church,

As I got older, I started going to different churches to see what it's like . . . and I feel, once you attend another church besides the Mar Thoma church, most people tend to walk away from the Mar Thoma church . . . Like our generation . . . most of them do not go. Yeah, they've all like pretty much started going to local churches and being involved.

My research on this phenomenon within the Mar Thoma church has also been corroborated by others. According to a 2013 study conducted by Mar Thomite Thomas Thazhayil, only about 20 percent of the second and third generation Mar Thomites continued to attend the Mar Thoma church on a regular basis. An older Mar Thomite man I interviewed, shared an unpublished essay on the Mar Thoma church that he had written in the mid-2000s. In the essay, he noted that out of the twenty-five children of the early Mar Thoma immigrants that he knew, only four remained in the Mar Thoma church.

In the early 2000s, however, some activist, evangelically influenced Mar Thoma youth began to return, with the goal of trying to minister to the second generation and to challenge and transform the church. Since then, younger members have been picking up evangelical ideas from within the Mar Thoma church. The youth leaders who teach in the Sunday School, and who lead youth and young family's classes are those who have attended (and in some cases continue to attend) evangelical campus groups like InterVarsity, evangelical Bible groups like the Bible Study Fellowship, or non-denominational churches. All the English oriented classes and organizations in the Mar Thoma church draw on resources provided by evangelical groups. For instance, the praise and worship songs sung in the Mar Thoma church are from large evangelical publishing houses like Indelible Grace and Hillsong, as well as contemporary Christian music singers; the young family's groups use the resources provided by the Family Life series, Our Daily Bread ministries, and Charles Stanley's In Touch Ministries. One of the churches that I studied was using leaders from the Child Evangelism Fellowship and its curriculum for its Vacation Bible School session, at least for that year. However, the theological assumptions embedded in these organizations, forms of worship, and education are very different from those of the Mar Thoma church.

As indicated, many of the American-born members contrasted the Mar Thoma church with non-denominational evangelical churches. For instance, Manju said, "You go to church to learn about God, to be closer to him, to feel his presence, and to be renewed. Not for the politics and the social stuff." What she appreciated about Millbury, the large non-denominational church that she and her family now attend, was that she could "just focus on God," since "I don't have to think about anyone else, I don't have to worry about what anyone else might think about me or is going to say to me." In short, the second generation viewed ethnicity and social bonds as being a distraction from achieving spiritual goals.

The language barrier was another obstacle to spiritual growth that several youths mentioned. Even second-generation members like Mary who knew Malayalam well mentioned the language barrier they faced during the Malayalam services:

> I know Malayalam, but when I pray deep down in my heart, it's like in English. . . You know, the parents always argue, well the kids should learn Malayalam. But you want to ask , "Mom, would you be able to really feel, you know, the Holy Spirit moving in you if you sang a song in English versus Malayalam?"

An Ethnic Church Is Not Christian: Heaven is Going to be Multicultural

Viju, who was in a non-denominational church, emphasized the value of worshiping with people of other cultures. When asked why that was important, he replied:

> The main reason is, I mean heaven's going to be multicultural. And so, you know, one of the things that we always say about our church is, we want people to get a foretaste of what heaven's going to be like and heaven's not going to be like you're worshiping with people that look just like you, but people from all different backgrounds. Like it says in the Bible, tribes, tongues, you know, of all nations.

Satish, a young man in his twenties who attended the Mar Thoma and a non-denominational church, was looking into seminary schools, since he was interested in going into full-time ministry and becoming a pastor. He said that in the long run he wanted to be at a mixed church based "just strictly on faith" since he felt that the "political aspect" in the Mar Thoma church was a barrier to spiritual growth. Like Viju, Satish emphasizes that heaven is going to be multicultural and that his generation recognizes the importance of having a "mixed" church comprising people from a variety of backgrounds, and not just Malayalis. We can see here that multiculturalism, as interpreted by both Viju and Satish, meant that churches should not be ethnic, but instead should be multiracial. However, a multiracial church would necessarily mean that many of the Mar Thoma traditions that are accessible only to the initiated would have to be abandoned.

Many of those who remained in the church also criticized its closed, ethnic nature. For instance, Jacob declared, "I believe in opening our doors to everyone. The Mar Thoma faith doesn't. It is very closed-door oriented. To me, that's not being Christian-like." Jacob is referring to the discomfort of the immigrant generation with members of the local community entering the Mar Thoma church.

Valuing the Social Benefits of the Church

Despite their criticisms of how the "ethnic" features of the Mar Thoma church hindered their spiritual growth, most second-generation Mar Thoma Americans, even those who had subsequently left for other churches, talked about how much they had enjoyed being part of the congregation when they were young, for social reasons. Since their parents often tended to be very restrictive, not allowing them to go over to the houses of their schoolmates, church was their one place of freedom where they could spend time with their friends. The church community had been like their extended family. Reeba remembers it this way: "You got yelled at by your parents, you got yelled at by your friend's parents, so it was very, very community oriented. And I loved it. I absolutely loved it!" Youth who were going to a local college, and

consequently continued to attend the Mar Thoma church, often spoke
enthusiastically about the nurturing youth group. The community
orientation and familial nature of the church were the primary factors
motivating some second-generation members to continue to attend
the services (sometimes in addition to a non-denominational church),
to return to serve the youth, or to want to raise their children in the
church. Alex said that he had stayed even though most of his cohort
in church had left for other churches, since his father had taught him
that "your church is your family" and that it was his responsibility to
mentor the "younger guys" in church. However, many American-born
Mar Thoma youth who have absorbed the individualistic paradigm of
evangelicalism feel a tension between their social and cultural needs
on the one hand and their spiritual needs on the other. Those that
remained in the Mar Thoma church appreciated the ethnic community
and social support the church provided but felt that the Mar Thoma
church and service did not provide an optimal environment for spiritual
development.

Valuing Ethnicity but in Secular Spheres

This tension was particularly acute because second-generation Mar
Thomites valued their Kerala heritage. Most married other Syrian
Christians and, like their parents, practically all their close friends were
from one of the Syrian Christian denominations. After telling me that
her Christian identity was more important than her Indian identity,
Sally went on to explain what she appreciated about Indian culture:
"Respect for elders, the family emphasis. I enjoy going back to India.
The food, the people, and all that. The values, I guess. I think the
culture is a lot different from the American culture and when I go
back to India I just feel right at home." Unlike their parents, however,
American-born Mar Thomites felt that their spiritual objectives would
be weakened if they mixed their religion with secular goals such as
learning the language and maintaining ethnic ties. Miriam, who had
mixed feelings about the Mar Thoma church and was staying in it
because it was her husband's wish, expressed the discomfort with
intertwining ethnicity and religion, clearly saying:

Don't get me wrong. I *love* my culture. I think I am more Indian than most of my friends. But I don't believe that culture and Christianity must go hand in hand. I think I can teach them [her daughters] the traditions of India and our ancestors without compromising their faith. And sometimes I feel that going to the Mar Thoma church that's really what I am doing.

In Miriam's understanding of the relationship between culture and Christianity, the concept of a "de-ethnicized" religion is clear: she argues that maintaining Mar Thoma traditions will compromise the Christian faith of her daughters. Similarly, Sarah, who had waxed eloquent about her appreciation for Indian culture, was adamant that when she did have children, she would send them to the Sunday school at the non-denominational church that she currently attended.

I wouldn't send them to a Mar Thoma church . . . because above the culture and the identity and all that, we have an identity in Christ and spiritual growth needs to be there. And I think that this [non-denominational] church would provide it. I would still do things with the Indian people. I have cousins. We do a lot of things, but you need to be grounded in the word of God and I think the Mar Thoma church doesn't provide it.

In other words, the second generation who left the Mar Thoma church tried to resolve the tension between their appreciation for their ethnic heritage and their opposition to ethnic churches by arguing that they did not need to go to an ethnic church to be around co-ethnics.

Intergenerational Tensions within the Church

Since the first and second generations had such a different understanding of the meaning of being Christian, the two groups were often at odds, both in the church and at home about religion. The second-generation youth were contemptuous of the "automatic Christianity" model of the older generation. Several of them talked about the fact that the older generation did not really know the word of God well or how to apply the Bible to their lives. However, the older generation were deeply offended when the youth stated or implied that they, the elders, were not true Christians because they did not have a "born again" experience and did not personally evangelize. Dr. Peters, one of the founding members of the Bethel Ville church, summed up the perspective of many of the older generation when he said, "We are a traditional church. . . We believe that it is the obligation of those who are Christians [by birth] to go to their church and become part of the church. And though we may not personally evangelize to people of other faiths, our church supports the activities of missionaries who do."

When talking to me, many members of the older generation spoke passionately about the hardships that they had experienced (and continued to experience) due to the process of immigration and relocation. In most cases, they justified these hardships by saying that it had been for the sake of the children (although it was not always clear that this was the original motivation for the migration). Thus, they found it particularly upsetting when the youth in the church were trying to take away the one place where they could recreate home and be validated, and when their children were rejecting all their cherished traditions and becoming strangers to them. The youth, on the other hand, felt that their parents were placing an undue burden on them. As one young man put it, "We didn't ask them to come here. But now that they are here, they can't expect us to act like we are still living in India in the 1960s."

Conclusion

The American-born generation had internalized the individualistic perspective of contemporary spiritualism and evangelicalism, and consequently viewed the social, cultural, and historical practices of the Mar Thoma church as a distraction from its spiritual mission. In embracing an evangelical orientation, American-born Mar Thoma youth separated their faith and their sociocultural identity. As a result, although most valued their heritage and eventually married other Syrian Christians, preserving the history and traditions of the Mar Thoma church was not a priority. At the same time, they appreciated friends and community that the church provided, and thus were caught between what they considered to be their spiritual needs and their social needs.

I identified four different strategies that such individuals adopted. There was an older group that had left the church in the 1990s (some attended evangelical churches, others became unchurched), who had few connections with the Mar Thoma community other than their immediate family, and only maintained their ethnic identity in the home (I was not able to speak to anyone in this group). There were individuals in their late twenties and early thirties who had left the Mar Thoma church but still maintained close relationships with people of their age in the church. A third group in this age category, remained in the church but, as we have seen, were critical about many of its central ethnic practices. Some of these individuals tried to transform it, failing which they attempted to create subgroups or organizations like the "young couples group" where they could connect with like-minded second-generation members. A fourth group comprised a younger demographic, those in their early to late twenties who were unmarried and were either studying or working. They attended both the Mar Thoma church and an evangelical church every week, probably because their lack of family obligations gave them the time to do so.

The situation of each Mar Thoma parish was somewhat different, depending on the composition of congregation and the nature of the area, so the long-term outcome may also vary. Regardless, the Mar Thoma North American diocese is likely to be substantially transformed through the influence of its evangelically influenced American-born members. A change within the American parishes will probably change some of the traditional doctrines and practices of the Mar Thoma church. This is particularly the case since American evangelical churches now have branches in India, and English-dominant Mar Thoma youth there are attracted to evangelical parishes in Indian cities that have links to American nondenominational churches.

Reference

Kurien, Prema. 2017. *Ethnic Church Meets Megachurch: Indian American Christianity in Motion*. New York: New York University Press.

'I Still Call Australia Home:' Indian Christians Negotiate Their Faith in Australia

Jonathan D. James

Introduction

Indians, Chinese and Arabs travelled to the Indonesian islands in search of spice and gold as early as the seventh century CE. In their journeys, some of these foreign traders noticed the coastline of Australia but very few settled in this foreboding island-nation (Coedes 1968 and Munoz 2006). The contemporary Australia, however, offers a different scenario. Recent studies indicate that migrant Hindus and Sikhs are flourishing as religious communities in Australia (Billmoria et. al. 2015) and their numbers have doubled between 2006 and 2016. The Christian Research Association (CRA) revealed this growth in comparative terms:

> The Hindu community is already much larger than the Pentecostal community in Australia, and the Sikhs are much larger than the Salvation Army. If their rate of growth continues the Hindus and Sikhs will surpass the number of Muslims and the number of Buddhists in Australia by 2016 making them the second largest religious community surpassed only by the Christians! (2016)

But what about Indian Christian communities in Australia? The title of this chapter is borrowed from the words of the iconic song, *"I Still Call Australia Home"* alluding to how Indian Christians practice ancestral faith while remaining loyal to their new homeland. My research was informed by academic studies, public records and personal interviews of Christian leaders and members from the two groups that form my case studies.

I begin by reviewing diaspora studies to provide theoretical foundations for the research on the Indian Christian diaspora and present an overview of Indian Christian communities in Australia and how they fit into the Christian landscape through the practice and propagation of their faith and culture. Then, I describe two brief case studies of Indian Christian communities located in Perth (Western Australia), one from a Pentecostal and the other from a Brethren background that meets outside the structured church. I conclude the chapter by drawing out the salient features and challenges of Indian Christianity in Australia.

Diaspora Studies

In the 1960s and 70s, sociologists regarded Indians in Europe as a subset of colonial multicultural European society. 'Ethnicity' and 'diaspora' were not used in these studies because Indians were regarded as a segmented sociological ethnic group, albeit with unique institutions and practices (Brereton 1982). During the 1990s and beyond, the terms 'Indian diaspora', 'Indian identity' and 'Indian groups' were prevalent because religion (Hinduism, Sikhism and Islam) was used for categorizing the Indian diaspora (Desai 1963; Rukmani 2001). At the same time, scholars started to analyze Indians in terms of their regional identities and based on languages such as Telugu, Tamil, Malayalee, Gujarati and Bhojpuri communities (Brack 1988).

Some scholars have used novel theoretical concepts about the Indian diaspora, such as 'imagined diaspora' (Anderson 2002), implying that Indians are a socially constructed reality. The image of India as a country of origin for the parents and as a place of ancestral heritage for descendants born in Western countries, are primarily based on shared memories. Whereas those called 'persons of Indian origin' (PIO), (a term used by the Indian government to categorize Indians born in India but living overseas) may consider India their homeland, they are raised and socialized outside of India. To these Indians, 'Indianness' is an imagined concept (Anderson 2002). This notion has gained traction because in many European countries, the host culture addresses Indians as "Dutch Indians", "German Indians" and the like (Gautam 2013, 9). And some scholars have introduced the term 'exemplary diaspora' to depict diaspora Indians who accept their minority status and identify with their adopted country (Barth 1969). Alternatively, Indians in the diaspora are sometimes compared to the Jewish diaspora as a transnational social group, in their valuing of education, professionalism and mobility. Framing the Indian diaspora in terms of a transnational social community is based on the perception that overseas Indians possess innate social values of Indian heritage which are transplanted everywhere they go.

Another finding that resonates with my study is the concept of 'twice migrants' or 'multiple migrants' (Bhachu 2015, 1-4). This refers to Indians who migrate to more than one country. Such migrants have typically learned new skills and developed networking opportunities that assisted in their overall integration with new territories and people groups. In the most recent decades, student migration and technology professionals constitute a significant share of new arrivals from India.

Indian Diaspora in Australia

The *Migration Act of 1966 ended the* 'White Australia' policy giving equality between British, European and non-European migrants and introduced multiculturalism in Australia. Today, Asian Indians are one of the fastest growing communities in Australia. According to the Australian Bureau of Statistics census report of 2016 shows that there were 468,800 people of Indian origin resident in Australia, constituting about 1.9 percent of the entire population. The large Indian Australians population is found in Victoria followed by New South Wales. Between the years 2011-2012, Indians constituted the largest source of permanent migrants to Australia, with Indians forming 15.7 per cent of the total migration program during that period.

In all Australian states and major cities, there are registered associations and organizations catering to Indian interests such as the Australia India Business Council. In addition, Indian ethnic publications, Indian language programs on radio, Indian language, dance schools and temples operate in all major cities. Indian evangelists and missionaries such as G. D. James of Singapore and Brother Bhakt Singh of India, travelled to Australia from the late 1950s onwards, and through these visits the Indian Christian community was encouraged and strengthened (Koshy n.d.). As a prolific church planter in India, Brother Bhakt Singh visited Australia with the goal of establishing churches, or what he called assemblies for Indian and Australian Christians. In early 1959, a *Jehovah Shammah* congregation (the denominational name for Bhakt Singh's churches in India) was formed in Padstow, a suburb of Sydney, New South Wales. This church started with a handful of Indians and has become an international church with people of many ethnic communities.

Further visits by Indian leaders of denominational churches led to the establishment of several denominational churches. The Indian (Syrian) Orthodox bishop visited in early 1970s and led to the creation of the first Syrian Church in 1980 in East Coburg, near Melbourne, Victoria. Currently it has more than 250 families. The Mar Thoma Church was established in Melbourne, Victoria in 1997 and the Church of South India (CSI) started its first church in Melbourne, Victoria in 2011 to cater for the Malayalam-speaking families. Under the leadership of Brother Rajan Varghese, the Melbourne Indian Brethren Assembly formed a church in 2006 after meeting as a non-formal group of worshippers for many years. Today, the church has around 100 members, but more importantly it has gained recognition from the national Indian Brethren movement through its annual Australia-wide conferences. It is not clear when the first Indian Pentecostal church was established in Australia and many different strands of Indian Pentecostal churches can be in most Australian cities today.

The Australian Pentecostal Assembly (APA) was started in 2009 in Brisbane, Queensland.

Perth Revival Center

Until 2000, there were no formal Indian churches in Perth, Western Australia. The Perth Malayalee Christian Fellowship (PMCF), an interdenominational gathering of Indian Christians met once a month, with attendees drawn from the various churches. Visits by Indian clergymen and denominational leaders from India such as bishops from the Church of South India (CSI), Syrian Orthodox and Mar Thoma Churches, eventually led to the formation of these denominational churches. Today, Perth has four Indian Churches. There are also several non-formal groups like the PMCF, who gather for fellowship.

One of the first Indian congregations in Perth was the Perth Revival Center (PRC hereafter), which was started in 2008 with four families. The pastor, James John is a 'twice migrant': he was born and raised in a Christian Pentecostal family in Kerala, India; then at the age of 21, he took up secular employment in Bahrain for several years. After sensing a call to Christian ministry, John returned to Gujarat, India and enrolled at a Bible College. After serving in India and through the network of Indian Christians overseas, he heard of the need for an Indian Church in Perth. His coming to Perth in 2006 was a "great relief to those who were longing for an Indian Church in Western Australia". Currently the PRC has 60 families, with an aggregate attendance of some 300-people meeting in a rented hall in Carlisle, near East Perth. The Church has bought a piece of land in Armadale and there are plans to construct and relocate to a church worship center within the next 3 years.

Theology and liturgy

Although PRC calls itself interdenominational, it has recently come under the umbrella of the Australian Christian Churches (formerly known as the Assemblies of God), which is a Pentecostal denomination. Interestingly, 80 per cent of the PRC attendees came from a non-Pentecostal background. The services at PRC are run on similar lines to the informal Pentecostal liturgical pattern of worship, combined with some aspects of the traditional Indian church worship style. A typical service on Sunday lasts for two hours, with elements such as prayer, reading of the Psalms and silent meditation drawn from traditional Indian churches, worship and praise (singing), testimonies from the congregation, sermon and prayer for healing, where church members come to the altar for personal ministry.

When I interviewed the pastor, he described the Sunday sermons as 'prophetic' which in Pentecostal and Charismatic parlance refers to specific and unique information "coming from the mind of God for a specific situation, an inspired word directed to a certain audience...a word from the Word" (Hamon 1987). So, the pastor's messages speak to real needs and real-life situations. This explains why a couple come to the service from as far away as Mandurah (1.5 hours by car) every Sunday. In the Church WhatsApp group, a social media platform, one of the members sent the following text message in anticipation of the upcoming Sunday service: "Sunday's message will be memorable."

Senior Pastor John mentioned that his theme for 2017 (preached at the Watchnight service on December 31, 2016) is the 'year of the supernatural' because "I feel every aspect of the individual will experience the miraculous intervention of God...our people will see this in health, finances, the mind, giving to God and all other dimensions." The pastor mentioned an example of how a lady was diagnosed with spinal cancer and was admitted to the emergency department of the local hospital. The church quickly organized a 24-hour prayer vigil via *WhatsApp* and two weeks later, the cancer patient came to the Sunday service and testified that whereas she was not healed completely, she felt a lot better and thanked the church members for their prayer and support. Clearly, the church operates through the manifestation of the Holy Spirit and in the realm of the supernatural.

Language, Demographics and Migration Patterns

Unlike churches in India which are structured based on caste, language and ethnic groups, at PRC they conduct multi-lingual services. All three services each Sunday are delivered in one of these languages: Malayalam English, Hindi with interpretation, so the attendees do not segregate according to language. There is also a fortnightly Tamil service to cater for the growing number of Tamil-speaking members. A few Gujarati people also attend the church and since they understand Hindi, there is no need for a separate Gujarati service. However, the pastor intimated that a Gujarati service would commence if there were more than 12 families. Most of the current members are Malayalam speakers and they also sing songs in Malayalam, English, Tamil and Hindi in their church services.

PRC is a young church with about 20 teenagers and most adult members in their 40s. There are many children attending Sunday school. The church leadership recently started a youth group that meets on Saturday mornings, which is a new approach because the PRC services have been structured as 'all in one' (as in India). Apparently, the PRC leadership has conceded that its Indian youth growing up in Australia need to be given special attention during these vulnerable times of their lives.

Around 65-70 percent of the congregation lives about 15-25 minutes away from the Carlisle location where the church services are held. But as mentioned previously, about 10-15 percent come from locations ranging from 45 minutes to 1.5 hours. The fact that there are people coming from such distances would suggest that PRC is meeting a need among the Indian Christian community, and one wonders whether more churches are needed to cater for the growing numbers of Indians scattered all over the Perth metropolitan areas. The migration patterns of the church show that 60 percent of the congregation are 'twice migrants' that is Indians who have come to Australia from locations other than India. Of these, 20 percent are from the Middle East, 20 percent from the UK, 15 per cent from New Zealand and 5 percent from South Africa. The remaining 40 percent are directly from India.

Leadership and Governance

The church used to have a governing committee, but the pastor intimated that this structure has proved to be a hindrance and so a lean governance model was adopted. The present structure consists of the senior pastor assisted by a team of three lay elders and one youth pastor. It appears that the senior pastor is the main decision maker, assisted by the youth pastor and the elders. Together, they help in the running of the services and the overall pastoral work.

Cultural Challenges

When PRC leaders were asked to identify the challenges their church members face living in Australia, they answered without hesitation that most members cannot fully accept the Australian culture, so they tend to adhere to a hybrid culture comprising the Australian culture, the Indian cultural pattern and the patterns informed by the Bible.

The main contention for the leaders seemed to be the permissive dress code for women. PRC expects that women veil their heads during the church service – a carryover from the Indian traditional Church pattern where, as the senior Pastor explained, "in India, women are veiled in churches during worship across the board, in *all* denominations." Also, white sarees and Punjabi suits are the preferred outfits for women because some traditional members are somewhat appalled by women who wear pants in Australia for church services. The pastor conceded that this is a cultural preference, not a biblical injunction. Nevertheless, the culturally appropriate dress code in Australia does seem to be an issue that will continue to challenge PRC.

The youth pastor who (who worked previously in para church organizations such as *Youth for Christ* and *World Vision*) added that: "the youth are struggling with the issue of identity". Many are aware of the 'old-fashioned' culture of their parents compared to the Australian ways and the way other churches conduct worship and are anxious for change. An example of the desired change according to the youth pastor, was incorporating dim lighting and modern musical instruments in the worship services. The youth pastor's goal is to find common ground in these and other issues and close the gap.

Surprisingly, when asked about the secularization of Australian society and the introduction of "Safe Schools" (a gender-friendly initiative by the educational authorities), and whether the Sunday preaching addressed such issues, the leaders' emphatic answer was "no". They explained: "our people know that males can only marry females so there is no issue...there is no need to address these matters in the Church". From this statement, we can infer that these Indian Christians are very conservative in nature and have already worked out the fundamentals of their faith. Thus, they do not see the need to give biblical teaching on the current redefinition of marriage, gender and other related issues, which the rest of Christianity is grappling with, especially in the West.

When asked: "Why do people come to PRC if they can speak English?" the senior pastor gave a one-word answer: "fellowship". He explained that Sunday attendance is the result of what takes place throughout the week which builds a sense of community. There are special weekday meetings, prayer meetings, personal visits by the pastor and elders and networking via chat groups. Another reason mentioned was the similarity to the way the church services and the fellowship is experienced in India - in a word 'culture'. The pastor explained that even though most of the congregation understand English, there is a greater ease of communication and understanding among Indian believers at PRC.

Outreach at home and in India

PRC is involved in local outreach at a disability center that caters for Australian children near the church's meeting place. PRC members conduct a worship service there once a month by leading in Christian songs and establishing rapport with the children. PRC also has a very large outreach in Rajasthan, north India where it has opened an orphanage and established more than 19 churches (10 are fully supported and the rest are partially supported). The senior pastor travels to Rajasthan at least three times a year for ministry. During the pastor's recent visit in January 2017, 63 baptisms took place in one of the church's mission points in a remote village in Rajasthan.

Brethren Indian Fellowship

The Brethren Indian Fellowship (BIF hereafter) is not a church as such. It is a non-formal group of Indian (Malayalee) families who, as members of other churches, gather fortnightly on Friday evenings for fellowship and Bible study. Most families live in the suburbs of East Victoria, Cannington and surrounds near Perth, Western Australia. This is a para-church gathering, a social nexus and spiritual home for Indians of the Brethren theological tradition.

BIF has a few distinct reasons behind its origin. Indian Christians do not follow the Australian custom of going to bar after work on Fridays to socialize. Especially, parents are concerned about young people going to nightclubs and BIF members planned to counter this culture with Bible studies and fellowship on Friday evenings. Furthermore, the churches that BIF members attend did not have gatherings for families on Friday evenings. Another reason for the emergence of BIF in 2011 was because Indian Christians felt spiritually deprived of deep fellowship and teaching in Australian Churches. It was reported by one of the members that prayer life in Australian churches is not as fervent as in the Indian Brethren context. One respondent said that in his opinion, the Australian church is 'asleep', bogged down by many issues including political correctness. Language is another major factor. Although most of the Indians at BIF speak English, they are not too conversant in the nuances of the Australian English. Also, some Australians do not understand their strong Indian accents. Other Indian believers felt that their spiritual gifts could not be fully used in Australian churches because they (believers) were not immediately accepted by the church members.

Demographics

BIF is a small fellowship involving 12 families, which translates to an attendance of 45-50 people in total. As in PRC, the Friday meetings at

BIF are for the whole family. The attendees come from 3-4 Brethren churches in Perth. All of them are Malayalam-speaking Indians. Meetings are held in member's homes on a rotation basis and nearly 80 percent live within a radius of 1-6 miles from the usual meeting locations. Unlike PRC, which is a young church, BIF members come from a wider age range with 40 percent over the age of 50. Only 5 percent of members are from India; the remaining 95 percent are twice migrants coming from countries such as the UK, New Zealand, Singapore and Malaysia.

Pattern of Fellowship

Using a 5-week calendar, the first two weeks are devoted for Bible study, week three is set aside as a prayer time, week four is organized as a time of sharing, thanksgiving and testimony, and week five is designated as a time of fellowship. Every meeting ends with an evening potluck meal while the host family provides rice and drinks. Every meeting starts with singing congregational Malayalam songs and sometimes a few songs in English are sung. Special services that are observed just as in India such as watchnight services on New Year's eve since most Australian churches do not hold any services at that time.

A core group of three leaders determine what books in the Bible to study and they appoint facilitators to lead the discussions and to give a summary of the passage of Scripture at the end of the meeting. During Bible study, all read aloud the selected biblical passage (some in Malayalam), even women and children. Women can ask questions, but they are not permitted to voice opinions or 'teach' in keeping with the Brethren interpretation of the New Testament. This is an exact replica of how group meetings are run in India among the Brethren churches. Leaders are appointed to lead the testimony time and the various prayers so that there is order in the group meetings.

BIF and Church Dynamics

BIF's Friday group has become influential in attracting people to join their respective Australian churches on Sundays, especially new migrants coming to Perth. This is seen positively by the church leaders because some of these churches are losing members and the presence of Indian believers is a boost to the overall weekly attendance and the vitality of these churches. However, there is an uneasy situation brewing. Some in the BIF have proposed that BIF should also conduct a communion service. The idea was well received and put into practice for a short period, but then some members who hold a literalist view of the Bible, questioned whether communion should be held on a Sunday (the first day of the week) and not a Friday when BIF meets. This led to the communion being shifted to a Sunday morning. But a further problem arose because many BIF members attend their respective churches for communion every Sunday, which meant BIF members were struggling to attend their church and then meet immediately for the communion time in a home. After a short trial, the communion services on a Sunday were abandoned by BIF. However, some members have sensed that the next step might be that BIF transitions into a full-fledged church to get around the problem of a clash between BIF's communion services on a Sunday and established church services. The Melbourne Indian Brethren Assembly has already established a model for a church, and BIF may use that model should it decide to become more structured. However, not all the BIF members are comfortable with this perceived move to become a church because this might cause strained relationships with their churches.

Cultural Issues

The transmission of culture (Indian culture and the Indian Church culture) to the next generation seems to be the main motivation for BIF's existence. One of the members shared that he believes the Australian Church has by and large, become 'worldly':

> ...there is a need to return to the traditions of our parents. Family values here are degrading. A strong sense of family values need to be passed on. The Brethren are strong in the word of God...so identifying with fellow believers in Perth is the only way.

One informant shared anecdotal details of the strong Brethren tradition in Kerala, south India. Back home in the early days the informant's grandfather would leave for church with the entire family and as they set out to walk from their home, the family members would start singing songs of praise and that would be a testimony to the whole village and even serve as a reminder to the village folk that it was time to go to church. Indian Christians aspire to remember these rich traditions in Australia and pass them on as a generational legacy. Another informant shared "I want my children to learn my culture and language and be comfortable when they visit India to see their relatives."

BIF members continue to meet because of two main reasons. First, their lack of proficiency in the English language. Second, the lack of acceptance by several traditional Australian churches which may stem, in part, from the residual effects of the 'White Australia' policy which the government enforced between the years 1901-1966.

Comparative Analysis

PRC, unlike the traditional Indian church structure, is a multi-ethnic and multi-lingual church with a distinctive Pentecostal heritage. BIF is a single ethnic, Brethren group that is a para church movement. PRC has a clear outward focus as evidenced in its outreach activities both in Australia and abroad. BIF exists in a more inward looking way to provide a cultural and spiritual ballast for its members. Whilst PRC seems to be more equipped to reach out to multi-lingual Indians arriving from India and other nations, BIF's single-language and denominational focus may exclude some new arrivals such as Telugu and Tamil IT professionals. PRC is a younger demographic than BIF. PRC is organized with a prophetic underpinning, emphasizing the specific word of the Lord as spoken by the pastor; whereas BIF is rooted in the written word of God and members spend time studying the Bible exegetically by using traditional hermeneutics as the means of interpretation.

Both PRC and BIF have a high percentage of twice migrants in these churches which helps them connect with the worldwide community of Indian Christians. It seems that foreign-born Indians are not as attracted to these churches as those who were born in India. The glue that binds PRC and BIF is that both groups exist to provide *the culture of India* and the *culture of the Indian Church* to their members. Both structures are, in their own ways, negotiating how to live in Australian society with an Indian Christian perspective.

Conclusion

Embedded within Indian migration to Australia over the years, are Indian Christians gathering to worship the Lord. Two types of worshiping communities have emerged – the structured church with a distinct denominational flavor, and the non-formal grouping of believers who meet for fellowship while maintaining membership in their respective Australian churches. The preservation of Indian culture and the traditions of the Indian Church are the main motivations for the emergence of these groups. Indian Christians are also troubled that political correctness has led to the point where the church is afraid to offend and now finds itself embracing values that are fashionable rather than what is instructed in the Bible.

The large number of Indians coming to Australia's shores means that the scope for outreach among Indians in Australia, and the establishment of new churches is greater than any other previous time in history. This is true in all the states of Australia, but especially so in Victoria and New South Wales where the largest proportion of Indians have made their home. The numbers of University students and technology professionals from India are increasing but there is little evidence to suggest that most Indian churches and groups are intentionally reaching out to these new arrivals.

A feature of the increasing migration of Indians, to Australia has been the growing internationalization of the Indian Christian community. The relatively high proportion of twice migrants has ensured that networks of Indian groups, churches and organizations have enabled Indians to move to Australia easily and establish links for arranged marriages, work, church life, missions and the like. However, the increased globalization and mobility are not trouble free. The challenges that Indian Christians in Australia face are centered, in a large measure, on how the young generation of Indians cope with the changing norms and values in Australia *vis-à-vis* the Indian Christian heritage of their ancestors. Therefore, more studies and research are needed to seek specific ways of addressing and encouraging the unique needs of children and young people who are socialized in Australian society.

Culture is both the instigator and the glue of the Indian Christian community in Australia. The somewhat threatening, prevailing culture motivates Indian Christians to gather in 'safe zones'. At the same time, when Indians gather, their activities help to strengthen and reinforce the Indian Christian culture. It would appear from this study that as Indian Christians continue to negotiate life in Australia, the reality is that they will continue to live in two worlds as a bicultural community. Therefore, in the case of Australian Indian Christians, the words of the well-known Australian song, "I still call Australia home" may need to be modified to *"I still call India (and Australia) home."*

References

Anderson, Benedict. *Imagined Communities*. London: Verso, 1983.

Australian Bureau of Statistics website, "Australian Social Trends". http://www.abs.gov.au/AUSSTATS/abs@.nsf/Previousproducts/4102.0Main%20Feat?opendocument&tabname=Summary&prodno=4102.0&issue=2007&num=&view=(Accessed July 1, 2017)

Australian Pentecostal Assembly - http://www.apabrisbane.com.au/apastory.php (Accessed July 1, 2017)

Barth, Fredrik. *Ethnic Groups and Boundaries*. Oslo: Jhansen and Nielsen, 1969.

Bhachu, Parminder. "Twice Migrants and Multiple Migrants," *The Wiley Blackwell Encyclopedia of Race, Ethnicity, and Nationalism*. 2015: 1–4.

Brack, La Bruce. *The Sikhs of Northern California 1904-1975*. New York: AMS Press, 1988.

Brereton, Bridget and Winston Dookeran. *East Indians in the Caribbean: Colonization and The Struggle for Identity*. New York: Kraus International, 1982.

Billmoria, Purushottama. Jayant Bhalchandra Bapat and Philip Hughes. 2015. *The Indian Diaspora: Hindus and Sikhs in Australia*. New Delhi: DK Printworld.

Church of South India (CSI) website. http://www.melbournecsichurch.org. au/ (Accessed Jul 1, 2017)

Coedes, George. *The Indianized states of Southeast Asia.* Canberra: Australian National University Press, 1968.

Christian Research Association website. N.D. http://cra.org.au/products-page/books/the-indian-diaspora-hindus-and-sikhs-in-australia/ (Accessed Jul 1, 2017)

Desai, Rashmi. *Indian Immigrants in Britain.* London: Oxford University Press, 1963.

Gautam, M.K. "Indian Diaspora: Ethnicity and Diasporic Identity". *Research Report CARIM-India* 29, 2013: 1-16.

Hamon, Bill. *Prophets and Personal Prophecy: God's Prophetic Voice Today. Shippensburg, PA: Destiny Image Publishers, 1987.*

Koshy, T.E. "Ministry in Australia—Taken from Bro Bhakt Singh of India". http://www.churchesinaustralia.org/te-koshy/ (Accessed July 1, 2017)

Melbourne Mar Thoma Church -http://melbournemarthomachurch.org.au/ (Accessed July 1, 2017)

Munoz, Paul. *Early Kingdoms of the Indonesian Archipelago and the Malay Peninsula.* Singapore: Edition Didier, 2006.

Rukmani, T. S. *Hindu Diaspora Global Perspectives.* New Delhi: Munshiram Manohar Lal, 2001.

St Thomas Indian Orthodox Cathedral - http://www.hcindia-au.org/indians-in-australia.htm

The High Commission of India in Australia - http://www.hcindia-au.org/indians-in-australia.htm (Accessed July 1, 2017)

Werbner, Pnina. *Imagined Diaspora among the Manchester Muslims: The Public Performances of Pakistani transnational Identity Politics.* Oxford: James Curry, 2002.

Global Telugu Christian Diaspora

Joseph Paturi

Diaspora, a biblical word, has a Greek origin and it means to scatter or disperse. The word was strictly used to refer to dispersal and exile of the Jews, but in recent decades the term has proliferated in usage and applied to migrants of all kinds (Kenny 2013; Cohen 1997). Diaspora is an apt term to describe the widespread dispersion of Telugu speaking people all around the world in recent decades. Telugu diaspora refers to the Telugu people who speak Telugu language and now live outside of India with sizable settlement in North America, Gulf nations, Southeast Asia, Europe and Australia.

Some scholars have used religion as the primary lens to scrutinize dispersed Indians such as Hindu Diaspora (Rukmani 2001 and Vertovec 2013) and Sikh Diaspora (Tatla, 1999), while others used ethnicity or language as primary viewpoint to research diasporic community such as Malayali (George and Thomas 2013) or Gujarati (Mawani and Mukadam 2012). In this study, I use language and religion as a primary lens to investigate Telugu speakers of India who are Christians living abroad. When the linguistic division of states in India took place after Independence, Telugu speakers were largely in one state of Andhra Pradesh, however, it was recently bifurcated into two states - Andhra Pradesh and Telangana. Thus, the subjects of this study origin in two states of India and both are adherents of Christian faith, but now live overseas in different regions of the world. They comprise of numerous sub-regional, caste, socio-economic and denominational distinctions within it.

The Telugu Diaspora

Telugus are also known as the Andhras. Andhra's were first mentioned in the Aitareya Brahmana of the Rig Veda (600 BC). The word Telugu is used synonymously with the words Andhramu and Tenugu. Telugus have the distinction of being the largest South Indian community to have migrated to different parts of the world since early 19th century. Andhra Pradesh and Telangana and they together form the third largest and most densely populated region of the Indian subcontinent. The official language of Andhra Pradesh and Telangana is Telugu and it is spoken in India by 83 million people constituting around 7.2 percent of the total population of India according to 2011 census. The Telugu language is spoken by nearly 90 percent of the population in the states of Andhra Pradesh and Telangana. The Telugu speaking population consists of 88 percent Hindus, 7 percent Muslims, 4 percent Christians, and 1 percent comprise of Sikhs, Parsees, Buddhists and Jains. Telugu is the third largest language spoken in India after Hindi and Bengali.

Telugu diaspora can be divided into two broad categories as the Old Diaspora and the New Diaspora. Others have used the same categories in analysis of the Telugu diaspora (Bhat 2007) as well as Lal (2006) in distinguishing the difference between pre-Independence migration under the British indentured labor system and more recent volitional migratory movements of educated professionals. The beginning of the Telugu scattering can be traced back to the colonial rule. It began at the abolition of slavery in 1833, when some unskilled Telugu speaking people were recruited to work in sugar, coffee and rubber plantations in the colonies. Telugus formed a major share of this recruitment and migrated predominantly to Mauritius, South Africa, Malaya (now Malaysia), Fiji, Burma (now Myanmar) and Ceylon (now Sri Lanka) during the colonial era. One of the earliest destinations for Telugus was Mauritius and between 1837 and 1880, nearly 20,000 Telugu people were taken there. Today, Telugus amount to nearly 60,000 on the island nation, and have a distinctive culture of their own in terms of language, festivals and temples. They are widely spread on the island and are involved in a variety of occupations.

Another major Telugu emigration occurred to South Africa as a part of the indenture system from the Madras Presidency, which ruled Andhra Pradesh during the British Raj. It was believed that the first ever-Indian migrant to the colony was a Telugu, who was taken there in July 1885, to work for an English farmer in Natal. There are many Naidus (Naidoos) and Reddys (Reddi) that migrated to South Africa. The migrants included peasants, farmers, clerical staff, teachers, Kummaras (potters), Kamsalis (gold smiths), Kamsala (weavers), and a few Komatis (traders). Except for a few families, most lost their identity or any linkage to their ancestral homelands over the course of many generations. Some Indo-Fijians traced their roots to Telugu people, but most in Malaya, Burma and Ceylon have merged with the dominant Tamil people.

However, the new diaspora of Telugus is very different in many ways. Accordingly, to Helweg and Helweg (1990, xii) the post-colonial migrations from the East to the West has two distinctive characteristics: First, the technological base of the receiving nation is not agrarian or industrial, but post-industrial, oriented towards the service sector; and second, the socio-economic level of the migrant community is primarily educated professionals, not uneducated peasants or laborers. During this period, migration was totally directed towards developed countries, and the migrants mostly constituted talented professionals, highly skilled workers, experts, entrepreneurs from the peripheral, colonial and underdeveloped countries. Today Indians are the richest ethnic minority in USA, and in the IT sector especially in Silicon Valley, Telugus constitute nearly three-tenths of the total Indian software professionals.

The new Telugu diaspora phenomena could be further divided into two eras – those that migrated in 1960s through 80s and those from 1990s to the present. The first wave of Telugu immigrants to the United States consisted of doctors, scientists and other medical professionals like nurses and lab technicians. The well-to-do elite of Andhra Pradesh were quick to realize the need of advanced education for overall development and established several technical colleges, universities and institutions which in turn produced a large number of doctors, engineers, scientists, software developers and other professionals. The second wave of Telugu immigrants arrived in the United States because of IT revolution and comprises engineers with computer software skills and now they constitute a large share of the entire Indian American community. In addition to the US, many of these young technology professionals migrated to other developed countries such as UK, Canada, Germany and Australia.

The migration of Telugus to the United States was facilitated by the Immigration Act, which made provision for skill-based immigration because of lack of sufficient engineering or computer science professionals in the US market. Most of the Telugus who immigrated to USA during that period were the best and the brightest, and their talents were immense in their respective fields. A recent study on Indian Americans confirms the trend of new influx of Indians after 1995 not only "brought new skills in a new industry (information technology), but also represented new language groups (Telugu and Tamils)" (Chakrovorty at al. 2017, 56). The American Community Survey 2014 report found that there were 270,000 Telugu speakers and surpassed Guajarati people and Telugu has become the second most spoken Indian language in the United States after Hindi. Asian Indians being the most educated group in the United States and among them Telugus stand out in educational achievement with most number of master's degrees in engineering and sciences.

Many Telugus in the United States hail from the coastal districts of Andhra Pradesh. Since Independence of India, the coastal Andhra was far more developed than the Rayalseema and Telangana regions. The difference is due to the availability of natural resources and fertile land on the coast. Moreover, those two regions were under feudalism which did not contribute to the growth and development. As a part of the Madras Presidency, the coastal districts availed the benefit of formal education with English as the medium of instruction in college and university education. It was initially from the coastal Andhra Pradesh that many doctors migrated to the United States during the late 1960s followed by engineers, teachers and students.

The Telugu Boom

The Information Technology revolution was a major catalyst to large scale dispersion of Telugu speaking people, often referred to as Telugu Boom in popular media, which helped thousands of Telugu speaking people to find their way to the United States and Canada in the mid-1990s. The economic liberalization of India in early 1990s and resulting policy changes in the state of Andhra Pradesh drew attention of many multinational software corporations to harness the latent potential of the Indian techies. The Prime Minister of India during the liberalization era hailed from Andhra Pradesh and the Chief Minister of Andhra Pradesh foresaw the emerging wave and provided visionary policy changes to attract overseas investment in the state. As of 2017, one out of every four Indians who are going to the United States is a Telugu person.

Many private engineering colleges sprung up all across southern India, particularly in Andhra Pradesh and Karnataka in the 1970s and 80s which attracted many high school graduates to take up studies with hopes of finding employment in the fledgling computer and software industry. The growing population of Andhra Pradesh with little prospects in agrarian economy due to repeated monsoon failures coupled with high unemployment and corruption, more and more families saw little prospects in traditional industries. Many parents preferred to send their children to reputed state technical colleges in India and those who could not get admitted there went to the private colleges. Armed with undergraduate degrees in science and technology, these graduates explored educational and job opportunities in developed nations. The decade of 1980s also marked an era that American universities started to target undergraduate students in India for their graduate studies and research in technical fields under its F-1 visa program which was followed by universities in UK, Canada and Australia.

However, the foremost boost to the dispersion of Telugu people came at the onset of the Y2K (numeronym for Year 2000) problem and state government's initiative to develop Software Technology Parks (STPs) in India. The turn of millennium posed a major challenge to legacy software that only had two digits to mark the year and computers could not distinguish between 2000 and 1900. The Y2K problem or millennium bug needed thousands of engineers and computer professionals to tweak software codes and reprogramming efforts that could be met through overseas workers and Telugu/Indian engineers and computer professionals were well positioned to exploit. Many manpower supply companies sprang up in technology centers of India to facilitate prospective employees with contract employment and H-1B visa program. Some have left corporate jobs to start software companies and consulting services and have become successful Telugu diaspora entrepreneurs, with elaborate backend operations in India.

A progressive vision of the state government to set up Software Technology Parks (STPs) in Hyderabad resulted in renaming a part of the city as Cyberabad, which further accelerated outflow of trained technical people from Andhra Pradesh. Many American companies established back offices, software testing and development centers in major cities of India to take advantage of cheap labor cost and time zone advantages. The Telugu people who went to colleges and worked in software industries in other cities of India became a pool for largescale emigration to overseas destinations. Those who returned after short assignments abroad were quickly sought by the Indian division of reputed global firms and Hyderabad became an important regional hub for technical prowess in the world. The fourth annual global convention of Indian diaspora (*Pravasi Bharatiya Divas*) was held in Hyderabad in 2006 and played a catalytic role in its engagement with dispersed Telugus. The establishment of the American consulate office in Hyderabad facilitated the visa processing and further aided migratory outflow of Telugu people.

Telugus have built a culturally vibrant, economically strong, socially conscious and politically savvy diaspora networks around the globe.

The Telugu diaspora represents the best of Indian culture, ethos and values with stable family lifestyle. The Telugus in general with their hard-working, disciplined, law-abiding and peace-loving nature have become role models to other immigrant communities around them. They are active in homelands as well as places of settlements. The Telugu diaspora emerged as a significant and powerful community in their adopted homelands and prospered in every realm. The initial brain drain has only helped to create a worldwide network of Telugu people and much brain gain in the following decades and a significant social and economic advancement through remittances, technology transfers, access to capital and global experience.

However, not everything is as rosy as it looks from the outside. The usual migratory disruptions have played havoc in the form of nuclearization of families, family breakdown and the abandonment of elderly parents who sacrificed much to send the IT generation to colleges and universities which helped them to enter the road to success. There is also much corruption arising out of hyper competition to get ahead at any cost and domestic violence has become too common in households in diaspora. The short-term nature of technology jobs, isolation from familial support system and unequal visa status of the dependents skew unfair power dynamics against women. The Indian cultural aspects such as patriarchal attitude, shame and success orientation have created much pain and despondency which remains invisible under the common perception of model minority. Several instances of financial scandals, exploitation of poor girls in the marriage market, illegal human trafficking and enslavement have been reported among Telugu diaspora community. There is also a widespread online porn consumption and production using minors and others among Telugu technology professionals which has eroded sanctity and stability of marriages in the community.

Telugu Language and Faith

The language and religion are a binding force for all diaspora communities and is also true of Telugu diaspora at large and Christians in particular. Hence, I use the double lens approach to study this community. The Telugu language has made inroads into different parts of the globe such as Mauritius, Singapore, Fiji, South Africa, Sri Lanka, Pakistan, Israel, USA, UK, UAE, Canada, France and Australia. Being a sweet and pleasing mellifluous language, Telugu is called *the Italian of the East*. It is generally common to assume that within a new cultural milieu, the old lingua franca would change its original fashion, but in the case of Telugus the vernacular is still well retained among the Telugu diaspora.

However, the western-born young adults who are in their twenties and thirties, the children of early immigrants to the US or UK, have lost linguistic skills in Telugu language. Lal notes that some of early immigrants in the Old Diaspora did not have sufficiently large number of speakers to survive beyond a generation in most territories (2006, 90). Also, disruption in subsequent migration hampered the development of language in diaspora. Some foreign-born children are able to understand simple conversations in Telugu, but unable to speak or read anything in Telugu. They have no avenue to learn their mother tongue at school nor did their busy immigrant parents have the bandwidth to teach them. Moreover, Telugu community was not large enough in the 1980s to undertake community wide initiative to teach their progenies the language in the western context. Nonetheless, in recent years many efforts have been made to ensure that foreign born children retain ancestral languages as well as pride in communal culture. Several community activists and organizations have started offering Telugu language lessons. Many temples and churches also offer Telugu classes and traditional dances to foreign born children. New software and apps have been developed to learn Telugu language and popular media are a key to language retention.

Telugu people have established cultural associations in many countries to promote cultural values and to bring dispersed community together. Telugu food, music, movies, television programs and newspapers made their way to far corners of the globe wherever Telugu people have scattered and knit a global identity for the community. The Telugu entertainment content is streamed into handheld mobile devices worldwide, while remittances from around the world flow into banks in the home states of Andhra Pradesh and Telangana. Regular financial help from the widely scattered Telugus help family members or invest in real estates or support various charitable organizations. Many Telugus in the West are active in business, cultural bodies and political activities both in homeland and places of settlement.

The caste identification remains subtly among the New Diaspora, as Bhat notes that cultural associations have been established in the United States along the lines of caste: Telugu Association of North America (TANA) is mostly Kamma, while American Telugu Association (ATA) is dominated by Reddys (2007, 111). However, caste sensibilities have considerably diminished among the current generation who are born and bred in foreign lands, as race becomes the principal social stratification category than caste. The numerous Telugu associations in different regions organize conferences and observe festivals to galvanize and cater to the collective issues of the community. Broadly there are two kinds of cultural associations: one that is local and primarily involved in bringing Telugus in the city or state together for common issues relevant to the community, and second transnational networks that bring together leaders from multiple countries. The local associations exist to preserve and perpetuate heritage of Telugu people and interface with local community and media. The global Telugu associations are involved in promotion of language and culture of Telugus and to interface with political entities back home and host countries. There are also many virtual networks of Telugus that connect dispersed masses.

The Telugu Christian Diaspora

Among the Old Diaspora, many early migrants of Telugu origin have embraced Christian faith at overseas locations and in subsequent generations as it can be seen in Fiji and South Africa. However, most early emigrants to Mauritius and Surinam have retained Hindu traditions. Many Christian leaders in Fiji and South Africa trace their roots to the Telugu ancestors, though they have lost much of linguistic or cultural linkages. Contrarily, the New Diaspora includes many Christians from among the Telugu speakers, from both Andhra Pradesh and Telangana region, and are widely scattered in Southeast Asia, Middle East, Europe, Australia, and North America. Telugu songs are sung, and sermons are preached in nearly every time zone on every Sunday. Telugu preachers and evangelists span the globe ministering to their scattered flock, while Telugu Christian music and television programs are streamed across the globe. These networks have supported many church and mission projects back home and are actively involved in reaching people in their adopted homelands.

No studies have been undertaken or any reliable reports exist about the faith of early Telugu migrants or those who switched religious affiliation and under what circumstances. But over many decades and generations, their religious rituals and beliefs have undergone substantial evolution. The Telugu Christians in the Old Diaspora were primarily evangelized by local Christians in respective countries or other international mission agencies. They did not know of any Indian Christians or establish any contact with them after conversion and relied solely on local Christians or foreign missionaries. They tend to merge with local customs and adopt prevailing religious practices, even intermarry local Christians more than those who have retained faith of the ancestors in India.

Today, there are Telugu Christian Fellowships and Telugu churches in every major city across North America and around the world including in Israel and the Middle East among the Telugu Christian Diaspora. They provide spiritual support and benevolent help needed for the Diaspora community. The Telugu churches in UAE, Kuwait, Bahrain, Qatar, Dubai and Muscat have greater freedom in assembling on a regular basis and seasoned leadership is in place as compared to Saudi Arabia. The Telugu Christian Fellowships meet in hotels in Singapore, while they meet in specially designated compounds or even in homes in some Gulf countries. They are affiliated to many denominations such as Church of South India, Reformed, Baptist, Mennonite, Brethren, Pentecostal, Charismatic and Independent. Some Telugu Catholics have joined local Catholic churches in different destinations such as Italy and Ireland. One distinctive Telugu spirituality is the Bakht Singh Assemblies, which began as a revival movement in Hyderabad and brother Bakht Singh was considered as a major church planting and missionary evangelist of the 20th century in India (Koshy 2008). Many who have grown up in these assemblies in Andhra Pradesh are scattered all over the world and are instrumental in starting similar assemblies in their respective places of settlements.

Over the last two decades or so, many Telugu churches have come up wherever Telugu techies have settled, particularly large industrialized global cities in the West. Though some prefer to go to local churches near them or find familiar denominations, most Telugu Christians seek membership in Telugu Christian churches and contributed to the forming of many churches across North America. Most of these churches began as small home fellowships and Bible study groups and were led by spiritually mature Telugu Christians. The Telugu churches conduct services in Telugu language and some have added services in English for the sake of foreign born children. They preserve many aspects of Telugu cultural Christianity by recreating their own version of spirituality and faith cultures to pass it on to future generations. Some of these churches are led by seminary trained professional pastors who came from India for theological studies and have stayed back to join denominational churches or minister to immigrant congregations, while others are brought in from India on religious visas, some of whom have become permanent residents. Some other pastors are bi-vocational techies who are self-taught or have obtained basic theological education locally.

Some Telugu Christians maintain dual associations by going to local Bible or evangelical churches for spiritual nurture and worship, even as they regularly or occasionally attend Telugu churches and fellowships to keep ties with fellow Telugu Christians from India. Among the recent Telugu immigrants to the United States, there is proportionately larger number of Christians and this reflects a major revival of Christianity among Telugus in India. Christian faith also brings a new level of mobility and breaks its adherents from deep-rooted traditional baggage. The recent converts, seekers and students coming to study in universities have shown remarkable openness and eagerness to join Telugu immigrant churches. Some immigrant churches offer marriage brokerage and hold common cultural festivities for their members.

Some Telugus desire to join American churches of the denominations they had growin up in like Baptist, Mennonite, Methodist, Brethren, Lutheran, and Pentecostal etc. As a result, Telugu Christians in US, UK, and Canada are highly fragmented among themselves, particularly in places which have attracted many Telugu Christians like in San Jose, Chicago, Atlanta, Dallas, Houston, New York, New Jersey and Toronto. Some of these churches are led and supported by respective denominational pastors from India and maintain close links to sister churches in India as in the case of Church of South India whose Moderators and Bishops make regular visits to churches in the United States. There is certain of degree of maneuvering for power and positions in immigrant churches and some incidents of church splits have happened because of personality clash and petty matters. The language and culture are a major attraction for several people in these churches but may be a hindrance to some. The Telugu immigrant churches oftentimes remain insular and fail to engage host societies or people of other cultures around them. Many associate with Telugu churches to keep their children connected to Telugu/Indian culture and community.

Some other Telugus prefer to remain loyal to the denomination and join local churches with American or Asian pastoral leaders and play an active role as deacons, elders or board members. There are some others who join local evangelical churches that are independent without any relationship to churches in India or any affiliation to a denomination. They consider that those churches have better suited in offering appropriate children and youth programs for those growing up in the United States as compared to Indian immigrant churches. Generally, some of them are concerned over Indian churches becoming an ethnic enclave with its overemphasis on culture and language. They are disgruntled over trivial conflicts and personality cults of immigrant Christians and so they prefer to enter mainstream Christian community in the host society and see their future being part of American Christianity instead of remaining stuck with a total ethnocentric mentality.

Many Telugu churches have developed Christian community associations which tend to establish networks and community wide ministries and services. They organize conferences, revival meetings, evangelism campaigns and festivals catering to the Telugu community settled in different parts of the world. Besides celebrating religious festivities like Easter and Christmas, they also organize parties at New Year, birthdays, anniversaries and festivals like Diwali to bring Telugus together and for evangelistic outreach. In addition to the local associations and assemblies, there are global networks like Global Telugu Christian Ministries (GTCM). Telugu Christian diaspora leaders have also established a seminary in Kuwait in 1998 called Telugu Krystava Vedanta Vidhyalam (TKVV) to provide theological training and prepare leaders for the church ministries in the Gulf region. This seminary was accredited by Asia Theological Association (ATA). The local associations play a crucial role in preserving and promoting Christian faith in a local context. The global associations provide a forum for participation of Telugus from all over the world. The local associations cater to a diaspora community and operate in the country of settlement, whereas the global associations are transnational in nature cutting across the national borders. GTCM conducted World Telugu Christian Summits (WTCS) recently in New Jersey, USA in 2014; Jerusalem, Israel in 2015, London in 2016 and Sydney in 2017.

The Telugu Christian leaders from India, well-known pastors, televangelists, dignitaries, and denominational leaders pay regular visits to the dispersed Telugu churches in the diaspora. Visiting Christian cine stars, gospel singers, Christian politicians and public servants from Andhra Pradesh and Telangana offer another form of transnational cultural network among the Telugus worldwide. This religio-cultural flow not only links dispersed Christians to their ancestral homelands, but also creates diasporic consciousness and provides evangelistic platform to reach Telugus in diasporic settings. Telugus abroad send a significant part of their savings back home in the form of remittances to invest in real estates, small businesses, and educational institutions and to contribute towards welfare activities such as church ministries, charities, old age homes and relief during natural calamities.

The development of electronic media, transnational satellite aided TV channels, Facebook and WhatsApp technology today has brought together Telugus from distant lands, creating a virtual Telugu community. A local event is globally witnessed, compressing both time and space. Virtual interaction between the homeland setting and the Telugu diaspora community is promoted through the Christian Channels like Aradana TV and Calvary TV, besides other TV channels, like Gemini TV, Maa TV, ETV and TV9. These TV networks now reach out to the Telugus worldwide and are dedicated to cater to their needs of information, communication and entertainment.

Conclusion

Today Telugus have emerged to be a distinctive transnational community, bringing the "local" and "global" together in new ways. While knowledge and skills in software technology has resulted in the widespread dispersion of Telugus worldwide, the modern advancement in communication, transportation and technology has facilitated effective networks among Telugus globally. This is manifested in the socio-economic, cultural and political networks of global Telugu communities with their homeland and their family and friends around the world. The relative higher share of Christians among Telugu migrants, revival of Christian faith in the diasporic setting and many new believers joining the Christian church have created a vibrant network of Telugu Christians worldwide. The Telugu Christians abroad are valued not just for their strength in numbers and financial abilities, but they are respected for the spiritual vitality and missionary passion through significant contributions they make for the advancement of the societies and the mission of God, both where they reside and in their ancestral land.

References

Bhat, Chandresekar and T.L.S. Bhasker. 2007. Contextualizing Diaspora Identity: Implication of Time and Space on Telugu Immigrants in *Global Indian Diaspora*. Ed. Gijsbert Oonk. Amsterdam: Amsterdam University Press.

Chakrovorthy, Sanjoy. Devesh Kapur and Nirvikar Singh. 2017. *The Other One Percent: Indians in America*. New York: Oxford University Press.

Cohen, Robin. 1997. *Global Diasporas: An Introduction*. Seattle: Washington University Press.

George, Sam and T.V. Thomas, 2013. *Malayali Diaspora: From Kerala to the ends of Earth*. New Delhi: Serials Publications.

Kenny, Kevin. 2013. *Diasporas: A Short Introduction*. New York: Oxford University Press.

Koshy, T.E. 2008. *Bakht Singh of India: An Incredible Account of a Modern Day Apostle*. Secundrabad: Authentic Publishing.

Lal, Brij. V. 2006. *The Encyclopedia of the Indian Diaspora:* Honolulu: University of Hawaii Press.

Mawani, Sharmina and Anjoom A. Mukadam. 2012. *Gujarati Communities across the Globe: Memory, Identity, and Continuity*. London: Trentham Books.

Oonk, Gijsbert. 2007. *Global Indian Diaspora: Exploring Trajectories of Migration and Theory*. Amsterdam University Press.

Rukmani, T.S. 2001. *Hindu Diaspora: Global Perspective*.

Tatla, Darshan Singh. 1999. *Sikh Diaspora: Search for Statehood*. Seattle: University of Washington Press.

Vertovec, Steven. 2013. *The Hindu Diaspora: Comparative Patterns*. London: Routledge.

Zomi Diaspora from Chin State, Myanmar

Jamang Ngul Khan Pau

Introduction

In this paper, I want to introduce you to the world of Zomi people and their recent global dispersion. I have drawn extensively from my doctoral fieldwork that I conducted in 2011 and more recent research work on Zomi diaspora at the Fuller Theological Seminary, USA.

Zomi is the name of an ethnic group of people that occupy Northwest Burma, Northeast India, and Northeast Bangladesh, and commonly known as Lushai, Chin and Kuki. However, a single name has technical limitation within its own context because the Mizo (Lushai), the Kuki, the Bawmzo and other ethnic groups would not normally accept a single identity collectively. When the British divided the Zomis' inhabitance with three international boundaries into India, Burma and Bangladesh, the above stated three main distinctive identities emerged, although those given names were not being used locally, and were initially unknown to the natives. The estimated 1.5 million Zomis speak a Kukish language of the Tibetan-Burman language group. The majority of Zomis are nominally Christian with sizable Theravada Buddhist and animists (Minahan 2015, 365).

There have been debates in different levels in trying to find the original name of Zomi families. They are known by different names in India, Myanmar and Bangladesh, there is no question that they are from a common ancestor. This is how they define their origin:

> The term 'Zomi' meaning, 'Zo People' is derived from the generic name 'Zo', the progenitor of the Zomi. In the past, they were little known by this racial nomenclature. They were known by peoples of Burma, Bangladesh and India as Chin, Kuki, or Lushai. British employed these terms to christen those 'wild hill tribes' living in the 'un-administered area' and was subsequently legalised to be the names for the newly adopted subjects by Queen Victoria of England. However, they called themselves Zomi since time immemorial. They are Zomi not because they live in the highlands or hills, but because they are the descendants of their great ancestor, 'Zo' (Zogam 2009).

The ancestral homeland of the Zo people was around the South-Eastern Tibet and Western China. They speak a common language belonging to Assam-Burma branch of Tibeto-Burman family having an affinity with Filipino, Brunei, Malaysia, Thai etc. both in language and culture. They form a group of Tibeto-Burman people inhabiting the Chin Hills in Myanmar, Mizoram, Meghalaya, Assam, Tripura, Nagaland and Manipur states in India and the Chittagong hill tracks in Bangladesh (Lalremruata 2011, 1a)

After the annexation of the British, the name Chin Hills was legalized by the colonial administration under Queen Victoria of England. Thus, the name Chin Hills came into use in 1886 as a governmental unit within the British Empire. The term Chin Hills meant that the hill country is being inhabited by Chin people (Khai 1984, 1). But the name Chin or Kuki was not the name that the people called themselves (Nawni 1990, 17). According to Carey and Tuck, the first ones who recorded the Chin tribes under a modern system of administration:

> Those of the Kuki tribes designated as Chin did not recognise that name which is said to be Burmese corruption of Chinese word "jin" or "Jen" meaning "Man" (1896, 3).

According to traditions, the forerunners of Mizo/Zomi hailed from a place called *Chhinlung Puk* (Chhinlung Cave) between 300 and 200 BC and came to Chin-Lushai Land to settle there between 2nd to 7th Century A.D. The Chin-Lushai Land, hereinafter referred to as Zoram or Zoland is situated between 92 and 95-degree longitude (East) and between 20 and 25-degree latitude North of the Equator. The whole area is roughly about 91,000 square miles with a population of about 5 million in 1991. The Zo dynasty or Zo kingdom was built between 200 CE and 700 CE (Lalremruata 2010, 1b).

Very little study or research has been conducted on Zomis in India or elsewhere. Gin Khan Nang wrote a thesis on Zomi Baptist churches in Indo-Myanmar who also claimed, "The people who live in the Chin state and the surrounding areas were called Chins by the British colonialists. Chin means "man" in Chinese. However, the people call themselves "Zomi," (Nang 1990, 7). The Chins in Mizoram were first known as Lushais, who lived in a more compact area than their neighboring tribes. "Lushai," meaning "taking human head," was a name given to them by the British. The Lushais knew that their name was given to them by foreigners and that it carried a certain negative meaning. By consensus in 1954, the name Lushai Hills was changed to Mizo hills (Nang 1990, 8-9). J. George Scott, a former British official in Burma, records:

> Like others, the people do not accept the name given to them by the Burmese and ourselves; they do not call themselves Chins, and they equally flout the name of Kuki which their Assamese and Bengali neighbors use. They call themselves Zho or Shu, and in other parts Yo or Lai (1932, 187).

The Identity Crisis

The Zo people are originally from the Mongoloid stock. They have physical resemblance with the Thais, Vietnamese, Cambodians, and the Filipinos. It is, therefore, very difficult to identify since we no longer use any of our traditional demarcations. Richard Zatu's article, "The Chin Identity Crisis," stated this problem as below:

Can you identify a Chin national in the streets of Yangon, Mandalay or elsewhere? Chances are that you can't. However, most of the time, you will be able to tell an Indian or a Chinese by the color of his skin. But it is difficult, sometimes impossible, to differentiate other racial groups of Myanmar from another by appearance since we all have similar skin color and roughly the same body build (Zatu 1999, 92).

Besides the physical resemblance becoming a source of identity crisis, the main struggles today are about by what name they should be known. Within the "Zo" families are Chin, Mizo, Kuki and Zomi. We are yet to settle a common nomenclature. This makes it very unsettling amongst us. Due to external dominance and influence, the Bengali called the Zo people Kuki, the Burmans called them Chin, the Indians called them Lushai, but traditionally they never called themselves by any of those names. Gin Khan Nang pointed out that in Burma Chin became an official name with the creation of Chin Special Division in 1948 and later Chin State in 1974. However, the people called themselves as Zo or Zomi. (Nang 2010, 24). Lian H. Sakhong's book *In Search of Chin Identity* points out this confusion of ethnic naming ourselves by saying:

> The common proper name of the Chin is inseparably intertwined with "the myth of common descent" and "myth of origin of the Chin." According to the origination myth, the Chin people emerged into this world from the bowels of the earth or a cave or a rock called Chinlung, which, as we will see below, is spelled slightly differently by different scholars, based in various Chin dialects and local traditions: Chhinlung, Chinnlung, Chie'nlung, Chinglung, Ciinlung, Jinlung, Sinlung, Shinlung, Tsinlung and so on (Sakhong 2003, 1).

Therefore, some continue to use the name Chin or Kuki within the Zo families. This has created a sense of alienation amongst them. There is a clear consciousness among different sections of the people like students, cultural organizations, social units, church groups, political segments and various organizations about the absence of a popularly accepted nomenclature for the Chin-Kuki-Lushai people. One name after another was propounded but failed to get popular acceptance. This happened although they belong to the same ethnic groups.

The terms, Kuki, Chin, or Lushai, or their combinations like Lusei-Kuki, Kuki-Chin, Kuki-Lusei-Chin or even acronyms like CHIKUMI (for Chin-Kuki-Mizo) or CHIKIM (for Chin-Kuki-Mizo) could not be firmly in the minds of the people, who intrinsically know that they are foreign terms having no meaning in any local dialects. Two wrongs or three wrongs cannot make right. They cannot but help resist because they were imposed upon them by rulers and outsiders to be their identity, without their knowledge and readiness to accept them (Zogam 2011, 1).

Since they cannot come to terms with one nomenclature and at the same time fear that they would lose one another, the struggle is far from over. They are aware that they are of the same ethnic origin. Vei Kho Ning stated this dilemma in this way:

This nation has been carrying different names, such as Kuki, Chin, Zo and is spread over many different parts of India, such as Manipur state, Assam state, Mizoram state, Nagaland state, Tripura state, and the Chittagong Hills of Bangladesh, and in Burma, such as Chin state, Arakan state, Sagaing division, and Maguai division. By 1985, the population of this nation was two and a half million. Though the original name of this nation may not be discovered, nor their origin convincingly traced, the fact that these peoples with different names belong to one origin is unanimously accepted. There are enough historical evidence and records proving that the Kuki, Chin, and Zo people are one nation (Ning 2009, 3).

Besides struggling to come to terms by having one collective nomenclature, the problem has been multiplied by the desire of many tribes under the Zo families who have preferred to be identified as distinct tribes according to their registration under the Government of India's Scheduled Tribes. Such movements against coming together under one umbrella have further complicated the dream to realize a collective identity. We cannot come together with a closed mind to discuss our future. Even though we cannot agree on one nomenclature, it is imperative that we keep our lines of communication open and that we accept one another despite division. Our survival as a people will largely depend on how soon we can nail down our differences and agree to pursue our destination with an open mind.

"The wind of national consciousness and ethnic resurgence did give insights and re-examination of their names. Zo tribes, who are recognized by the Indian government under the Scheduled tribes in India, would like to have a common nomenclature by which they should be known." (Pau 1995, 11).

In a similar vein of exploring to foster unity among our families, Rev. Khup Za Go has made a compilation of the documentary study, history and culture of the Kuki-Chin-Lushai tribes into a single book, *Zo Chronicles*. In the acknowledgement section he expressed the reason for taking up this project:

> It is also my belief that through a study of socio-religious, cultural and political history of Zo people past and present, a spirit of unity and harmony and realization of their unique oneness among themselves will be fostered and strengthened in spite of their being politically and administratively divided and found in different districts, states and countries of India, Burma and Bangladesh (Go 2008, ix).

The problem of identity crisis is far from over, yet it cannot be solved by others except the Zo people themselves. At the present rate, the road to their destination will be far away and rough. It may take many years to come together under a common nomenclature. However, the journey may be long, they should be willing to take a step at a time. Haokip made this observation in his article "Contesting Nomenclatures: The Kuki-Chin-Mizo of India and Burma":

> There cannot be a common identity so long as they have the mentality of Cain and go Judas' way. So long as they define their socio-cultural boundaries in much narrower terms than in the past without shedding old clannish baggage and promoting a positive sense of nationalism, proposing new common nomenclatures at this stage would lead to partition of minds. The Kuki-Chin-Mizo must be willing to negotiate on issues concerning the names of their collective identity, their lingua franca, etc. seriously. However, no collective identity would emerge so long as identity negotiation takes place within limited groups and space. The road map ahead, unlike in the past, should be all-inclusive in which all the Kuki-Chin-Mizo groups of India, Bangladesh and Burma should be involved as equal players (2009, 31).

The Colonial Mistake

Since Zo people were divided by hills and rivers, in Chin Hills, Chittagong hill-tracks and in Lushai hills, there was no common front organization through which they could fight against any invader. As a result, they were easily annexed under the British rule. Their areas of habitations were brought under the administration of the East India Company, and they were divided into four administrative units. The complexity of the governance of the region was rightly observed:

> The Chittagong Hill Tract, the South Lushai Hills District, the North Lushai Hills District, and the Chin hills. The first two regions were initially put within Bengal. In 1898 the southern and northern parts of the so-called Lushai hills were united and put in Assam. The Chin Hills of Burma could never be effectively controlled and, at the time of transfer of power in Burma and India, a small tract of territory remained actually 'unadministered' between them (Vabeihmosa 2009, 1).

L. Lam Khan Piang highlighted what happened to them when the boundary lines were drawn across their territory:

> The melon cutting of the Zo inhabited area or territorial homeland ethnified them and they become ethnic minority in every side of the boundaries. Among the boundaries, the Indo-Bangladesh (East Pakistan), the Indo-Burma, and many administrative units or state boundaries, the Indo-Burma boundaries have divided them in such a way that they began to develop a sense of distinct identity to have an existence as a different entity (Piang 2008, 51).

The political unrest and ethnic conflicts in the African continent and Asia go back to the mistakes made by the Colonial rulers. Before leaving colonial outposts, the demarcation of the boundaries was made according to their convenience not according to the ethnic affinity and conglomeration. Since the Zo people are divided into three nations, till today they cannot accept the political boundaries. Chaube in his writing, *The History of Mizo Politics* stated:

> The territorial demarcations were never accepted by the people. The separation of Burma from India in 1937, the partition of India in 1947 and the extension of administration over the entire Indian part

of the area completely stopped their pristine mobility, which had begun to be curtailed from the time of the imposition of the British rule. On the other hand, since the British days, the different groups were slowly losing their sub-ethnic identities to the extent that, in the late British period, the census reports started classifying them broadly into Lushai, Kuki, Pawi, Lakher and Hmar in India (2010, 1).

In the Chin Hills area of Burma, the British put Zo tribes under a single administrative area and administered it with an act known as the Chin Hill Regulation 1896. This regulation was replaced by the Chin Special Division Act of 1948, which was adopted on October 22, 1948. There were six sub-divisions in the Chin Special Division: Tedim, Falam, Haka, Mindat, Paletwa and Kanpellet. The Chin Special Division was changed to Chin State under Section 30 (B) of the Constitution of the Union of Burma adopted on January 3, 1974 (Dal 2010, 7).

After India and Burma gained their independence, the international boundary between them ran through the Zoland, separating the Zo people into two nations. There was no protest about what happened, and people inherited a Colonial mistake, leaving us with a problem that cannot be solved just by ourselves. The British rulers made the demarcation to introduce the modern administrative system, but it resulted in dividing people into three countries of India, Burma and Bangladesh. In his article, "Ethnic nation building: Chin-Kuki-Zo Trail" Keivom discussed one of the greatest damage committed by the British Rulers to the Zo families by dividing them into three countries:

> The greatest harm the British Raj did to us was the bifurcation of our inhabited areas into different administrative units under their divide-and-rule policy. This seemed to matter little until formal borders were drawn up and we suddenly found ourselves all divided up as we are today in three different countries. On the eve and immediately after India's independence, the newly formed political party with common agenda to bring our ethnic group under one roof in the form of "Greater Mizoram" raised strong voices against this unholy divide but to no effect. This was followed twenty years later by a much louder armed protest which plunged Mizoram into darkness and miseries for twenty years. In fact, an unpardonable damage had already been done to us in 1935 when the Government

of India Act was passed by the British Parliament which completely separated not only Burma from India but our people living across the borders of the two countries (2010, 1).

The Zo families although stuck into the present situation admittedly will not accept it as their fate. History will not forgive if they recoil in to say, "What else can we do?" They realized that they have every right to raise their voice in protest against the divisions. He reasons:

> Our fate was decided without our consent and we have been stuck with it ever since. Can we undo it? It is the dream of every self-respecting people to have freedom to decide and determine their own fate. There is no permanent boundary on earth. Histories are written and re-written and boundaries are drawn and redrawn at the bidding and will of the people. The mighty Soviet Union was undone in 1990 and 15 States including Russia came out from its gigantic ruins (Keivom 2010, 1).

On the one hand, there is a deep longing to unite the Zo families into one nation. We are divided against our will and today the hope of coming together is a dream yet to be realized. On the other side of the coin, there is a belief that the Zo families in Bangladesh, India and Burma are almost hundred percent Christians and theye become the bearer of the good-news of salvation in these three nations, calling people to reach all everywhere.

The Scattering of Zomis

In my research on Zomi diaspora, I attempted to find reasons and extent of the scattering of Zomi people around the world. Using a questionnaire, I asked Zomis about various reasons that led to their dispersion and where Zomi people have migrated from their ancestral lands to many different parts of the world. According to my respondents, the top five reasons that led to the Zomi diasporization are given below in the order of prominence:

- *Poor economic condition* in Chin state, and in Burma in general. Economic hardship and the government negligence for the development of Chin state in transportation, infrastructural or economic development. Authorities are not interested in lack of valuable natural resources and developmental work is left to the initiative and free labor of local people. The market is at the whim and pleasure of select businesses who can grease the palms of the authorities. Therefore, the economy of the region is very unstable and does not allow people to risk investing their resources. Going overseas to work is the only way to survive whose motivation is purely economic. They are not fighting about human rights or concerned about political issues, but primarily seeking livelihood. They walk across the border of Burma to survive and support family back home. With the inflation skyrocketing, it is impossible to live in Burma, without help from family members who are abroad.

- *The suppression of freedom of speech and restriction of the expression of faith.* Being marginalized and discriminated as a minority ethnic group creates a desire for democratic government where they can express their rights and enjoy freedom. The military junta is not interested in protecting and safe-guarding its citizens. Zomi ethnic people now keep going out of the country for fear of the Burma military's "Burmanization" scheme by means of military and religion, religious oppression, ethnic discrimination and forced labor without payment. In general, the desire to stay on and cultivate their own farms and land is no more appealing to the younger generation, because those who continue in this occupation are barely surviving.

- *Political and economic instability.* The disparity between the "rich and the poor," due to inequalities in the socio-political system is ever widening. The political instability in the country is because the military government who wants to stay in power. For them, all other issues are secondary. The lack of adequate planning to meet the rising needs of the younger generation by the government compelled the younger generation to go abroad by all means. After the 1988 uprising, many schools, colleges and universities were closed and students were left with no choice but to seek refugee or political asylum status in foreign nations.

- *To find freedom and new life.* Zomis are going abroad seeking better and brighter future for them and their children. Even if one obtains a higher academic degree there is no guarantee that their employment will adequately support their families. The government is not creating new jobs matching with their degree. To pursue higher theological education, there is no alternative but to go to the US, Europe or other Asian developing countries. Most of those who go abroad for studies do not return resulting in brain drain among Zomi people. When one studies for a longer period and is well adjusted to the affluent society, there is no desire to return to their home country.

- *The Lord must have a plan.* Since the Lord wanted to use and lift up Zomi, He called them out from their ancestral land and scattered them. Just as in biblical narratives of Abraham, Jacob and Moses who are called out of their places, God is scattering Zomis because of bad government, poor economic situation, rat infested famine and other innumerable hardships out of their villages and towns.

Zomis were rooted in the land until very recently and migration was never an option. One respondent observed, "As far as I know, there were only a few or handful of Zomi who left Burma before the 1988 Democracy crack-down.... One of the main reasons of such insignificant numbers is because we don't know anyone who would support us." Only the educated and fortunate people who have an idea and vision had the rare privilege of migration. In general, the uneducated masses didn't know anything and lacked in imagination or connection to explore livelihood beyond land-based economy. Another respondent said, "The poor farmers in Chin state would not even move to other states within the country or border states such as Mizoram or Manipur states in India."

As there was a general awakening around South East Asia due to political instabilities and developmental neglect of northeast India, many people were looking towards the West or elsewhere in India for better opportunity. Zomi who left Myanmar before the democratic movement crack-down joined others in their migrations to developed nations. Most of them left Myanmar seeking better educational avenues in the West or the Far East, and from the Northeast India, young people moved to other major cities of India for higher education and employments. Many Zomis left their homelands to work as sailors in merchant ships in Japan, Australia and the US and they were much better off when they returned home. A few left for higher theological studies abroad with the hope to return and serve the people (including reaching the Burmese).

A mass exodus is taking place out of the Zomiland. The churches in Chin state are suffering for want of educated personnel. The *Khonumthung News* estimated that there are about 4,000 Chin people in Malaysia and 3,000 in New Delhi waiting for their opportunities to other countries under provision of United Nations Refugee agency. Every day the number increases at the rate of 10 to 20 persons. The article titled as "Church leaders and Politicians Request Chin people not to Migrate", further reported that:

> Chin people are leaving their home-town daily, so the population is decreasing year by year. The bad thing is that teenagers cannot attend formal school as they must work in other countries for their livelihood.... A record shows that there are two hundred thousand Chin people residing in foreign countries over the past 20 years. Currently, our church members are very few compared with last year. If one of our members die, there are no workers for burial activities. Some are very lazy as they get financial support from their relatives in foreign countries. It will certainly have bad consequences for our future. Indeed, Chin people have no desire to settle in their home town (2009).

Zomis scattered all over the world are seeking any possible status to stay in the new places. In the present context of political instability, lack of educational or economic prospects, the desire to migrate to the developed nations to have a better life is very high. They even make dangerous attempts to go to Malaysia, Thailand or India where they enroll themselves as refugee or political asylum seekers at United Nations offices or other countries. My research found that Zomis are living in some thirty-five countries in all continents of the world, most are in US and UK while a few even in Israel and Finland.

Concerns and Challenges

While taking Bible studies with a dozen young people in Pasadena, California, whose parents are Zomis from Myanmar, I found out that they are struggling with their cultural and national identities. They are saying that most American young people will not know where Burma or Myanmar is. They also expressed their difficulties in telling Americans their names, because they are difficult to pronounce and often their names are long. Zomis cannot pick up their names because Zomi names are a family historical record and represent lineage. Since the society is patrilineal, the eldest son of the eldest male member is named after the paternal grandfather.

Language remains a major challenge for Zomis in new countries of settlement. For those who know Basic English, they have a better chance of adapting themselves faster than others. Most Zomi immigrants arriving in the United States speak little or no English and their children hardly have any primary education or medium of instruction in English. The fortunate ones know some older Zomi immigrants who can guide and assist them to navigate through life in the new country. Zomis also face much racial misunderstanding and discrimination as immigrants in foreign lands. Many in the host countries are unaware of the regions of the world that Zomis hail from or not kept up with current happenings there. Because of their appearance, they are often mistaken for Asians and considered as Indians or Bangladeshis. The monster of race raises its ugly head even after Zomis obtain citizenship and have all privileges in the adopted homelands. They are often seen as a perpetual foreigner and stereotyped especially because of their skin color, race and religion.

Zomis also experience various kinds of cultural shock and loneliness as immigrants. They have been living under the "cloud of inferiority" for so long that they are accustomed to it. It is very normal to be looked down upon by the citizens of the host country as the new arrivals are economically and educationally backward. Being despised by others comes in different forms. If one is not prepared to face hardship or ill-treatment, they may end up in depression. Hardship in adjustment is part of the challenge everyone faces in any new country.

Conclusion

As dispersion of Zomis is a more recent phenomenon - over last twenty years or so and their global scattering have brought many closer to the gospel of Jesus Christ. They stand to benefit by learning from other emigrants from South Asian and South-East Asian nations to thrive in foreign lands. Zomi Christian Fellowships around the world are facilitating the practical needs of the immigrants, without which the Zomi society could disintegrate and lose their identity. Many Zomis see the purpose of their dispersion to be God's witnesses to the ends of the world.

References

Carey, Betram S. & H.N. Tuck. *The Chin Hills Vol I*. Rangoon: Government Printing Press. 1896.

Chaube, S.K. "History of Mizo Politics" http://mizoramexpress.com/index.php/2010/05/history-of-mizo-politics/. (Accessed on February 27, 2011).

Dal, Thang Za. 2010. *The Zo People of Bangladesh, Burma and India*. Hamburg, Germany.

Go, Khup Za. 2008. *Zo Chronicles* New Delhi: Mittal Publications.

Khai, Sing Khaw. 1984. *The Theological Concept of Zo in Chin Traditional and Culture*. Unpublished thesis at Myanmar Institute of Theology, Rangon, Myanmar, 1984.

Haokip, Thangkholim 2009. "Contesting Nomenclatures: The Kuki-Chin-Mizo of India and Burma" *Ahsijolneng Annual Magazine* Kuki Student Organization of Shillong, Meghalaya.

Keivom, L. 2010. "Ethnic Nation Building: Chin-Kuki-Zo Trial" Unpublished paper presented on "Ethnic Nation Building: Chin-Kuki-Zo Trail" at School of International Students (SIS), JNU, New Delhi on April 5.

Khonumthungnews 2009. "Church Leaders, Politicians request Chin People not to Migrate" http://www.vaphual.net/church-leaders-politicians-request-chin-people-not-to-migrate/ (Accessed on February 2, 2010).

Lalremruata, C. 2011. C. "Who are the Zo People?" http://zoindigenous. blogspot.in/2009_02_01/archive.html (Accessed on February 7, 2012)

Minahan, James. 2015. Ethnic Groups of South Asia and the Pacific: An Encyclopedia. Santa Barbara, California: ABC-CLIO.

Nawni, Khuang. 1990. *The History and Growth of the Churches in Chin State, Myanmar.* Unpublished Master of Theology dissertation at Fuller Theological Seminary, Pasadena, California.

Nang, Gin Khan. 2010. *Zomi Christianity and Cultural Transformation.* Unpublished Doctor of Philosophy dissertation at Fuller Theological Seminary, Pasadena, California, 2010.

Ning, Vei Kho. 2009. *Understanding and Practicing the Sabbatical for the Kuki/ Chin/Zo in the United States: Cultivating Wholeness through Self Care for the Service of the World and Ministry of God.* Unpublished Doctor of Ministry dissertation at San Francisco Theological Seminary, California.

Pau, Ngul Khan J.M. 1995. *When the World of Zomi Changed.* Unpublished Doctor of Missiology dissertation at Western Seminary, Portland, Oregon.

_____, 2011. *Zomi in Diaspora for World Evangelization.*

Piang, Lam Khan L. 2008. "The Process of Ethnification of the Zo People" *Prism of the Zo People.* Lamka: Thawnsau Printing Works, 2008.

Sakhong, H. Lian. 2003. *In Search of Chin Identity: A Study in Religion, Politics and Ethnic Identity in Burma.* Nordic Institute of Asian Studies Press.

Scott, George J. 1932. *Burma and Beyond,* London: Grayson and Grayson.

Vabeihmosa, K. 2009. "The Past & Present Condition of the Maras: A Brief Review" www.maraland.net/articles/english-articles/114-the-past-a-present-condition-of-the-maras-a-brief-review.html (Accessed on Feb 25, 2011).

Zatu, Richard. 1999. "The Chin Identity Crisis" in *Thinking about Christianity and the Chins in Myanmar.* Cung Lian Hup (Ed). Yangon: Chin Evangel Centenary (1899-1999).

Zogam 2011. "Who are the Zomi?" http://www.zogam.org/history. asp?article=history_116 (Accessed January 26, 2011).

Sindhi Christians in Diaspora:

A Global Review

Celia Mahtani, Deepak Mahtani, and Suneel Shivdasani

Introduction

The Sindhi people are an ethnolinguistic group native of the Sindh province, one of the four provinces of Pakistan, lying in the northwestern region of the Indian subcontinent which was named after the river Sindhu (Indus). As ancient Persians pronounced "s" as "h", Sindhi and Sindhu were also called as Hindi and Hindu, which evolved as Hindustan as the name of a northern region of the subcontinent and was anglicized to "India" during the British Colonial era. Sindhis speak the Sindhi language and most Sindhi peoples were originally Hindu or Buddhists, but after the arrival of Muslim Arabs in the seventh century, Sindhi culture and religion were influenced by Islam. After gaining independence from the British and partition of India and Pakistan, most Sindhi Hindus migrated to India and other parts of the world, while Sindhi Muslims remained in Sindh, Pakistan.

This chapter is a global review of Hindu-background Christ-following Sindhis outside India and Pakistan. We begin by describing how the Sindhi Diaspora was established and what provides its cohesion.

We then explore those who follow Christ in this diverse diasporic context. Our research involved discussions with Sindhis around the world to gain their local insider perspectives and links to Sindhis elsewhere. We identify issues that remain a concern, factors that have been significant for growth, and conclude there is still tremendous need to reach Sindhis around the world.

A brief word about the authors: *Celia Mahtani*, is a Sindhi, born in London where her father managed the UK office of an international family enterprise. Her mother ran one of the first saree shops in London. Growing up as a Hindu, yet surrounded by Christianity, she chose to follow Jesus Christ in 1984. She is married to Deepak and they have two married sons. *Deepak Mahtani* was born in Hong Kong and lived in Japan where his father was a Sindhi businessman. He grew up in a Hindu home and followed Jesus in Geneva when he was 25. He is a management consultant based in the UK. Deepak and Celia are editors of *Sindhi Journeys of Faith* (2010). *Suneel Shivdasani* was born in a Sindhi Hindu family in the UK and started following Christ during his university days. He worked for several years with Satya Bhavan, running training courses at Bible colleges and churches, helping people reach out to South Asians. Currently based in London, Suneel facilitates the International Sindhi Partnership and is the International Coordinator for Christian Vision for Men.

Christian missionary work has been going on among Sindhis since the early 1800s and portions of Bible were translated into the Sindhi language by William Carey's team in 1820. Yet, there were only a small number of baptized believers of Sindhi background. The estimates of the number of Sindhis and Sindhi believers vary widely. This is partly because of who is being described. By the end of the twentieth century, in Pakistan, there were about 28 million ethnic Sindhis from a Muslim background with under 500 believers and an estimated 200,000 ethnic Sindhis from a Hindu background with a handful of believers. Moreover, Hindu communities from other backgrounds who live in rural Sindh and speak Sindhi, of whom thousands have come to Christ. This chapter focusses on Hindu-background Sindhis outside South Asia but there are also many Muslim-background Sindhis working in the Middle East. In 1997, I (Suneel) visited Sindhi Christian fellowships around the world (Shivdasani, 1998) and estimated that about 230 Sindhis followed Christ in Southeast Asia compared to a total of about 350 Sindhi Christian believers globally. After twenty years we now estimate that there are around 1,000 Sindhi believers in the diaspora. However, in India, the number of Sindhi Christians has grown from 50 in 1997 to an estimated 40,000 in 2017.

The History of Sindhis and the Sindhi Diaspora

Sindhis originated around 3000 BC as an Indus Valley aboriginal tribe (Quddus 1992, 56) and they have 3 distinct *jatis* (community groups): Lohanas, Bhatias and Brahmins, which operate individually, with some intermarriage and association between them. Sindhi Panjabis are another significant group, who remained in Punjab after the partition. The global Sindhi Diaspora is estimated at 241,000, which some regard as the most widely dispersed South Asian Diaspora and second only to the Gujarati Diaspora in terms of wealth (Markovits 2007, 270). Today, most Sindhis live in Pakistan and are predominantly Muslim. During the Partition, a smaller section of Hindu background Sindhis migrated to India and subsequently around the world. Thus, the global Sindhi Diaspora is predominantly Hindu.

Between 1400 and 1860, Bhatia traders established a colony in Muscat, leading to Sindhis living in Bahrain and other Gulf ports (Markovits 2007, 271). Sindhis also established themselves in Indonesia around 1840 (Partogi 2017). Migration to Central Asia followed, with a network between Afghanistan, Iran and Chinese Sinkiang, along with Sindhi moneylenders who moved to Ceylon and Burma. The Hyderabad Sindworkis are Sindhi merchants, mostly Hindus, who established global trade links of Sindhi crafts. Sindhis were established in Mozambique in the early 1900s, and by the time of the Partition it is estimated that 10-15,000 Sindhi traders and moneylenders lived in at least 11 countries around the world in communities of 100-200 members. Between 1940 and 1970 there was another significant move of Sindhi traders, together with a stream of professionals to countries with or without established communities.

Bhavnani found that at India-Pakistan Partition the Bombay Presidency became the "preferred destination for many Sindhi Hindus" (2014) and being a port city, Bombay helped further outmigration to newer destinations. Many Sindhis felt uprooted and stateless, and consequently took the opportunity to leave the region, resulting in a global scattering of Sindhis. Falzon has tracked members of the *Manghnani brahdari* in nine countries outside India: in Africa, Europe, the USA and the Middle-East, reflecting global dispersion within families (2005). *Jhulelal.com* specifies 149 countries with Sindhis, including locations as remote as the Falkland Islands (Malkani 1984, 169).

Different elements provide a Sindhi cultural identity or 'Sindhayat' in the diaspora: language, food, the "ani" ending of many Sindhi names, the way that Sindhis make a hotchpotch of spiritual and religious ideas, their common heritage, and the blend of all the above. Haller concludes that diaspora cultural identity is determined "by the independent quality of the multiple links between individual communities" (2004, 202), noting that the Sindhi global network itself is a component of Sindhayat.

Markovits reflects that the Sindhi Diaspora has its own identity since it does not primarily relate to India, economically or politically. However, where the local (non-Asian) community is not able to differentiate between the South Asian communities, Sindhis describe themselves as Indians but remain culturally closer to the Sindh, Pakistan in elements such as language and food (2007, 273). According to Bhikhu and others, international family bonds among diaspora Sindhis are strong, serving emotional, social, personal and economic interests. As a diaspora, Sindhis have sought to make the most of their opportunities for survival and prosperity. Family connections provide a credibility that is called upon when in need, or to gain access to funds. Support is not always forthcoming, which can lead to disappointment and resentment.

Diaspora Sindhis have switched increasingly to English or Hindi plus the local language, such as Mandarin or Spanish to engage with the local community (Oonk 2007, 273) while retaining their cultural heritage by continuing to value their language, food, and religious customs within their family (198). Moving with their husbands, women have found themselves living in a culture that was totally foreign to them, causing a stronger bond to develop with other Sindhis they meet (Raina 2002, 123).

Religion of Sindhi Diaspora

Religion remains a distinguishing feature for diasporic people everywhere and there is heightened awareness and differentiation in overseas locations. Baumann notes that for some, "religion has become the defining characteristic for people whose initial objectives in migrating were primarily financial, educational and social' and argues about its significance for providing cohesion in diaspora communities (2004, 174). Some Sindhis confidently claim, "I am proud to be a Sindhi, but I follow only one religion, that of humanity." (Falzon 2005, 72).

Many Sindhis follow gurus such as *Sai Baba, Radha Soami* or the *Chinmaya Mission*. The *Sadhu Vaswani* mission, now led by *Dada Jashan, (JP Vaswani)*, himself a Sindhi, has 37 mission centers on five continents. It should be noted that his work has promoted 'Sindhayat' (Falzon 2005, 38). *JP Vaswani* was also known to bring cohesion across the diaspora. He claimed that "Though Sindh is not on the map of independent India, Sindh is wherever Sindhis live." Uderolal Jhulelal continues to be a bond of unity between Sindhis all over the world. *Jhulelal* is seen by many as the community deity, and women are usually the ones who maintain religious practices in the household.

Hindu Sindhis are known for tolerance and assimilation. Unlike other Hindu communities, it is not unusual to see the Sikh scriptures and a picture of Guru Nanak in a Sindhi temple since he is viewed as a reincarnation of Vishnu. Similarly, Hindu Sindhis may include elements of Sufism as part of their Hindu worship (Haller 2004, 189). Some Sindhis in Malta attend Mass, follow Catholic fasts and

Saint worship, or accept Catholic burial rites, but view themselves as Hindu. As one Sindhi said at a meeting, "This is a typically Sindhi hotchpotch of different religions!" So many Sindhi families have a mix of Hindu gods and goddesses, Sikh gurus, Hindu gurus and sages, and even some Sufi traditions. This is not seen as a contradiction to the Sindhi mind but rather complementary. Consequently, Sindhi weddings and funerals can take place in Hindu temples, Sikh Gurdwaras or in Christian churches.

Celia and Suneel's parents moved to the UK in 1951. They spoke Sindhi to one another but encouraged their children to use English. Cultural identity was retained through their name, religious customs, such as being vegetarian on Mondays, and regular contact with Sindhi relatives. The role definitions were clear: men were responsible for income generation, and the women were responsible for social and family activities, keeping the traditions, and bringing up the next generation. Because of cultural assimilation and loss of language skills among foreign born subsequent generations of Sindhis, there is a noticeable shift in attitude in spirituality, religious sentiments and greater openness to other faiths.

The story of many Hindu Sindhis after Partition is a story of people on a journey full of hardship, leaving homes and businesses, feeling unwelcome in their homeland. Many were forced to leave with only the clothes they had on or whatever they could carry in a suitcase. They travelled by foot, road and rail to safer places in neighboring countries. Most stopped in India, but many, including Deepak's family, found India so different that they left South Asia completely. Many Sindhi families today are still in the ports where they arrived seventy years ago. In Deepak's family, there were those who went to Yokohama, Hong Kong, Malta, Guam and Gibraltar.

In the diaspora, Sindhis came together because of language, food, culture and history. It was crucial for their success and survival in foreign countries. Often, they lived together on the same street reflecting their solidarity and need for community. They set up Sindhi Associations with temples which became a community center to gather in an otherwise foreign environment, which are often still the first point of call for newcomers to the country and ongoing networking and support.

Followers of Christ in the Sindhi Diaspora

In 1997 there were about 350 Hindu-background Sindhi believers in the world, of which 50 were in India, and 300 were in 12 countries outside South Asia. Today there are an estimated 40,000 Sindhi believers in India (out of an estimated 3.6 million Hindu Sindhis), and about 1,000 Sindhi believers of an estimated 241,000 in 21 countries outside South Asia. There has been a growth of Christianity in the diaspora, but it is small in comparison to the overall number of Sindhis. For example, in Indonesia, the growth has been nearly four times over last two decades, from 120 Sindhi Christians in 1997 to 450 in 2017 out of an estimated Hindu Sindhi population of 20,000 and 98 percent remains unreached. Likewise, in Hong Kong the Sindhi Christians grew from 7 in 1997 to 125 in 2017 out of a total Sindhi population of 12,000 and 99 percent are still unreached.

In India, the growth has almost completely been in Charismatic churches, with Sindhis coming to Christ in search of peace, and responding to supernatural intervention such as personal healing or miraculous provisions. The pastor of a large Sindhi church in India found that it is important to remove misunderstandings, such as seeing devotion to Christ as conversion to another religion, and avoiding terms such as "Christian", using instead the phrase "follower of Christ". Regular prayer and fasting undergird their activities. Many have been baptized, but many are secret believers. While miracles are recognized as accompanying the Gospel, the focus in some churches is to spread the Bible's message rather than seek the miraculous. Many Sindhis report visions and dreams of Jesus and need believers to help them process these experiences.

Outside South Asia, most of the growth has been in Southeast Asia, particularly in Indonesia where a fellowship has been established that focusses on being culturally consistent with the local Sindhi community. The Fil-Indian fellowship in Manila has seen several people come to

Christ as they engage with the community through prayer and Bible study. The number of countries with Sindhi believers outside South Asia has nearly doubled in twenty years. This corresponds to family networks and migration rather than outreach by local churches. For example, 4,000 copies of *Sindhi Journeys of Faith* have been distributed through family networks and fellowships in 102 countries.

The biennial International Sindhi Partnership Consultations, held in Southeast Asia, have developed trust between fellowships and leaders in the region, providing a springboard for prayer and resource collaboration, with evangelistic events in homes and central venues. Contextual approaches such as *Satsangs* have been introduced in many countries. Sindhis with a Mission International events (SWAMI), held primarily in North America, but also in India and Southeast Asia have also provided greater networking among Sindhi Christians.

One of the Sindhi ministry consultation held in Southeast Asia in 1997 identified some of the major issues facing Sindhi fellowships: reaching unsaved husbands or wives, finding believing marriage partners, speakers and leaders who are Sindhi, the formation of Sindhi fellowships or churches. All these issues continue to be a challenge even today. Where Sindhi believers are on their own in a country, some report a lack of confidence and difficulties in being consistent with Bible reading or attending a local church. This reflects the need for effective discipleship through family networks. For example, in Japan, 20 young Sindhis came to faith, but due to lack of fellowship and pressure from spouses and in-laws, they no longer follow the Lord. Sindhis may not attend church since they view the culture as foreign and some are willing to go to an Indian fellowship as it is culturally similar. Since the literacy level in the diaspora is high, new believers benefit from discipleship materials produced in English or the host language. A common question is *Can I change my faith and keep my Sindhi culture?* One contributor, a Hindu vegetarian, wondered if she would be cursed by eating chicken, reflecting the significance of cultural issues for those who are seeking Christ.

Many churches have a high expectation of attendance at their meetings, so Sindhis who attend all the meetings are likely to spend correspondingly limited time with Hindu family members. Many are willing to share their faith with their family or in the city where they live, but few are known to have served Christ overseas. Some have visited fellowships or ministries in India, but very few have attended prayer events in the Sindh. Fear, personal discomfort or inconvenience are cited as reasons for not attending.

Sindhi believers generally live comfortably, and the personal wealth of the overall community is substantial. It is understandable for a displaced community to prioritize their stability and a basic level of comfort; however, a measure of discipleship is the willingness to serve the gospel beyond personal comfort and at personal cost. One good example of outward orientation is the Fil-Indian fellowship which has planted four Punjabi churches in Manila, each with 25-90 members.

A long-term concern of Sindhi fellowships is the provision of believing Sindhi marriage partners for women, and to a lesser extent for men. It is also an important concern of Hindu parents of a believing daughter. In one family, the Hindu father visited several churches to find a potential life partner for his daughter, through which he found Christ. A Sindhi believers' marriage bureau was started by International Sindhi Partnership and is being operated by Jeevan Jal Church in Indonesia who had been successful in bringing several couples together.

Some believers have married Hindus that are supportive and attend church only at special events. Some partners have come to the faith once their own identity as a couple has been established. Some single believers, only known to their family as believers, have been brought together as a couple in an arranged marriage. But many believers are still single. This is an important pastoral issue as marriage is a significant life stage for adults, as well as a sensitive issue since those who are called to singleness, need support in their calling.

Sindhi women who refuse to submit to their in-laws are seen as very disrespectful and, in some cases, the close family may insist that the faith of a daughter-in-law should not reveal to others. Baptism is often not allowed as it is a public act and may bring shame to the family. Attending church regularly for a believing wife may be difficult although participation in other ways may be possible. One interviewee in this study told us,

> "Six months after accepting Jesus, I returned to live with my parents, who knew of my decision but were unhappy with it, worried I would not find a husband. Within a few weeks, my mother commented that she had seen a great change in me – I was more loving and patient than before – which she attributed to Jesus."

The women are usually responsible for looking after the household temple and religious tasks, or accompanying older family members to the temple, which can raise discipleship challenges:

> After accepting Jesus, I struggled to change and bathe the gods as I felt I was betraying Him by caring for the idols. But my mother-in-law insisted I take my turn, calling me lazy and disrespectful. Confused, I asked Jesus for a way out, and He showed me how to care for the idols as though I was caring for Him. My Christian friends did not understand when I told them, as they had said I should refuse to bathe the idols.

Where Sindhis have embraced Christian faith, there is always a family dimension and many challenges involved. The travelling family members take the Gospel with them naturally. The family movement caused by marriage, retirement, life-events, or even visits to overseas family members that may not be intentionally missional, have provided opportunities for the Gospel to spread. Irvine has identified the significance of a believers' family network rather than individuals for the growth of the Gospel amongst South Asians (1996). We found some Sindhi Christians hold regular prayer meetings over Skype or Internet for their extended family which has brought many to Christian faith. The concern of how family members would respond is often cited as a leading factor for those who have not responded to the Gospel. Many believing adults teach stories about Jesus to their children and some are supportive of their believing spouses.

Many Sindhis who follow Christ adopt a "Christian" identity, using language and metaphors that can alienate them from family members. Some recognize that calling oneself a Christian can be a barrier to the gospel since Christianity is perceived as a western religion. It is also seen as alienation from family and heritage or being westernized and not care of one's own people and culture. Out of much zeal and without wisdom, some new Sindhi converts have a strained relationship with family and community. In our family, I (Deepak) discovered that Jehovah's witnesses had visited my father and realized the term "Christian" did not communicate to my family one who follows Christ. One interviewee told us, "A Christian identity in the overwhelmingly Hindu circles of *Sindhiyat* here in the New York City is more a hindrance than a help. What we need is an approach that focuses on spirituality and truth-seeking rather than religious identity." In Japan, Christianity is associated with being Western, and the example of military who live an ungodly life are examples of Christianity.

Much has been written about "Churchless Christianity" with discussion as to whether those who follow Christ should be baptized, and whether they should be part of a visible community that meets regularly (Tennent 2005, 171). One large church in India does not avoid baptism or visibility but deals with misconceptions such as the difference between following Christ and calling oneself a Christian, undergirded by practices such as prayer and fasting. Terminology such as "following Christ" is intentionally used in Sindhi circles. For many churches, the main discipleship event is the Sunday service or evening Bible study. Clearly, these are important times for the whole community of believers to gather. However, for Sindhi businessmen a more significant form of discipleship may be a midweek lunch or Skype call. In Hong Kong, the Asian Fellowship had a significant response to an event entitled *"Integrity, Wealth, and the Meaning of life."* than an invitation to a church event. And over eighty people came to an evening called *"Who wants to be Millionaire?"* a spiritual talk on money, wealth, success and purpose, when many asked deep spiritual questions.

While there are examples of relationship-building events such as cooking classes and ladies' groups, evangelistic approaches often rely on bringing a person to a church service. For some, authentic evangelism is event-based, with a proclamation of the Gospel or a testimony. A potluck supper with unchurched Sindhi friends would not be considered worthwhile. For women who are married to Hindus, a vital form of discipleship may be a home Bible-study group with other Sindhi ladies rather than a church service. The growth in Jeevan Jal, Indonesia reflects the value of running events that are consistent with local Sindhi culture. The Fil-Indian fellowship has run Valentine's dinners drawing in Sindhis who do not normally attend their fellowship, reflecting that resonance with the diaspora does not need to be limited to areas associated with *Sindhiyat*. Identifying analogies relevant to the teachings of Guru Nanak, Sai Baba or Radha Soami would be particularly helpful to those reaching out to Sindhis who follow those spiritual leaders.

Many Sindhis profoundly identify with anything Sindhi, and so fresh resources that are consistent with their culture need to be regularly produced and distributed. The faces of many Sindhis who read the New Testament in Sindhi for the first time, or hear a Sindhi worship song, tell a story as they realize that the Gospel is not foreign but something for them. The traditional model for following Christ involves saying a "Salvation prayer" as the key moment is when the person commits to Christ. It is apparent that for many from a Hindu mindset the commitment is more of a gradual process.

Conclusion

In many countries, there has been a growth in the number of followers of Christ in the Sindhi Diaspora, but it is small compared to the local Hindu Sindhi population, and also small in comparison to the growth of the gospel amongst Sindhis in India. The Sindhi Partnership Consultations have helped this diaspora community to develop and expand further but several issues identified when it was formed still need work. If Sindhis had a better understanding of their identity in Christ, learnt how to use their family networks more effectively, developed links between the diaspora and South Asia, as well as learnt lessons from the past, there could be significant growth amongst them in the next twenty years.

References

Baumann, Martin. 2004. "A diachronic view of diaspora, the significance of religion and Hindu Trinidadians" in *Diaspora, Identity and Religion, New Directions in theory and Research*, Editors: Carolin Alfonso, Waltraud Kokot and Khachig Tölölyan. New York: Routledge.

Bhavanani, Nandita. 2014. *The Making of Exile: Sindhi Hindus and the Partition of India*. Chennai: Tranquebar Press.

Davda, Sonal, Suneel Shivdasani, Robin Thomson, Margaret Wardell. 2006. *Looking for Directions*, London: South Asian Concern.

Pollock, Doug. 2009. *God space: Where spiritual conversations happen naturally* Colorado Springs: Group Publishing.

http://www.jhulelal.com/sindhispopulation.html (Accessed May 18, 2017).

Haller, Dieter. 2004. "Let it flow: Economy, spirituality and gender in the Sindhi network" in *Diaspora, Identity and Religion: New Directions in Theory and Research*, Editors: Carolin Alfonso, Waltraud Kokot and Khachig Tölölyan. New York: Routledge.

Kesavapany, K., A Mani, P Ramasamy (Eds.). 2008. *Rising India and Indian Communities in East Asia*. Singapore: ISEAS.

Falzon, Mark-Anthony. 2005. *Cosmopolitan Connections – The Sindhi Diaspora, 1860-2000*. Leiden: BRILL.

Mahtani, Deepak and Celia Mahtani (eds.) 2010. *Sindhi Journeys of Faith*. London: South Asia Concern.

Malkani, K.R. 1984. *The Sindh Story*. New Delhi: Sindh Academy.

Markovits, Claude. 2007. "Afterword: Stray Thoughts of a Historian on "Indian" or "South Asian" Diaspora(s)" in *Global Indian Diaspora: Exploring Trajectories of Migration and Theory*. Editor Gijsbert Oonk. Netherlands: Amsterdam University Press.

Irvine, Matt. *Compelling encounters with the good news of Jesus: Emphasizing Koinonia Embodied in Ekklesia as Essential to bearing Witness to the Gospel in Hindu Contexts*. (USA: Cornell University, 1996)

Naylor, Mark. 2004. *Towards Contextualized Bible Storying: Cultural factors which Influence Impact in a Sindhi Context*. M.Sc. Thesis, University of South Africa.

Naaman, Samuel. 1999. *Revisioning outreach to Sindhi Muslims: Proposals for Christians in Pakistan*. D. Miss Dissertation, Asbury Theological Seminary.

Oonk, Gijsbert. 2007. *Global Indian Diasporas: Exploring Trajectories of Migration and Theory*. Netherlands: Amsterdam University Press.

Partogi, Sebastian. "Sindhi Community in Indonesia: Keeping strings connected" in *The Jakarta Post* dated Jan 26, 2017. http://www.thejakartapost.com/news/2017/01/26/sindhi-community-indonesia-keeping-strings-connected.html (Accessed July 1, 2017).

Paul Stock, *Yesu Nasiri Zindabad* (Pakistan: Shama Studio, 2009) Paul Stock has produced several CDs and audio-visual resources for the Sindhi diaspora community.

Quddus, Syed Abdul. 1992. *Sindh: The Land of Indus Civilisation*, Karachi: Royal Book Co.

Ramey, Steven W. 2008. *Hindu Sufi or Sikh, Contested Practices and identifications of Sindhi Hindus in India and Beyond*. New York: Palgrave Macmillan.

Shivdasani, Suneel. 1997. *"Isn't it time you were married, Suneel!" – An apologetic for Singleness*. (UK: Essay for D.Th, Spurgeon's College, 1997)

_____, 2015. *Men and Women reaching Men, a presentation at Latvia Bible College*, 2015.

_____, 1998. Sindhi Fellowships in Asia (London: South Asian Concern).

Salvadori, Cynthia and Andrew Fedders. 1989. *Through open doors: a view of Asian cultures in Kenya*. Nairobi: Kenway Publications.

Tennent, Timothy. "The challenge of Churchless Christianity: An Evangelical Assessment" *International Bulletin of Missionary Research*, 29, no. 4, (2005): 171-176

Thapan, Anita Raina. 2002. *Sindhi diaspora in Manila, Hong Kong and Jakarta* Quezon City: Ateneo de Manila University Press.

Table 1: Estimated number of Sindhis Followers of Christ in 2017								
By location						**By background**		
Location	Pakistan	India	Diaspora	**Total**		Muslim	Hindu	**Total**
Sindhi followers of Christ	Under 500[1]	40,000	1,000	**41,500**		Under 500	41,000	**41,500**
Total number of Sindhis	28.2 million[2]	3.6 million	241,000	**32 million**		28 million	4 million	**32 million**
Followers of Christ (%)	0.002%	1.11%	0.41%	**0.13%**		0.002%	1%	**0.13%**

Table 2:Sindhi Population and Sindhi Christians in 2017)			
Country	Sindhi Population	Sindhi Followers of Christ	
		2017	1997
Pakistan	28,200,000	500	5-8
India	3,550,972	40,000	50
U.S.A.	40,109	25	20
Hong Kong	12,000	125	7
UK	30,000	20	20
Singapore	28,029	90	40-55
UAE	25,000	25	
Canada	23,090	3	1
Indonesia	20,000	450	120
Philippines	8,000	150	50
Australia	7,516	5	
Thailand	7,056		
Spain	6,000	4	
South Africa	3,168	5	1

---

[1] These are Muslim background believers.

[2] This includes an estimated 200,000 Hindu background Sindhis

Japan	2,725	25	25
Aruba	2,500	1	
France	1,822		
Jamaica	1,516		
Bahrain	1,508		
Austria	1,410		
Chile	1,250		
Nigeria	766	30	
Malaysia	716	25	7
St. Marteen	700	8	
Ghana	366	1	1
Panama	366	1	
Kenya	76	1	1
Egypt	51	14	
Belize (Dahomy)	26	12	
Totals	31,976,738	41,520	348-366
Less India / Pakistan	225,766	1,020	293-308
Global Total	31,991,704	41,520	348-366
Global Total less India / Pakistan	240,732	1,020	293-308

Source: International Sindhi Partnership Consultation 1997, 2010 and 2017. All the believers are from a Hindu background except those in Pakistan.

Persecution and Pakistani Christian Diaspora in Canada

Rashid Gill

Pakistan: An Overview of Religious Minorities

As of 2016, Pakistan had a total population of 195 million people, a vast majority of whom (nearly 97 percent) are Muslims, and most of whom are Sunni and a sizable Shias (6 percent according to Pew Survey). Pakistan has the second largest Muslim population in the world after Indonesia. Christians are considered as one of the major religious minority in Pakistan with a population of 3-4 million people. Other minorities include Hindus (2-3 million), Zikris (700,000), Ahmadiyya (285,000), Sikhs (50,000), Baha'i (30,000), Buddhists (20,000), Zoroastrians (5000) etc. It must be noted that there has been no official census report in Pakistan since 1998 and these numbers are based on other sources.[1] The Christian population in different regions also vary greatly such as Islamabad (4 percent), Punjab (2.3 percent), Sindh (1 percent) and Balochistan (less than 0.5 percent) (Mandryk 2010; Gabriel 2007).

Pakistan was formed as a home for the Muslims of the British

---

[1] This demographical information are collated from United Nations, Library of Congress Country Profile, Operation World and Pakistan Census Bureau reports.

Raj in South Asia in 1947 and its creation led to a bloody partition and many wars with neighboring India. In recent years, the war in Afghanistan and nuclear escalation have resulted in protracted strained relations with her neighbors. The Constitution of Pakistan maintains that Islam as a state religion, however, it provides freedom of religion to all her people. The Constitution states, "every citizen shall have the right to profess, practice, and propagate his religion." The making of a separate nation was not originally intended as an Islamic state and founders pledged that Hindus, Christians, Parsis and other minorities would enjoy protection and equality with the Muslim majority.

However, Pakistan has not embraced pluralism and has moved away from secular principles of its founders and constitutional provisions. When Pakistan was founded, nearly 23 percent of the population were non-Muslims which have now dwindled to less than 3 percent (Ispahani 2013). The military rule, widespread corruption, extremist violence and sociopolitical instability have led the successive governments to establish *sharia* into civil and criminal law. The failure to investigate, arrest, or prosecute those responsible for religious abuses cultivated an environment of impunity that fostered intolerance and acts of violence against religious minorities. The government policies did not afford equal protection to members of minority religious groups, because of the discriminatory legislation such as blasphemy laws and laws designed to marginalize, making them afraid to freely profess their religious beliefs. Moreover, the Christian population was not large enough and had no steady income except employment. A few of them were working as teachers, nurses, doctors, technicians but mostly Christians were working as sweepers because of poor education.

The religious minorities have faced continual attacks and oppressive treatment by the majority communities. It was not just against Christians and Hindus, but also groups such as Ahmadis who are not considered as Muslim. All non-Muslim minorities such as Christians, Hindus and Sikhs have been the targets of suicide bomb attacks and their houses of worship attacked at several locations each year. Many well-to-do Hindus minority have faced a steady barrage of forced conversions and kidnappings for ransom. In recent years many Hindu families have migrated to or sought asylum in neighboring India. The preferred destinations for Pakistani religious minorities tends to be the prosperous Arabian Gulf nations or Western countries in Europe or North America.

The government does not recognize civil marriages and all marriages are performed and registered according to one's religious group. There is no legal mechanism for the government to register the marriages of Hindus and Sikhs, causing women of those religious groups' difficulties in inheritance, accessing health services, voting, obtaining a passport, and buying or selling property. The marriages of non-Muslim men remain legal upon conversion to Islam. If a non-Muslim woman converts to Islam and her marriage performed according to her previous religious beliefs, the government considers the marriage dissolved. Children born to non-Muslim women who convert to Islam after marriage to a non-Muslim man are considered illegitimate, and therefore ineligible for inheritance. The only way to legitimize the marriage, and render the children legitimate, is for the husband to convert to Islam. The children of a Muslim man and a Muslim woman both of whom convert to another religious group are considered illegitimate, and the government may take custody of their children.

Pakistani Christianity

The origins of Christianity in Pakistan go back to as early as the first century CE and was established by St. Thomas the Apostle. Bishop John Malik, the Moderator of the Church of Pakistan, are among many Christian historians who believe that the apostle had come to Taxila the ancient university of the region and who established a church before going to Kerala for his missionary endeavors and establishment of St. Thomas Christianity in the southern parts of India in AD 52 (Gabriel 2016, 9; Thomas 1954; Moffatt 1988). Pakistani Church has adopted Taxila Cross as its symbolic icon, pointing to the ancient presence of Christianity in Pakistan. But it declined and faded away over subsequent centuries and particularly after the arrival of Islam in the north-western regions of South Asia. The impetus for the growth of Christianity came in the nineteenth century through the missionary movement of Christians from Europe and the US. The initial response was in Punjab province and later the entire villages had embraced Christian faith.

During the British colonial period becoming a Christian had a number of advantages, not least because it gave members of this impoverished minority access (at least in principle) to basic educational support from European missionaries, and a priority for employment (in junior positions) in maintaining churches and schools, and above all as nurses in mission hospitals – jobs which members of the upper 'clean' castes regarded as being wholly beneath their dignity. According to the *Oxford Encyclopedia on South Asian Christianity*, Pakistan's Christian community is one of the few in Asia which on the whole ranks socially, economically, and educationally below the national average. For example, whereas the national literacy rate in Pakistan is about 43 percent, only 20 percent of Christians can read and write. Although nearly 65 per cent of Pakistani children between the ages of five and eighteen attend school, the percentage of Christian children in school is only half of that, and a mere 0.4 per cent of Christian young people get as far as college. So, despite the huge number of Christian educational institutions, the present status and progress of the Christians, taken as a whole, remains abysmal. This is somewhat understandable in terms of the extremely depressed background from which most of the early Pakistani Christians came.

Today, Christians remain a very small and struggling community in Pakistan. Their social discrimination and economic isolation, especially of those of polluting occupations and so-called untouchables who have joined the Christian fold, continue to face much stigma and resistance to overcome the resentments of majority Muslims. The current world events and foreign policy of Western nations have undermined the Christian minority and have failed to buttress development or growth for Pakistani Christians. The long-standing dispute with India over Kashmir and conflicts in Afghanistan coupled with radical Islamic ideology, Pakistani Christians feel marginalized and alienated from mainstream life. Since it was not formed as an Islamic state and legal provision of equality and protection of minority group, there is much hope despite ongoing constitutional amendments to erode the rights of minorities.

Christians in Pakistan experience many stringent rules and constant monitoring because of their religious affiliation. They face chronic sectarian and religiously-motivated violence from both terrorist organizations and individuals with political connections within their own society. Pakistani Christians are incessant targets for rape, murder, bombings, abduction of women, forced marriages and eviction from home and country. Unjust and arbitrary blasphemy laws are used to punish Christians and prevent any evangelistic or missionary activities.

Religious Persecution

After the separation of Bangladesh in the 1970s, Pakistan strengthened its ties with the Gulf States, particularly Saudi Arabia, the United Arab Emirates and Kuwait as a source of trade and financial aid. Later in the 1980s under a military ruler, a policy of state led Islamization was adopted, which outlawed alcohol, gambling and night clubs. The ordinances prescribing amputation, stoning and whipping for theft, robbery, unlawful sexual intercourse etc. were also introduced. Shariat benches were established at the High Courts, Federal Courts and the Supreme Court to implement Sharia criminal laws.

It was in the 1980s that Pakistan's infamous "Blasphemy Law" were introduced which targeted religious minorities all over the country on a regular basis. The key section of Pakistan's Penal code relating to Blasphemy is Section 295. "Damaging or defiling a place of worship or a sacred object," and "defaming the Holy Prophet of Islam" are among the crimes under these laws with penalties ranging from a fine to death. Marshall and Shea claim that Pakistan now "enforces some of the world's strictest anti-blasphemy laws" (2011, 86). These legal provisions apply only for blasphemies against Islam, not any other religion. Islamization of laws also meant anyone who leaves Islam could be killed as well, although the legal system does not include apostasy. Prominent political figures like Salmaan Taseer, the former governor of Punjab province, and former Federal Minister for Minorities, Shahbaz Bhatti, were assassinated in 2011 for their opposition to the blasphemy laws.

The US International Religious Freedom Report 2014 found widespread religious freedom abuses an environment of impunity that fostered intolerance and acts of violence against minorities. As per the latest Open Doors world watch list of persecution against Christians, Pakistan occupies the fourth position in the top fifty countries in the world, scoring a high 88 points out of 100 (2017). Government policies did not afford equal protection to members of minority religious groups, and due to discriminatory legislation, such as blasphemy laws and minorities were afraid to profess freely their religious beliefs. The discrimination against Christians in employment are common and it is difficult for Christians to find jobs other than those involving menial labor, although Christian activists stated the situation had improved somewhat in the private sector and in the military in recent years. Other minorities like Ahmadis, who are not considered as a sect within Islam, have also come under severe religious persecution. But the majority Sunni Pakistani Muslims deemed them as heretics and are persecuted severely using the blasphemy laws. Even Shia groups were treated as enemies of Islam and when they were attacked by majority groups, they are being congratulated by radical terrorist groups in the region. On several occasions, the terrorist groups have taken responsibility for attacks on Islamic minority sects and other religious minorities in Pakistan.

In March 2013, a mob attacked and burned down more than 40 houses in Lahore belonging to Christians while the police stood watching. The attacks on Christians followed a rising tide of attacks on Pakistan's Shia Muslims and were often mischaracterized in the media as the products of sectarian conflicts. These increasingly ferocious attacks reflect the ambitious project of Islamists to purify Pakistan, making it a bastion of a narrow version of Takfiri Islam. Pakistan literally translates as "the land of the pure." However, what started in an imperceptible way in the 1940s has picked up momentum in the 1990s to purify and transform Pakistan into a land of the pure.

Asia Bibi, a poor Christian woman from Punjab, was the first woman in Pakistan's history to be charged with blasphemy and sentenced to death. In August 2010, in Punjab, 7 Christians were burnt alive, 18 others injured and at least 50 houses set on fire by a mob that accused the victims of blasphemy. In early 2012 a young Pakistani Christian girl, Rimsha Masih, was accused of blasphemy though fortunately the case was dismissed in November 2012. Despite the case's dismissal by the court, Rimsha Masih and her family had to be kept in a safe house in Pakistan to prevent vigilante actions against her. Rimsha and her family now live in Canada.

Scattering of the Persecuted

In recent decades, the religious minorities have come under severe persecution in Pakistan and Christians in particular, have felt the brunt of the religiously motivated violence. This has caused pervasive dispersion of Christians to other secure parts of the world. It is natural for people when feel attacked or subjected to the oppressive environment, they choose to find refuge elsewhere or suitable surroundings where they can find gainful employment and raise their family in relative safety. Various denominational and Pakistani Christian leaders have brought attention to the ill treatment in the hands of the majority and radical Islamic elements in the society. Many lawyers and international human rights advocates have continuously challenged the order of abuse of blasphemy laws and apostasy in Pakistan. Gregory analyzed the murders of two national figures in 2011 that shocked the international community, closely scrutinized the blasphemy laws of Pakistan and concluded that some Christians were forced flee after violent incidents perpetuated against a community repeatedly in different parts of the country.

Just as in early Christian history and throughout centuries in the Middle East and elsewhere, persecution of Christian has forced scattering of believers and resulted in the spread of Christianity itself. In a few decades after the birth of Christianity in Jerusalem, we see persecution breaking out on Christians in the city (Acts 8:1) and many followers of Jesus were imprisoned and killed. The natural response of the victimized community was to flee to neighboring regions which provided refuge, in turn fulfilling the mandate to go from Jerusalem to Judea, Samaria and the ends of the world as witnesses of Jesus (Acts 1:8). When Emperor Nero destroyed the city of Jerusalem in 70 CE, Christianity spread across the Mediterranean world and the Jewish diaspora became a foundation for the establishment and growth of Christianity beyond the ethnic and geographic confines.

The Christian and Missionary educational establishments in South Asia were some of the finest institutions that have provided not only economic and social mobility within the society, but also opened doors for outmigration for further studies in institutions around the world. As a result, a large share of educated Christians of Pakistan has migrated, leaving Pakistani Church without necessary intellectual strength to face the growing Islamization of the Pakistani society. Some minority activists have alleged that school textbooks contain many hate materials against minority such as defining Pakistan as a Muslim country and indirectly making non-Muslims feels they do not belong there. Such depiction sow seeds to leave the land of their birth when potential avenues emerge, and it requires a strong sense of call and mission for the younger generation to stay back in Pakistan.

Pakistani Christian Diaspora

Historically, the migration out of Pakistan has been driven primarily by political, economic, or religious circumstances. Since its formation in 1947, after gaining independence from colonial rulers and partition from India, many leveraged past colonial linkages to go abroad. Migration grew substantially in the 1970s, mostly to the Middle East for better employment and economic prospects because of the Oil Boom in the region. In the recent decades or so in the new millennium, much of the emigration out of Pakistan is attributed to the conflicts in the region, political instability, economic stagnation and religious persecution.

The rising military tension with India and ongoing support to war in Afghanistan have ensued continual economic stagnation and political instability. Being a strategic military partner with the United States in the war against Taliban and other terrorist groups in the region has led to many uncertainties for businesses as well as minority communities. The growing Islamization of legal framework and socio-religious sentiments have created fear in the hearts of all minorities in Pakistan. Some of these reasons have forced many to leave their place of birth and upbringing to explore options outside of the homeland and to face uncertainties in foreign lands. It could not be strictly considered as a forced migration like in countries devastated by famines as in Somalia or political turbulence as in Iraq or wars as in Syria. Nevertheless, a combination of multiple reasons of political, economic and religious dimensions have converged to motivate people to look overseas. For some, a push factor could have been more decisive factor than others in fleeing their homelands.

Pakistani Christians in the diaspora have relatively higher educational attainment as well as aspirations and are generally quicker to explore opportunities and migrate overseas. Since its independence, the first wave of emigrants pursued colonial connections and went to the UK and other commonwealth nations in the 1960s and 70s. They had the advantage of English language skills and pursued opportunities in Colonial institutions and businesses. Many of them were professionals like doctors and nurses and thrived in their adopted new homelands. They also brought family members and friends through family sponsorship provisions in immigration laws in many of those countries.

In the subsequent decades, many explored employment opportunities in the Gulf States such as Saudi Arabia, UAE, Kuwait, Qatar etc. because of the oil boom in the Middle East. Some also explore higher educational opportunities in Europe, North America and Australia. The state sponsored Islamization of Pakistan in the 1980s forced many Pakistani Christians to look for opportunities abroad, while others stayed back to fight for their rightful place in a secular democratic pluralistic society and political order. The support from the moderate majority, enlightened elected officials and community leaders and Pakistani diaspora are paramount factors for the future improvement of inter-faith relationship and well-being of Christians in Pakistan.

In fact, educated immigrants had no problem to mingle with others in gatherings, meetings or Churches but their spouses, parents and children needed a company of people who had same culture, background and language. They did not feel at home while dealing with Caucasians. A gap was felt, and authorities tried to fill this gap by encouraging new immigrants to have their own cultural organizations and worship places. Caucasian efforts were not very generous to accommodate the new immigrants and at the same time, new immigrants were scared to become part of the host culture. There was reluctance from the new and old immigrants. Unfortunately, it created a gap between them and it has not been fully filled up. That could be one of the reasons why South Asians felt the need to establish their own churches. With the passage of time, different denominational churches helped new immigrants to form their own congregations. The churches advocated that all new immigrants must conduct church services in their language and cultural particularities. They encouraged immigrants to have their own pastors who can speak their language and offered their facilities free of charge to encourage new immigrants. These churches were treated as an outreach of the denominations and incorporated within its structures. When there were no qualified pastors in a immigrant community, the denomination helped interested persons to have free theological courses. Government and churches offer English classes free of cost to all immigrants and every kind of counselling to encourage settlement in the country.

In short, it can be said the cultural shock, language barrier, lack of South Asian food, entertainment and living style were the main factors which forced South Asians to have their own worship places. For immigrant Christians, the church became a meeting place where all believers could gather and discuss their problems with others. To quell isolation in a new society and culture, and preserve cultural values, need was felt to establish neighborhood faith community. As per one community pioneer, Pakistani and Indian Christians want a meeting place for socialization and separate gathering failed the immigrants to become a part of the host societies. "When you come to a new country, you are supposed to integrate wholeheartedly and not to create division in society by creating your new groups."

Initially, Pakistani Christians join North Indian Christians to form a South Asian church. Conducting service in English was not enough as some wives and children do not understand English and preferred Urdu and Hindi songs and sermons. Christians of different regions wanted their distinct cultural elements incorporated in the worship as South Asians did not like giving up their culture easily. Professor Younas Wahab, who has in depth knowledge about this issue says, "Pakistanis or Indians Christians failed to realize that their future generation is not going to like it. The real need was to get immersed with mainstream Canadian church. By having a South Asian Church, we did not get any positive outcome. Our youth need a well-equipped pastor who could take Sunday school classes." At the time, there were no well-trained pastors to run South Asian Churches offering all functions of a regular church and meeting the needs of various regional groups. Due to lack of vision, funds and discipline, South Asian church failed to achieve their goal. They also did not find financial support to run a South Asian church on regular basis.

Pakistani Christians in Canada

It is very difficult to trace detail of the Pakistani Christians in Canada, but I was able to locate a few pioneers of our community in Ontario who provided some valuable information about the history of our community in Canada. North America remains a preferred destination for Pakistanis at large, Christians in particular. Though many Pakistani have settled in the United States, a significant number have chosen to pitch their tents north of its border. Pakistani Christians could be found in every province of Canada and each province has a different story regarding the establishment of South Asian churches. For this study, I limited my survey to Pakistani Christians in the province of Ontario and the city of Toronto where I live and pastor a South Asian church.

Though some Pakistani Christians have migrated directly from Pakistan to Canada, while many tend to take a circuitous journey over many years either through the Middle East or the UK. Some arrive for educational purposes by securing admissions in graduate programs in reputed universities, while others enter through work visa in professional careers in science, medical or technological industries based in large cities. A select few migrate owing to marriage or family sponsorship provisions of Canadian immigration laws. On account of English language familiarity, Pakistani Christians prefer English speaking provinces as compared to French speaking regions of Canada. The cultural and political framework of the Commonwealth helped Pakistanis to adapt well to life in Canada. A closer relationship between Canadian and Pakistani governments have been fostered in recent decades with regular flights to Toronto from Karachi, Lahore and Islamabad which is the most profitable route in the entire airline network. This has helped Pakistanis in Toronto to maintain very close ties to ancestral homeland, people and culture. Several weekly Urdu newspapers, radio stations and television programs provide necessary glue and support to the Pakistani Canadians in Toronto. Telephone and Internet help to maintain close connections with family and friends in Pakistan and with Pakistani diaspora at large.

Pakistani Canadian Christians live as nuclear families in predominantly ethnic or multi-cultural neighborhoods near a city or in the suburbs of a large city. This truncation of family life in diasporic settings has many benefits but also has produced many distinct problems that most immigrant families are not prepared to handle adequately. Most live a comfortable suburban life, with the vast majority living in the middle class and upper-middle class lifestyle. The need for two incomes to maintain a family's standard of living has required many women to leave the cloistered life at home that had been customary in Pakistan and seek work for wages outside of their homes. They highly value home ownership and have a strong emphasis educational achievement for their children.

Pakistani Christians can be found in all major cities of Canada such as Toronto, Montreal, Vancouver, Calgary and Edmonton. With nearly 70 percent of all Pakistanis in Canada live in Toronto, making it as the nerve center of Canadians of Pakistani heritage and descent. Among all Pakistanis in Canada, Christians are more dispersed as they have no fear of any religious persecution in Canada as share in the religious life of the dominant Christian culture of Canada. Most Pakistani churches in Canada, like most immigrant churches, have begun as fellowship meetings at homes under lay leadership. Upon reaching some level of regularity and critical mass, these groups start looking for public places to meet on Sundays. The group leader of these fellowships explores local churches, first along denominational lines and then the geographical proximity of its members. Over a period of time and sustained immigration, these home-based fellowship groups evolve into an immigrant church, conducting services in Urdu and according to various liturgies and worship formats most people are comfortable with. Language and Pakistani immigrant culture seem to be the glue that binds these groups together. They also become a support system to each other with strong bonds of affinity and mutual obligations.

Some Pakistani Christians prefer to stay away from such homogeneous groups and instead go to local Canadian churches, while occasionally visiting Pakistani fellowships or churches for cultural reasons or to maintain links with their old friends. Some make this choice in view of attending English services for the sake of their children who do not have the opportunity to learn Urdu and in order to better integrate into the host society. They also enjoy the broader offering of services available in Western churches and tend to be better-educated professionals. A few churches where Pakistani Christians participate tend to be Indian in its origin, but gradually evolved into a South Asian fellowship or church. They tend to comprise mainly of North Indian Hindi or Punjabi speakers who are comfortable with Urdu as well. A few churches offer contextualized worship experience in the form of *Masihi Satsangs* such All Peoples Church and some offer traditional Christian worship forms in a mix of Hindi, Punjabi and

Urdu languages such as All Nations Bible Church. Some have included English songs and preaching into their worship services.

Other churches have grown much broader to include some Southeast Asian or East Asians as well, while others have flourished to include people of many ethnicities, cultures and nationalities. Most have either a Pakistani or Indian in its leadership. They tend to follow a blend of South Asian values for the congregational life and pastoral leadership. There is strong thrust on fellowship at Sunday gatherings, mostly informal during which much support and encouragements are extended are received by church goers. Some of these maintain ties with denominations back home and others switch to similar ecclesial bodies such as Anglicans or Pentecostals. Still others seek ordination and affiliation with Western church structure or remain independent. Some maintain strong cultural branding such *Behta Darya* Asian Church, while others prefer generic names such as New Covenant Church of Canada. Other churches in Toronto where Pakistani Christians attend are First Asian Canadian Bible Church, Cornerstone Asian Church, New Life Asian Christian Centre, Light bearers of Christ Church International, South Asian Bible Church, The Warriors of the Cross Asian Church, New Life Gospel Temple etc. Other local denominational Churches that have attracted Pakistani Christians include Bramalea Baptist Church, Rexdale Alliance Church, Morningstar Christian Fellowship, Toronto International Celebration Church etc.

One of the major challenges that the Pakistani immigrant churches and community faces in Canada is in regard to the second generation. Young people who are born and raised in Canada, having lost linguistic and cultural competency due to assimilatory tendencies Most Pakistani and South Asian churches in Toronto has a strong emphasis on children and youth ministries. Congregations with a sizeable population of children and adolescents have adopted English more in their church service and some even offer entire service in English. Intergenerational conflicts abound in most Pakistani Canadian households and high expectations are set on weekly church gatherings and from pastors of ethnic churches.

Conclusion

The Pakistani Christian dispersion arose out of persecution of religious minority and pursuit of better education and economic prospects. Having come with a background of religious persecution, they possess high sensitivity to fellow Christians in their ancestral homelands and elsewhere in dominant Islamic nations. Pakistani Christians in North America is found to pray for persecuted church and Christians regularly as well extend practical and financial help for family and churches of persecuted Christians worldwide.

References

Ali, Charles Amjad. 2011. "Pakistan" in *Oxford Encyclopedia on South Asian Christianity*, Eds. Roger Hedlund, Jesudas Athyal, Joshua Kalapatti and Jessica Richard. New York: Oxford University Press.

Gabriel, Theodore. 2007. *Christian Citizens in an Islamic State: The Pakistan Experience*. Burlington, VT: Ashgate.

Gregory, Shaun. 2012. "Under the Shadow of Islam: The Plight of the Christians Minority in Pakistan" in *Contemporary South Asia*, Vol 20 No 2, 195-212. Routledge, London, UK.

Ispahani, Farahnaz. 2013. Cleansing Pakistan of Minorities, Jul 31. https://hudson.org/research/9781-cleansing-pakistan-of-minorities (Accessed Apr 15, 2017).

Mandryk, Jason. 2010. *Operation World*. Downers Grove, IL: Intervarsity Press.

Moffett, Samuel. 1998. *A History of Christianity in Asia*. New York: Orbis Books.

Marshall, Paul and Nina Shea. 2011. *Silenced: How Apostasy and Blasphemy Codes are Choking Freedom Worldwide*, New York: Oxford University Press.

Open Doors World Watch List. 2017. https://www.opendoorsusa.org/christian-persecution/world-watch-list/ (accessed Apr 15, 2017).

Pakistan Bureau of Statistics. Census Report. www.pbs.gov.pk (Accessed June 1, 2017).

Pew Survey. 2013. http://www.pewforum.org/2013/05/10/pakistani-views-on-religion-and-politics-as-election-nears/ (Accessed June 1, 2017).

Thomas, P. 1954.*Christians and Christianity in India and Pakistan.* London, George Allen & Unwin.

US State Department Religious Freedom Report. 2014. https://www.state. gov/documents/organization/238716.pdf (accessed April 15, 2017).

Walbridge, Linda S. 2003. *The Christians of Pakistan: The Passion of Bishop John Joseph,* New York: Routledge.

Diaspora Dilemmas:
Moral Issues of
Indian Christians in North America

Thomas Kulanjiyil

Introduction

Asian Indians are reportedly the third largest Asian immigrant group in the United States and the community continues to grow. It is the so-called "American dream" that attracts Indians to emigrate, with greater educational, employment and business opportunities, and today Indians are among the most successful immigrant groups in the United States. Having displaced from their native settings, many of these immigrants find the new socio-cultural environment quite strange and unfamiliar. They find many of the western societal values conflicting with their cultural and religious values. Consequently, they are faced with moral dilemmas on many issues that affect their lives. We shall try to identify a few of those moral dilemmas and suggest strategies to deal with them effectively.

The Dilemma of Parental Responsibility

With the kind of freedom people have in the western world, it is the concern of every Indian parent as to how much of personal freedom and autonomy they must grant to their children in matters of lifestyle, sexual preferences, dating and marriage choices versus how much control they must exercise on their conduct and behaviour. Indian parents are generally said to be authoritarian in their parenting style, and that mind-set does not change even after children have grown up to be adults. Parents feel morally responsible for how children turn out to be, especially, as it relates to their character and life choices.

Perhaps, with some exception, most Indian immigrants are conservative in their moral position, especially the first-generation immigrants. As to sexual orientations and preferences, they tend to be heterosexual. However, with the more liberal attitudes of the American society toward sexual orientations, it is a moral dilemma for the Indian parents that their children could be Americanized to such an extent that they could be either accepting of or attracted to bisexual, homosexual, transgender orientations. They dread about their children engaging in any kinds of risky sexual behaviors, including premarital sex and cohabitation. Most Indian parents generally avoid conversations on topics such as sexuality, sex education, and contraception (considered as taboo), and children feel inhibited discussing them with parents. Consequently, parents live in constant worry and suspicion of their children, resorting to their controlling and overprotecting behaviours that force children to be defiant and to detach themselves from any meaningful communication with parents on these vital issues. Children hide details of their personal life from parents and parents allegedly operate from a position of double standards of morality as Divya Kakaiya points out:

> For the Indian girl, the dilemma is multifold. She is taught what it means to be a "good" Indian girl who listens to her family, does not ask questions or challenge authority, and is dutiful in assisting her mother with daily household responsibilities preparing her for her adult role as a marriage partner. While this girl from a young age is being trained on how to be a good wife and daughter-in-law for when she is older, her brother is doted on by their parents and afforded greater leniency and fewer restrictions in his daily activities. These gender differences are ingrained in both genders and are constructed by the cultural values of their ethnic origins.

This dynamic sets the theme for a girl to be subordinate, and for her husband to dominate (7).

Furthermore, dating and intermarriages are not an accepted practice in the Indian community, and most Indian parents prefer traditional arranged marriages. It's a moral impasse for the Indian parent to learn that their son or daughter is dating someone. It is generally presumed that dating normally involves sexual intimacy between dating partners, something parents must guard their children from. It is primarily for this reason that parents are especially protective of girls.

> There is a strong disconnect between the daughters and parents since the girls will date and will not inform their parents about a huge part of their intimate life. The major reason why parents seem to fear their daughter's dating is intermarriage. The parents are fearful of sexual encounters as well as sexual assault (7).

The Dilemma of Marriage Choices

The mindset of most Indian immigrant parents is that it is their moral responsibility to arrange their children's marriage in a timely manner. Biological age is a deciding factor in this, and these days most people marry between 23 to 28 years of age. Within the limits of culture, religion, caste, and community, parents know that finding a suitable match for someone over 30 years is not an easy task. Parents worry when children delay marriage. There are many Indian households having more than one or two children, who have passed customary marriageable age because they could not find suitable matches within the community. Often, these factors force some to remain single and it is a great concern for parents. Marriage is traditionally arranged by parents based on religion, caste, social class and compatibility of the couples in matters of education, occupational status, income and physical appearance. As romantic marriages within Indian community is usually discouraged, most immigrant parents prefer the old fashioned arranged marriage. However, the second and third generation immigrants, and some new immigrants are largely opposed to that idea. Their preference is to date someone and to make their own marriage decisions (Manohar 171-588; Dhingra 41-63). Consequently, the topic of marriage not only brings conflicts between parents and children but also generates confusion in the minds of parents as to what procedure of marriage they must approve of. Some parents, having no other option, consent to children's choice. Still, there are those who are bent on arranged marriages that they either by pressure or trickery take their children to India to have arranged marriages. Such marriages hardly ever succeed. Some parents these days have found a middle path between the two extremes, which is "supervised dating" and which in turn allows "semi-arranged" marriage. In whatever way children are married, Indian immigrant parents are anxious if their children's marriage will last long enough in a society, where divorce is common.

Marriage between an Indian immigrant and someone born and raised in India is a matter of apprehension for parents from both sides. Cultural compatibility, educational status, and employment qualifications in the U.S. are the main concern for immigrant parents. For Indian parents, the chief concerns are immigration status, education, employment, qualification, psychological health, and marital status. More recently, sexual orientation has surfaced as a new issue for the parents to be beware of. Then there is the so-called "marriage of convenience" that results in a man or woman getting married to please parents, only to find out later that he or she is a gay or a lesbian. There are also other forms of convenient marriages, where migration to the West is the only motive for marriage with an American or Canadian citizen. In spite of these serious concerns, there are parents who rush through marriage proposals and eventually find out that there was some sort of deception involved in the marriage and that not all relevant information on the bride or the groom was disclosed at the time of proposal. For example, there are cases of marital separation and divorce in the Indian community because of serious psychological problems with a partner, which was not disclosed before the wedding.

Another moral quandary for Indian immigrant parents is inter-caste, inter-racial, inter-religious marriages that are becoming common these days among Indo-Americans. Parents are apprehensive of such marriages because of the fear that children might change their religious, cultural practices and beliefs systems. They also worry that such marriages will create "distance between grandparents and their grandchildren" (Inman, et al. 93–100). In spite of this, Indian parents are relatively tolerant of an inter-racial marriage with someone from the Caucasian race than a Hispanic or African race. Some parents are pugnaciously opposed to a marriage outside of their caste or community, in the fear of dishonor, such a marriage can bring to the immediate and extended families besides the entire community (Kay 79–98).

The Dilemma of Divorce

Divorce is a great moral dilemma for most Indian immigrants because almost every Indian religious tradition considers marriage as a sacred institution. Although there are religious and legal provisions for divorce in India under certain conditions, historically divorce has been rare. Despite the fact that, in recent times, there has been a steep surge in the divorce rate in India as well as in the U.S. among Indian immigrants, the Indian community is not yet ready to fully embrace divorce as a socially acceptable moral choice. In the Indian religious and cultural context, divorce is a stigma. A divorcee brings shame to the entire family and the community. Divorce has social consequences for both men and women, but especially women in arranged marriages suffer the most. Sharadha Bain narrates the costs of divorce for an Asian Indian immigrant:

> Husbands and wives are forced by social pressure originating 8,000 miles away to stay in emotionally unhealthy and abusive relationships. While parents and siblings might show sympathy over an unhappy marriage, divorce is often considered beyond the pale. Divorcees often are isolated from their families, an object of mingled pity and disdain. Sometimes, they stop receiving invitations to family functions, and when they do attend, they're made a target of relatives' shaming. In conservative families, a divorced woman is often viewed as pariah or harbinger of bad luck. The divorce taboo has particularly severe consequences for women who have no financial resources of their own (79–98).

The Dilemma of Sex Selective Abortion

Although sex selective abortion is not unique to Indian immigrants, such occurrences are being reported of some Indian immigrants in the U.S as well as Canada (Puri et al. 1169-1176). Cultural preferences for male and past history of infanticide continue to influence these Indian immigrants to practice sex-based abortion, which is deemed as unethical and banned in most progressive societies. Regarding selective sex-based abortion among Indian immigrants in the U.S., Higgins states:

> An ingrained cultural preference or belief can still permeate the lives of people in prosperous, free societies. I was recently told by an Indian-American doctor... although the cultural preference for sons varies in severity across economic, regional, and educational backgrounds, it is "no doubt" still an issue among Indian communities here in the US (2017).

Similarly, sex selection is prevalent among certain Canadian Indian immigrant communities as well. Women with two female children are likely to have an abortion if they can determine the sex of the fetus. There are noticeable differences in the male-female infant ratio among these immigrants, according to a recent study by Urquia and his colleagues:

> We evaluated most registered live births to Indian immigrants in Canada for more than two decades and compared these births to nearly all live births to Canadian-born parents. Among Indian immigrants, high M: F ratios were observed at third-order and fourth or higher-order births, which did not vary considerably across provinces. We conservatively estimated that 4472 daughters of Indian immigrants to Canada were unaccounted for over the last 2 decades—so-called "missing girls" largely among couples of two Indian-born parents (89.4 percent), but also among couples including one Canadian-born parent (2016).

Access to technology for sex selection, easy access to abortion clinics, and public health assistance for abortion available in the US and Canada benefits these immigrants in selective abortions. In Canada, health insurance coverage for abortion is offered with no co-payment. The moral ramifications for this selective abortion are many. It is alleged that frequently women are coerced into abortion by the family, rather than they themselves choose to do it. This contributes to their moral guilt for ending a human life and is discriminatory to women, as observed by Douglas and his associates (2010).

The Dilemma of Seeking Mental Health Needs

Asian Americans generally keep mental health problems private and seldom seek professional help, and this is the case with most Indo-Americans. They know that seeking timely help is the right thing to do for themselves and others when there is a mental health need in the family. Nonetheless, the stigma associated with mental health, cultural proscription against talking about personal problems with anyone other than family members, lack of mental health education, and ignorance regarding the benefit of counseling, hinder them from making use of the psychiatric counseling services (Kulanjiyil 21-28). While some assume that the mental health issue will slowly disappear, there are others who hope that their prayers will bring healing by God's miraculous intervention. Parents keep in secret their children's psychological conditions until a time when it's too late to provide any effective treatments or interventions. In many cases, children end up with some form of mental disability for a life time. Similarly, help is not sought after when there are generational conflicts with children, drug and alcohol addiction of a family member, or marital problem between spouses. The other psychological issues that Indians must seek professional help include substance abuse, depression, Schizophrenia, and mood, anxiety and psychosomatic disorders. With a timely diagnosis, many of these problems are treatable or manageable. However, long history of unattended problems ends up with devastating consequences for the individuals and their families. An Indian psychologist in California describes her experience working with Indian university students and families:

> Most of the conditions that will bring Indian families in for psychotherapy would be at points when the conditions are very severe, such as bipolar disorder, mania, severe immobilizing depression,

and severe behavioral conditions with teens such as out of control self-harm or drugs (Kakaiya 8).

The Dilemma of Elder Care

A very practical moral dilemma facing the Indian diaspora is that of caring for the elderly as the first-generation Indian immigrants are growing old. In major cities like New York, it is reported that between 2000 and 2010 the population of older immigrants from India grew by 135 percent or about 8000 people (Nair 2016). According to Pallassana Balgopal, Indo-American elderly can be classified into three groups: (1) Those who came prior to 1965, who are generally educated, employed and well-settled, (2) those who came after the 1965 Immigration Act, primarily immigrated because of professional and economic opportunities, and (3) those who came to the US as elderly immigrants on the sponsorship of their children. While the first and second group are generally economically independent along with retirement benefits, the third group lack any source of income and are completely depended on their children for physical and financial support (56, 60). Regardless of their financial status, all three of these groups need the support and care of their children and their families. He claimed that aging is a challenge for the Indian immigrants:

> For Asian immigrants because of drastically different value systems getting old in the U.S. poses a number of dilemmas. For the Indo-American elderly and their families, a major dilemma is whether to expect and abide by the value orientation of collectivism or follow the main stream American value of individualism (57).

For the aging, the moral dilemma is whether to stay on in the U.S. or to return to India, not wanting to be a burden to their children. At the same time, they want to be closer to their families in their advanced years. Celebrating the aging process, aging gracefully and stress-free are basic to Indian culture. While a smaller percentage of these older immigrants choose to return to India, they end up going back and forth between the U.S. and India, if they can. Resettling in India is not always practicable because there is no one to take care of them there either. With advancing age, these elderlies are quite helpless.

Elder care is a moral dilemma for the immediate family because they are to choose between home-based or institutionalized care. The Indian cultural norms expect children, especially sons, to take responsibility for their aging parents and to have them live with them. Parental care in old age is part of the filial duties and moral responsibilities of children in the Hindu, Christian, and Islamic religious traditions. Although a small percentage of aging immigrants are open to the idea of institutionalized care, it is considered a stigma to the Indian community even today, for that will be perceived as parental abandonment. The Indo-American elderly are relatively less prepared psychologically to give up the security and comfort of their homes and the network of friends and families, who are their basic source of social support. Besides language, food, lifestyle, cultural sensitivity, and socialization are major barriers to adapting to the American system of institutionalized care, rooted in an individualistic cultural orientation. Pallassana Balgopal explains this complex situation:

> For the Indo-American elderly and their family, a major dilemma is whether to expect and abide by the value orientation of collectivism, which implies dependence and nurturance from family and kinship networks, or to comply with the dominant value of their new environment, which is individualism (implying minimal dependence on others). This conflict or dilemma creates turmoil both in the elderly as well as in their family members. For example, placing a family member in a nursing home is not an easy decision, but for an Indo-American family, this option simply does not exist. Even if these families believe in such options they have tremendous difficulty in implementing it. Such decisions are unacceptable on an emotional level, including the fear of alienation by the social and kinship networks (51-52).

A study on elder care among Indo-Americans in Dallas area found that most educated Indians with high income were likely to find in-home services for their parents rather than sending them to a nursing home (Gupta and Pillai 7). However, the home-based elder was not easy for most Indian families with an average income, especially for working women who were typical caregivers. Besides the difficulties in balancing work and parental responsibilities, elder care added to their financial, emotional and physical stress and burden. The matter of elder care also had the potential to create conflicts between family members and particularly between caregivers and the elderly. Many caregivers reportedly experienced a high degree of 'role conflict' and 'role overload' that further contributed to their stress and burnout. Interestingly, it was found that those caregivers who believed in elder care as a moral duty (*dharma*), experienced lower levels of burden than those who treated it as something forced upon them.

Conclusion

In the discussion that preceded, we have identified six areas of moral dilemmas for the Indian diaspora in the United States, and Canada and they included, parental responsibility, marriage choices, divorce, sex selective abortion, seeking mental health needs and elder care. This is not an exhaustive list of issues but some of the most outstanding ones that are collectively experienced by most Indian immigrants. Although all these issues are to be resolved by each individual or family, some general perspectives and strategies can be offered.

About parenting, effective parenting should aim at helping children develop moral agency, to be able to choose for themselves healthy life choices. Parents must inculcate in children an appreciation for moral values, shaped by their culture and religion. Rather than being over protective of their children, parents must learn to provide them with moral guidance and counsels in a gentle manner. Parents must maintain open communication with children so that they are safe to share with them their feelings and thoughts. The right defense against the perils of abusing sex is educating children the sacredness and the responsible use of sex within marriage. The Indian immigrant parents must be open to provide sex education to their children, at an appropriate development stage, perhaps by the adolescence. The Indian community is yet to face the full moral weight of dealing with LGBT-related issues. Because of the cultural and religious inhibitions, many are afraid to come out openly. Rather than condoning the choice of a child to be gay or lesbian, parents may keep the communication with that child unhindered. It is the strength of the parent-child relationship that can motivate a child to seek out specialized counseling services and spiritual resources that could help address the issue effectively.

As regards to marital issues, the immigrant parents must know that the outlook of the younger generation in the matter of marriage is quite different from theirs. In the western context, parents cannot force children to marry someone they are not willing. Today's youth assert greater personal freedom to choose one's life partner, and generally, they are not in sympathy with traditional arranged marriages (Kulanjiyil 170). With some exception, their preference is to marry someone that they have known for over a period, preferably, in a dating or semi-dating relationship. Intellectual, psychological, and cultural compatibility are central to their choice of a life partner. As Manohar correctly points out, for the first-generation, marriage is often "a partnership between families, rather than solely between the couple, with the possibility that love might develop after marriage" (588). But in contrast, for the second-generation, it is "a relationship characterized by emotional commitment, psychological gratification, love and compatibility between partners, and one where their personal desires have been accounted for" (585). This is more reflective of the American value system. The second generation tends to be more flexible with caste, class, heredity, ethnicity, religion and occupation. Hence, parents must learn to be flexible to negotiate on many of these areas. The best approach is one of openness, understanding, compromise and support, rather than confrontation or sheer avoidance.

As far as divorce is concerned, as pointed out in our discussion earlier, the Indian community is not yet prepared to accept it unreservedly. The cultural and religious objections cannot be easily dismissed. Those who choose to divorce may continue to face resistance from the family and society. Perhaps, identifying signs of marital distress early and working through them, even by seeking professional help, is the way to prevent a divorce from happening. Also, since most break ups in Indian marriage is due to compatibility issues, a key factor

Indian immigrant must pay serious attention to is cultural compatibility in marriage, particularly, marriage between an Indian immigrant and someone born and raised in India.

An effective strategy to deal with sex selective abortion is community education, which can generate awareness of the value of life so that the right of the unborn can be protected. Communities susceptible to the past cultural preference for male children could be taught to value both male and female offspring equally. Regarding mental health, it is vital that the Indian immigrant community overcomes the taboo associated mental health and mental health services. They will benefit from the various counseling services that are available in North America. Today an increasing number of mental health professionals from Indian cultural backgrounds are available, who could offer culturally sensitive counseling. Individual counseling could help deal with psychological problems that limit or impair personal, interpersonal, and social functioning. Family counseling could help to identify behaviors that contribute to conflicts between family members, improving family communication and strengthening an emotional bond. The marital counseling could help couples alleviate marital distress and improve communication between spouses and problem-solving skills. Addiction related counseling could help with alcoholism, drug abuse, and pornography.

Concerning elder care, the long cultural tradition of respect and care for the elderly must be preserved within the Indian diasporic community, so that our seniors can gracefully age. If a parent decides to settle in India, having adequate support system established there, that choice may be honored. However, that does not exclude children and immediate families from caring for their welfare. Those choosing to remain in the US or Canada must be fully supported by the immediate family. However, families independently cannot handle the task of dialling care-giving without community help, especially from the diasporic Indian community. In addition to educating the families on various social services and community programs accessible for the elderly in their cities and neighborhoods, the Indian community must come forward with social programs that can assist the elderly. Creating a support group for the elderly within the Indian community, promoting senior centers for day-care, and establishing culturally sensitive living facilities that consider factors such as language, food, life-style, heath, spirituality, socialization and recreational needs may further the cause of elder care. These initiatives are more critical because the current American elder care system is not adequately prepared to meet the unique needs of the aging Asian Indian population. The needs of care-takers, who are mostly women, will also have to be attended to, to avoid burnout from care- giving. Individual families, identifying friends and families who can offer some type of help (visitations, taking the seniors out for a walk, helping the family with some day-to-day chores, and so on) to allow some release time for the care-takers, will be a helpful strategy. When physical and emotional conditions necessitate institutional care must be considered.

In the final analysis, the moral dilemmas encountering Indian diaspora in North America is reflective of the clash of cultural values between the East and the West. It is also representative of the inter-generational struggles within the Indian diaspora. Because these are collective experiences, continued engagement of the community with culture and society is crucial. Together with critical moral appraisal and effective practical strategies, the community can be better equipped to face the challenges of the changing times and the diverse socio-cultural realities.

References

Almond, Douglas et al. 2010. "O sister, where art thou? The role of son preference and sex choice: evidence from immigrants to Canada, National Bureau of Economic Research" *NBER* Working Paper, No. 15391, Massachusetts.

Balgopal, Pallassana. "Getting old in the U.S.: dilemmas of Indo-Americans." *The Journal of Sociology & Social Welfare*, Volume 26 (1), 1999, pp.56, 60

Bumgarner, Ashley. 2007. "A right to choose? Sex selection in the international context." *Duke Journal of Gender Law & Policy*, Volume 14:1289, p1299.

Dhingra, P. "Committed to Ethnicity, Committed to America: How Second-Generation Indian Americans' Ethnic Boundaries Further their Americanisation." *Journal of Intercultural Studies*, 29 (1), 2008, pp. 41–63.

Gupta, R. and V. K. Pillai. 2012. "Elder caregiving in South-Asian families in the United States and India." *Social Work & Society*, Volume 10 (2), p7.

Higgins, Anna. 2017. "Sex-selection abortion: the real war on women." Charlotte Lozier Institute, https://lozierinstitute.org/sex-selection-abortion-the-real-war-on-women/ Apr 24

Inman, A.G., Howard, E.E., Beaumont, L.R., & Walker, J. 2007. "Cultural transmission: Influence of contextual factors in Asian Indian immigrant parents' experiences." *Journal of Counseling Psychology*, Vol.54, pp.93–100.

Kakaiya, Divya. 2003. "Treatment issues among first and second generation Indian (South Asian) women and families in the United States." *Santiago Psychologist*, Vol 28 (5), p7.

Kay, Adam. "Reasoning about family honour among two generations of Hindu Indian-Americans." *Journal of Moral Education,* Vol. 41 (1), 2012, pp.79–98

Kulanjiyil, Thomas. 2013. "Malayali Family Life in Diaspora". *Malayali Diaspora*, edited by Sam George and T.V. Thomas, New Delhi: Serials Publications, p170.

————. 2010. "Landscape: Mental health needs of South Asian Indians." *Caring for the South Asian Soul-Counseling South Asians in the Western World,* edited by Thomas Kulanjiyil and T.V. Thomas, Bangalore: Primalogue, pp. 21-28.

Manohar, Nirmala. "Sshh...!! Don't tell my parents": dating among second-generation Patels in Florida, *Journal of Comparative Family Studies*, Vol. 39 (4), 2008, pp571-588

Nair, Meera. "Are South Asians prepared to age in America?" *Huff Post,* July. 27 2016.

Puri, S et al. 2011. "There is such a thing as too many daughters, but not too many sons": A qualitative study of son preference and fetal sex selection among Indian immigrants in the United States. *Social Science & Medicine*, *72* (7), pp1169–1176.

Sharadha, Bain. 2017. "The divorce rate is falling. Here's why that's bad news for some Americans." *Washington Post*, March 10. 2015, May 05.

Urquia, Marcelo, et al. 2016. "Variations in male-female infant ratios among births to Canadian- and Indian-born mothers, 1990-2011: a population-based register study." *CMAJ Open.* Apr-Jun: 4(2): E116–E123.

Remittance Trends in South Asia:

An Empirical Analysis

Jeffry A. Jacob

Introduction

Remittances are defined as the transfer of money or goods from migrant workers to their families living back in the home countries. In 1990, remittances going into the developing countries stood at $28.6 billion. This was nearly 52 percent of the Official Development Assistance (ODA) or foreign aid ($55.6 billion) received by these countries. By 2015, foreign aid received by developing countries had increased three folds to $152.4 billion. In contrast, over the same time period the amount of remittances received by these countries increased fourteen-fold to $422 billion. This trend is even sharper when we focus on the South Asian countries. In 1990, this region received $5.9 billion of foreign aid in contrast to $5.5 billion of remittances. Over the next twenty-five years, while foreign aid increased at an average annual growth rate of 6.4 percent to total $15.5 billion, remittances grew at a staggering average annual growth of 80.4 percent and stood at $117.6 billion, or nearly eight times that of foreign aid. This trend underscores the importance of remittances as a means of meeting various domestic expenditure needs, especially for families of migrant workers.

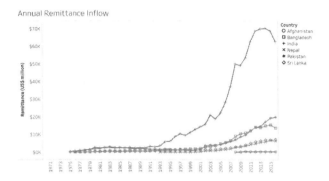

Figure 1: Inflow of Remittances in South Asia

Figure 1 shows the trends in remittances received among the six major South Asian economies: India, Pakistan, Bangladesh, Sri Lanka, Nepal and Afghanistan. All remittance data are taken from latest World Bank report, unless otherwise mentioned and details are given in the reference at the end of the chapter. India continues to be the largest destination of remittances and accounted for more than half of the region's total remittances. Considering the large amount of remittance inflows in South Asia, a report by the Asian Development Bank dubbed the region as a "remittance economy" (Ozaki 2012).

The amount of remittances received by a country are a direct function of the number of migrants the country sends out. Figure 2 examines the stock of migrants originating from the above six countries. From an initial number of 18 million migrants in 1960, the number of migrants sent out each year more than doubled over the next fifty years. As of 2013, this number stood at 37 million of which India accounted for more than a third of the migration- 13.9 million migrants- followed by Bangladesh at 7.6 million.

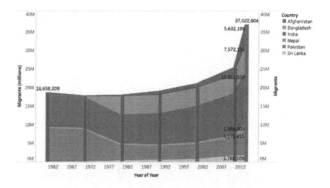

Figure 2: Stock of Migrants Sent out from South Asia, Selected Years

Another interesting fact from the above chart is that from 1960 to 2000 the stock of migrants grew very gradually from 16.6 to 20 million but then almost doubled to 37 million in 2013. This period saw a quadrupling of migration from Afghanistan- 1.8 to 5.6 million, doubling from Pakistan and a 50 percent increase from Indian and Bangladesh. Contrasting Figure 1 with Figure 2, we see a very strong correlation between remittances and migration.

In the remainder of this essay, I will summarize some of the economic benefits of remittances discussed in the literature and discuss the trends in migration and remittances of the above South Asian economies. Then, I will conduct an econometric analysis of the impact of remittances on the economic growth of selected South Asian economies and conclude with major findings.

Impact of Remittances

In one of the earliest studies on remittances, Lucas and Stark (1985) argued that tempered altruism is a critical motivation for remittance. They developed a theoretical model whereby migrants derive utility not just from their own consumption, but also from consumption of their household members in the home country and found evidence to support this hypothesis in Botswana. Another reason for remittances could be risk sharing whereby a household may send a migrant to a region having a better economic outcome, thereby having access to a stream of income. Developing on the idea of insurance, Yang and

Choi (2007) found that remittances enabled households in Philippines to have a steady level of consumption even in the presence of income shocks. Using a data set on Guyana households with multiple migrants to test altruism vs insurance motive for remittances, Agarwal and Horowitz (2002) found evidence to support the former hypothesis. In a qualitative study of 19 twice migrant Australian residents, Singh (2010) developed an argument that remittances are like a currency of care. She found that among South Asian migrants, sending money home is often seen as an expectation by the home family. She also found that routine remittances were often sent to the home country while the migrant parents were still alive and living in the home country. If the parents eventually moved with the migrant family, remittances as a medium of care were replaced by actual physical care-giving.

Analyzing a large scale household survey from India, Zachariah and Rajan (2015) concluded that household in Kerala receiving remittances had higher consumption levels, had a higher quality of life and possessed more consumer durables than non-remittance receiving households.

At a macro level, several studies have examined the impact of remittances on economic outcomes like poverty, inequality and economic development. A significant contribution in this area is by Adams and Page (2005) who constructed an extensive dataset on remittances, migration and poverty for a sample of 71 developing countries. Their results indicated that while both migration and remittances decrease the incidence as well depth of poverty, remittances have a much larger impact on these variables as compared to migration. Focusing on a sample of 20 Asian countries, Vargas-Silva, Jha, and Sugiyarto (2009) estimated that the elasticity of economic growth with respect to remittances is in the range of 0.02 to 0.032. They also found that remittances reduced the severity of poverty in these countries. This finding was also confirmed by Imai, Gaiha, Ali, and Kaicker (2014) in a more recent study on Asian economies. Focusing on a sample of South Asian countries, Cooray (2012) showed that remittances increase economic growth and also aid in financial development and higher educational attainment.

Bilateral Remittances and Migration in South Asia

As we saw in previous section, there is a very strong correlation between remittance and migration among the countries considered. At an aggregate level, both these variables have been increasing at a rapid pace over the past 50 years. However, the composition of the destination on migrants and the source of the inflow of remittances has changed substantially. We will examine these changes closely in this section.

Table 1 contrasts the top destination of migrants from India. One immediate observation is that only 15 countries account for more than 90 percent of migration from India. Overall, the stock of migrants from India was 8.2 million in 1970 and increased to 13.4 million in 2013.

Table 1: India's Changing patterns of migration-
Top 15 Destinations in 1970 and 2013

	1970			2013	
Rank	Destination Countries	Migrants	Rank	Destination Countries	Migrants
1	Pakistan	4,858,023	1	United Arab Emirates	2,268,200
2	Sri Lanka	1,080,645	2	United States	2,060,771
3	Bangladesh	704,574	3	Saudi Arabia	2,000,000
4	United Kingdom	336,567	4	Pakistan	1,395,854
5	Nepal	322,152	5	Nepal	810,172
6	Malaysia	150,723	6	United Kingdom	756,471
7	Myanmar	100,011	7	Kuwait	730,558
8	Saudi Arabia	70,109	8	Oman	644,704
9	United States	69,997	9	Canada	547,890
10	Congo, Dem. Rep.	67,967	10	Qatar	545,000
11	Singapore	50,875	11	Australia	364,764
12	Indonesia	48,166	12	Sri Lanka	309,489
13	Canada	45,737	13	Bahrain	262,855
14	Oman	31,427	14	Singapore	138,177
15	Afghanistan	26,242	15	Italy	120,224
	Total (Top 15)	7,963,215		Total (Top 15)	12,955,129
	Share of Total Migration	96.40%		Share of Total Migration	93.33%

In 1970, the top three destinations of migrants from India were within the South Asian region with Pakistan accounting for 60 percent of India's migrant stock. By 2013, UAE emerged as the largest host. Another interesting observation is that in 1970, only two of the Gulf countries – Saudi Arabia and Oman were among the top – 15 destinations of Indian migrants and together they accounted on only one million migrants. By the 2013, the Gulf region countries accounted for 6.4 million, or almost half of India's stock of migrants. United States with 2 million, UK with 0.76 million, Canada with 0.55 and Australia with 0.36 are the top 4 western nations with regards to the stock of Indian migrants.

The above patterns of migration can help explain the broad trends in remittance inflows in India. After posing a very robust growth, remittances declined for the first time in several years in 2009 because of the global financial crises (figure 3). However, they rebounded very quickly, growing at 8.7 percent in 2010 to the then highest level of $53 billion. The next five years saw a very sharp increase in remittances and they reached an all-time high of $70.4 billion in 2014. Since India has been the largest recipient of remittances in the world for the past decade, this number is the highest value of remittance inflows by any country in a year since data has been collected. This peak was followed by a dampening of inflow when annual remittance growth was negative in India two consecutive years for the first time since 1980. Remittance dropped by 2.1 percent in 2015 and an unprecedented 9 percent in 2016. These depressed remittances were in large part due to the declining global oil prices and weakening of several countries exchange rates versus the US dollar (Parussini, 2016; World Bank, 2017a). With the global economic conditions improving over the past year, the World Bank predicts that remittance inflows to India will post a slight rebound in 2017, growing at around 2 percent over the previous year for South Asia.

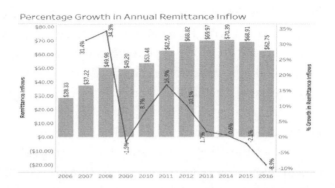

Figure 3: Annual Remittance Inflows in India in billions, 2006-2016

It is instructive to examine the trends in bilateral remittances inflow into India. Unfortunately, detailed data on this is currently available only for 2010-15. Figure 4 shows the top sources of remittances flowing into India from 2010 to 2015.

Given that the Gulf countries accounted for more than 60 percent of India's stock of migrants, it is no surprise that five of the six Gulf countries feature in the top 10 sources of remittances. They were the origin for $37.2 billion of the $68 billion total remittances received by India in 2015. The rate of growth of remittances was the fastest from Saudi Arabia, which increased from $6.5 billion in 2010 to $11.3 billion in 2015. This fact underscores the strategic importance of gulf countries for the Indian economy. United States has emerged as the second largest source of remittances to India and sent $11.7 billion. This is unsurprising as a recent study on Indian diaspora in the US found that Indian origin households have much higher educational attainment, have household incomes above the median US household income, have a larger share of population in professional or managerial occupation and have higher employment level than the average US population (MPI, 2014). There are a couple of recent events which may further increase the role of US and other developed countries as a source of remittance inflows compared to the gulf countries. Migration of Indians to OECD nations has been steadily increasing. In 2016 India became the top country of origin of migrants acquiring citizenship of OECD countries (OECD, 2017). On the other hand,

Saudi Arabia will be imposing a dependent tax on foreign workers (Sinha, 2017). This is expected to adversely affect the number of migrants going to Saudi Arabia. Juxtaposing these two facts with the overall depressed oil prices, may result in OECD countries becoming a more important origin of remittances than the Gulf region.

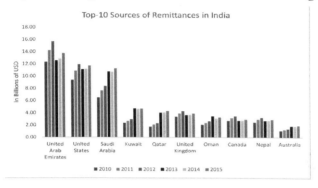

Figure 4: Top-10 sources of remittances received in India from 2010-2015

Remittances have become an important source of inflow of foreign funds. While the past two decades have witnessed rapid growth in India's GDP, the growth in remittances has been even faster. This can be gauged by Figure 5 which plots remittances as a percentage of GDP overtime.

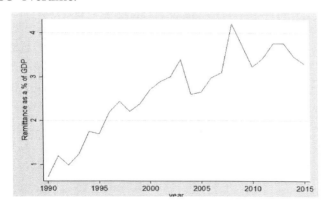

Figure 5: Share of remittance in GDP, 1990-2015

As we can see, remittances were under 1 percent of GDP till 1990 and from then they increased steadily, peaking at 4.2 percent in 2008 and have been above 3 percent since 2007. Remittances are even larger than Foreign Direct Investment (FDI). In 1991, net inflow of FDI into India was $3.3 billion while remittances were four times more, at $32.8 billion. With the liberalization of the Indian economy, FDI into India has steadily increased to $44 billion in 2015 but remains only 66 percent of the total remittance inflows.

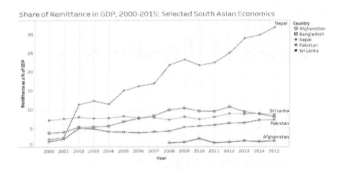

Figure 6: Remittance as a percentage of GDP in selected South Asian Economies

Remittances are even more important as a flow of external funds in the other five South Asian countries considered here (Figure 6). Remittances as a percentage of GDP in Nepal increased from 1.3 percent in 2000 to an astounding 31.7 percent in 2015. In Bangladesh, Pakistan and Sri Lanka, this figure was around 7 percent for 2015. Below we will examine the broad patterns in migration and remittances of these countries.

Table 2: Top Five Migration Destinations of South Asian Countries, 2013

Origin Country	Destination Country	Migrants
Afghanistan	Pakistan	2,326,275
	Iran, Islamic Rep.	2,299,676
	Saudi Arabia	500,000
	Germany	129,023
	United States	69,709
Bangladesh	India	3,230,025
	Saudi Arabia	1,500,000
	United Arab Emirates	1,000,000
	Kuwait	279,169
	United Kingdom	239,608
Nepal	India	553,050
	Saudi Arabia	500,000
	Qatar	341,000
	United Arab Emirates	200,000
	United States	88,109
Pakistan	Saudi Arabia	1,500,000
	United Arab Emirates	1,346,984
	India	1,126,796
	United Kingdom	476,144
	United States	339,076
Sri Lanka	Saudi Arabia	550,000
	India	158,083
	United Arab Emirates	150,000
	United Kingdom	134,140
	Canada	124,137

Table 2 gives the top five countries having migrants from the various
South Asian countries. Beginning with Afghanistan, it is two neighboring
countries of Pakistan and Iran were the top two destinations for its
migrant, around 2 million each. Migration into the US has also picked
up over the past decade and US is home to around 70 thousand
migrants. For Bangladesh, India had more migrants, at 3.2 million,
than the next four destinations combined. India is also among the
top-5 destinations of migrants from Nepal, Pakistan and Sri Lanka.
The other two major destinations for all these South Asian countries
are the two Gulf nations of Saudi Arabia and UAE.

The migration patterns for these South Asian countries are also
the prime determinants of remittances. Table 3 presents the top-5
sources of remittances for selected South Asian countries from 2010-
2015. Afghanistan has the least amount of remittance inflow among
these countries. Its main source has been Iran though the amount has
been decreasing successively. In contrast, Saudi Arabia has become an
important source of remittance for Afghanistan. Saudi Arabia is also
the leading source for Pakistan and Sri Lanka and the second highest
source for Nepal and Bangladesh.

**Table 3: Top-5 Sources of Remittances in 2015 for selected South Asian
Countries (in '000 USD)**

	2010	2011	2012	2013	2014	2015
Afghanistan						
Iran, Islamic Rep.	232.50	305.19	294.36	221.08	262.04	123.86
Pakistan	0.00	0.00	0.00	164.48	194.11	91.88
Saudi Arabia	6.28	4.34	4.19	80.12	94.19	44.43
Germany	37.79	25.81	24.89	18.88	22.73	10.79
United States	33.06	22.40	21.61	11.19	13.38	6.31
United Kingdom	28.03	18.79	18.12	8.14	9.87	4.72
Bangladesh						
India	5,041.31	5,681.81	6,619.82	3,854.15	4,354.59	4,450.37
Saudi Arabia	1,190.43	1,328.04	1,547.28	3,504.34	3,679.37	3,778.46
United Arab Emirates	368.24	400.39	466.49	2,427.29	2,631.65	2,773.65

| Kuwait | 817.95 | 878.97 | 1,024.07 | 829.42 | 857.34 | 832.99 |
| United Kingdom | 674.66 | 732.36 | 853.27 | 474.34 | 517.24 | 536.63 |

Nepal

Qatar	1,368.72	1,691.82	1,987.24	1,590.24	1,703.35	1,951.13
Saudi Arabia	74.68	89.03	104.57	1,509.78	1,562.06	1,783.91
India	1,167.31	1,391.31	1,634.26	786.36	847.30	961.80
United Arab Emirates	0.00	0.00	0.00	629.55	676.96	796.21
United States	236.17	276.62	324.92	266.47	280.18	320.09

Pakistan

Saudi Arabia	2,040.65	2,596.79	2,966.76	3,848.91	4,438.61	5,690.41
United Arab Emirates	1,195.37	1,494.01	1,706.87	3,559.13	4,220.18	5,526.60
United Kingdom	1,067.82	1,331.17	1,520.83	1,078.96	1,272.22	1,644.32
United States	762.09	957.47	1,093.89	871.01	1,015.99	1,302.85
Kuwait	343.60	425.35	485.95	756.56	869.63	1,064.54

Sri Lanka

Saudi Arabia	819.83	1,033.80	1,256.55	2,047.80	2,226.14	2,209.30
United Arab Emirates	407.69	504.46	613.16	569.64	630.22	634.20
Qatar	262.13	334.57	406.67	466.45	513.84	510.42
United Kingdom	265.00	328.24	398.96	459.98	508.55	507.40
India	258.36	329.46	400.45	445.06	494.76	491.40

After India, Pakistan had the second highest volume of remittance inflow. For Pakistan, Saudi Arabia and UAE accounted for $11 billion of its $19 billion total inflows in 2015. United States and Kuwait have also become important sources for remittances. Inflows from the United States doubled from $0.7 billion in 2010 to $1.3 billion in 2015. Over the same period, remittances from Kuwait tripled ($0.3 to $1 billion). The third largest recipient of remittances in the region is Bangladesh. Its inflow of remittances increased from $10 billion in 2010 to $15 billion in 2015. Inflows from India stood at $4.5 billion, Saudi Arabia at $3.7 billion and UAE at $2.7 billion. Thus far, we have seen that remittance inflows into South Asia have been growing substantially, both in absolute terms and as a percentage of GDP. We now turn our focus to investigating the economic impact of remittances on the growth rate of these South Asian economies.

Impact of Remittances of Economic Growth

Data: In this section we examine whether remittance had any impact on economic growth, controlling for other macro-economic policy and institutional variables. The main independent variable is the ratio of remittances to GDP. The dependent variable is growth rate of GDP per capita. Our study covers twenty-five years of data from 1991 to 2015. Due the lack of data for some countries, we focus on India, Pakistan, Bangladesh, Nepal and Sri Lanka. As we have seen before, these five countries account for the bulk of remittances coming into the region and are also the source of the largest outflow of migrants to other countries. Our choice of other explanatory variables is driven by the literature (Akobeng, 2016; Cooray, 2012). Following the growth regressions (Barro, 1991; Mankiw, Romer, & Weil, 1992), we begin with a simple model of including human and physical capital along with remittance and a determinant of economic growth. Physical capital is captured by gross fixed capital formation (GFCF) to GDP ratio, while human capital is captured by gross secondary enrollment rate. We then extend our empirical specification to include a measure of corruption, trade to GDP ratio and FDI to GDP ratio to measure a country's openness to international trade. We also include two macro-economic policy variables-ratio of government consumption expenditure to GDP and inflation rate. The variables are included following the "deep-determinants" of economic growth literature (Acemoglu, Johnson, and Robinson, 2001; Dollar and Kraay, 2003; Rodrik, Subramanian, and Trebbi, 2004).

Method and Results: We make use of the longitudinal nature of the data by employing panel data methods. Based on the existing literature examining the impact of remittances on economic growth (Chami, Fullenkamp, and Jahjah, 2005; Imai et al., 2014), our estimating model is given by:

$$\Box y_{it} = g remitt_{it} + b X_{it} + n_i + e_{it}$$

where $\Box y_{it}$ is the growth rate in GDP per capita, *remit* is log of remittances to GDP ratio, X is vector of other explanatory variables, n_i is the country fixed effects and e_{it} is the idiosyncratic error terms.

Table 4 : Impact of Remittances on Economic Growth

VARIABLES	(1) Pooled OLS	(2) Fixed Effects	(3) Fixed Effects IV
Ln GFCF to GDP ratio	0.038***	0.036*	0.022
	(0.010)	(0.013)	(0.016)
Ln Gross Secondary Enrollment	0.002	-0.009	-0.019
	(0.012)	(0.021)	(0.015)
Ln Remittance to GDP ratio	-0.007**	-0.001	0.008
	(0.003)	(0.003)	(0.005)
Observations	79	79	75
Number of Countries		5	5
D-M Exogeneity Test p-val			0.00
Hansen's Exclusion Test p-val			0.05
K-P Test of Underid p-val			0.00
K-P rk Wald F stat			28.41

Robust standard errors in parentheses

*** p<0.01, ** p<0.05, * p<0.1

We start with a pooled OLS estimation of our simple model in Table 4. Results in Column 1 indicate a positive and statistically significant effect of GFCF to GDP ratio but a slight negative impact of remittances to GDP ratio on economic growth. To account for cross-country heterogeneity among the South Asian countries, we use fixed effects estimation in column 2. While physical capital continues to remain positive and significant, remittances do not have a statistically significant impact on growth. One drawback of the OLS and fixed effects model is that these models do not control for endogeneity of the explanatory variables resulting from reverse causality. To correct for this, a fixed-effects instrumental variable approach is used in column 3, where GFCF and remittances are instrumented by their first and second lagged values. The identification assumption is that while current level of physical capital and remittance may be impacted by current levels of economic growth, resulting in reverse causality, past levels of these explanatory variables are not correlated with current GDP per capita but are highly correlated with their own current levels. Results of fixed-effects instrumental variable approach are presented in column 3. In this model, none of the variables are statistically significant. The various diagnostic tests however reveal that column 3 has the correct specification and this approach will be used for the extended model as well. These results are presented in Table 5.

In column 1, trade share is entered as an additional variable. Both, trade share and remittance share have a positive and significant impact on GDP per capita growth rate. Somewhat puzzling is the negative impact of human and physical capital. In column 2, the two government macro-economic policy variables are included. These variables are not statistically significant. Remittance and trade share continue to have a positive and statistically significant impact on growth. Column 3 includes FDI to GDP ratio as an additional variable. Remittance and trade still have a positive impact on growth. The first stage diagnostic tests however suggest that this model is not correctly specified. In column 4, FDI is dropped but Corruption Index is added to measure government's institutional quality. In this model, Remittance and trade share are still statistically significant.

Table 5: Remittances of Economic Growth: Fixed Effects Instrumental Variable Regressions

Dep Variable: GDP Growth Rate	1	2	3	4
Ln GFCF to GDP ratio	-0.077*	-0.076	-0.113	-0.063
	(0.043)	(0.049)	(0.079)	(0.045)
Ln Remittance to GDP ratio	0.024***	0.025***	0.037**	0.024**
	(0.009)	(0.010)	(0.015)	(0.010)

Ln Trade to GDP ratio	0.065***	0.061**	0.066**	0.058**
	(0.024)	(0.026)	(0.030)	(0.024)
Ln FDI to GDP ratio			0.016	
			(0.025)	
Ln Gross Secondary Enrollment	-0.035*	-0.031*	-0.039*	-0.015
	(0.019)	(0.018)	(0.020)	(0.022)
Ln Inflation		-0.000	-0.006	0.003
		(0.006)	(0.009)	(0.006)
Ln Govt. Exp to GDP		-0.046	-0.052	-0.049
		(0.039)	(0.042)	(0.038)
Corruption Index				-0.004**
				(0.002)
Observations	75	75	73	71
Number of Countries	5	5	5	5
D-M Exogeneity Test p-val	0.00	0.00	0.00	0.00
Hansen's Exclusion Test p-val	0.22	0.08	0.15	0.08
K-P Test of Underid p-val	0.02	0.01	0.17	0.01
K-P rk Wald F stat	5.99	4.49	0.96	5.5

Robust standard errors in parentheses

*** $p<0.01$, ** $p<0.05$, * $p<0.1$

In terms of economic impact, the elasticity of remittance with respect to GDP per capita growth is 0.024. Thus, a 1 percent increase in remittance to GDP ratio increases economic growth by 0.02 percent. The economic impact of trade to GDP ratio is even greater with its elasticity being equal to 0.06. The anomalous negative impact of secondary enrollment on growth is not statistically significant. Moreover, corruption has a negative and statistically significant impact of economic growth in the sample of South Asian countries. Taken collectively, these results indicate that countries that are more open to foreign trade, have higher remittances and lower corruption levels will experience faster economic growth.

Conclusion

This essay has examined the trends in remittances and migration in South Asia. This essay confirms the findings of previous literature that remittances exert a positive impact on economic growth. Along with remittances, openness to trade improves economic growth while corruption has a negative impact. Though the Indian diaspora continues to be the most generous in terms of sending money home, the past two years have seen a decline in remittances received. This decline in mainly attributable to the falling oil prices resulting in depressed inflows from the Gulf countries. In general, though, remittance continue to be an important source of external funds for South Asia. In fact, remittance inflows even exceed the foreign direct investment inflows in these economies. Given the important role remittances play in economic growth in South Asia, governments in these countries should take measures to encourage their diaspora to save and send their money to their home countries.

References

Acemoglu, D., Johnson, S., & Robinson, J. A. (2001). The Colonial Origins of Comparative Development: An Empirical Investigation. *American Economic Review*. https://doi.org/10.1257/aer.91.5.1369

Adams, R. H., & Page, J. (2005). Do international migration and remittances reduce poverty in developing countries? *World Development*, *33*(10), 1645–1669. https://doi.org/10.1016/j.worlddev.2005.05.004

Agarwal, R., & Horowitz, A. W. (2002). Are international remittances altruism or insurance? Evidence from Guyana using multiple-migrant households. *World Development*, *30*(11), 2033–2044.

Akobeng, E. (2016). Out of inequality and poverty: Evidence for the effectiveness of remittances in Sub-Saharan Africa. *The Quarterly Review of Economics and Finance*, *60*, 207–223. https://doi.org/10.1016/j.qref.2015.10.008

Barro, R. J. (1991). Economic Growth in a Cross-Section of Countries. *The Quarterly Journal of Economics*, *106*, 407–443.

Chami, R., Fullenkamp, C., & Jahjah, S. (2005). Are Immigrant Remittance Flows a Source of Capital for Development? *IMF Economic Review*, *52*(1), 55.

Cooray, A. V. (2012). The impact of migrant remittances on economic growth: evidence from South Asia. *Review of International Economics*, *20*(5), 985–998.

Dollar, D., & Kraay, A. (2003). Institutions, trade, and growth. *Journal of Monetary Economics*.

Imai, K. S., Gaiha, R., Ali, A., & Kaicker, N. (2014). Remittances, growth and poverty: New evidence from Asian countries. *Journal of Policy Modeling*, *36*(3), 524–538. https://doi.org/10.1016/j.jpolmod.2014.01.009

Lucas, R. E. B., & Stark, O. (1985). Motivations to Remit: Evidence from Botswana. *Journal of Political Economy*, *93*(5), 901–918. https://doi.org/10.1086/261341

Mankiw, N. G., Romer, D., & Weil, D. N. (1992). A Contribution to the Empirics of Economic-Growth. *Quarterly Journal of Economics*, *107*(2), 407–437.

MPI. (2014). *The Indian Diaspora in the United States*. Retrieved from www.migrationpolicy.org/sites/default/files/publications/RAD-IndiaII-FINAL.pdf

OECD. (2017). *International Migration Outlook 2017*. Paris. Retrieved from http://dx.doi.org/10.1787/migr_outlook-2017-en

Ozaki, M. (2012). Worker migration and remittances in South Asia.

Parussini, G. (July 31, 2016). Cheap Oil Squeezes South Asia's Cash Lifeline. *The Wall Street Journal*. Retrieved from https://www.wsj.com/articles/low-oil-prices-stanch-flow-of-cash-to-south-asia-1469988880

Rodrik, D., Subramanian, A., & Trebbi, F. (2004). Institutions rule: The primacy of institutions over geography and integration in economic development. *Journal of Economic Growth*, *9*(2), 131–165.

Sinha, S. (June 21, 2017). Saudi imposes family tax: Here is how it will hit Indians hard. *The Financial Express*. Retrieved from http://www.financialexpress.com/money/saudi-imposes-family-tax-here-is-how-it-will-hit-indians-hard/729187/

Teorell, J., Dahlberg, S., Holmberg, S., Rothstein, B., Hartmann, F., & Svensson, R. (2015). The quality of government standard dataset, version jan15. *University of Gothenburg: The Quality of Government Institute*.

Vargas-Silva, C., Jha, S., & Sugiyarto, G. (2009). Remittances in Asia: Implications for the fight against poverty and the pursuit of economic growth, Asian Development Bank (ADB). *Economics Working Paper Series*, *182*, 1–37. Retrieved https://ssrn.com/abstract=1618025

World Bank. (2016). *Migration and Remittances Factbook: 2016*. Washington, DC. Retrieved http://www.worldbank.org/en/topic/migrationremittancesdiasporaissues/brief/migration-remittances-data

World Bank. (2017a). *Migration and Development Brief 27*. Washington, DC. Retrieved from http://pubdocs.worldbank.org/en/992371492706371662/MigrationandDevelopmentBrief27.pdf

World Bank. (2017b). World Development Indicators. Retrieved from http://data.worldbank.org/data-catalog/world-development-indicators

Yang, D., & Choi, H. J. (2007). Are remittances insurance? Evidence from rainfall shocks in the Philippines. *World Bank Economic Review*, *21*(2), 219–248. https://doi.org/10.1093/wber/lhm003

Zachariah, K. C., & Rajan, S. I. (2015). *Dynamics of Emigration and Remittances in Kerala: Results from the Kerala Migration Survey 2014* (No. 463). Thiruvananthapuram, Kerala.

Cultural Hybridity:
Freedom and Faith in Diaspora Literature

Reena Thomas

Though globalization has arguably ushered an age of great diversity, contemporary diaspora literature documents the consequences of marginalized cultures encountering dominant ones – the negotiations, compromises, and concessions that underline the psychological struggles of the formerly colonized, migrant, and refugee in a condition of displacement/exile. To that end, faith often becomes a point of contention in a diaspora figure's endeavor to adapt and assimilate into a foreign culture, a marker of cultural loss, preservation, or integration. Ayub Khan-Din's play *East is East* (1996), Ruth Prawer Jhabvala's short story "An Experience of India" (1986), and Jamaica Kincaid's novel *Lucy* (1990) each feature protagonists living away from their native home, and each text presents faith (Islam, Hinduism, and Christianity, respectively) as a critical aspect of diaspora experience and identity.

The story of diaspora is a story of explicit and implicit confrontation as traditions and customs collide in a shared space resulting in cultural difference and hybridity, a new mixture of varied practices, histories, and beliefs. Postcolonial and diaspora literatures are often characterized by an overwhelming feeling of mourning, rooted in a perception that the "pure" indigenous identity of the exiled or migrant individual must inevitably cease in the new culture. Recently though, the diaspora experience has been conceived more as a bittersweet transition, acknowledging the hardships of displacement but also the thrill of opportunity cultural hybridity can offer. Regarding the formation of culture and identity, Homi K. Bhabha describes hybridity as a third space that "enables other positions to emerge ... [which] sets up new structures of authority" (211). Bhabha continues, "The process of cultural hybridity gives rise to something different, something new and unrecognizable, a new area ... of meaning and representation" (211). Similarly, Stuart Hall's "Cultural Identity and Diaspora" examines how narratives of cultural displacement affect identity. Hall puts forth two contrasting views of cultural identity that cause internal tension. One view believes identity to be stable, homogenous, and fixed, rooted in a shared history and shared cultural codes. According to Hall, the displaced migrant may feel he or she has lost a cohesive self and then pursues a futile journey to unearth or preserve a buried, suppressed cultural identity. Hall, however, proposes an alternative definition that is transformative, a "matter of becoming as well as of being" (112). Identity is not waiting to be "found" in a hidden history or past; instead, identity is a "production, which is never complete ... and always constituted within, not outside, representation" (110). In postcolonial and immigrant literatures, the diaspora or postcolonial self-gains prominence and agency through reclaiming an identity that is both hybrid and fleeting. These texts emphasize that with diaspora comes a certain amount of freedom as the displaced person, liberated from a single dominant or hegemonic culture, can create a more authentic identity by *choosing* cultural practices rather than blindly inheriting or reproducing them. Thus, a diaspora figure's relationship with faith and religion has significant social consequence.

Christianity too is not static and even urges both migration and displacement through the Great Commission. The Apostle Paul acknowledges the challenges of integration which J. Brian Tucker addresses in his study of 1 Corinthians 1-4. Tucker observes that not only does Jewish identity continue to factor in the development of early Christianity but also Greek and Roman social identities, denying a universalistic approach to Christian identity that discounts difference. For Tucker, Paul does not wish to eradicate or de-value ethnic difference; instead, Paul envisions communities living out the Gospel through distinct cultural practices (84). Thus, Christianity does not ask for a single homogenous culture, but it does ask that traditions reflect principles that uplift and honor Christ, that is, grace, humility, and unconditional love.

Khan-Din, Jhabvala, and Kincaid focus on issues of displacement and hybridity in their works, and while religion may not play an exclusive role in the texts discussed here, religion and religious worldviews do intervene in each text's representation of cultural difference. The texts portray the process of cultural negotiation diaspora communities undergo as straining and complex, and faith is part of this difficult yet necessary process of new understanding for the displaced individual. The degree to which characters come to accept or reject the faith of their homeland or adopted country signifies the freedom of choice cultural hybridity brings, and it is this freedom that the texts ultimately celebrate.

Khan-Din's *East is East* is a semi-autobiographical play about a Pakistani-Islamic father desperately trying to preserve his traditions while being married to a British woman in 1970s England. Taking its title from a Rudyard Kipling poem, the play through dark humor relates the unique familial dynamics at work when East and West attempt to join together within the private sphere. As they raise their seven children, George and Ella fight about Islamic customs that appear stifling in English society, George is constantly worried about his family in Pakistan undergoing a regional war rather than the battles raging within his immediate family, and the children try to appease both parents (and both cultures). As the lone source of Islam, George shoulders the responsibility of ensuring his culture of faith remains strong in competition with an English society that is both Christian and atheistic. Ella is not religious, but it is assumed that any religious knowledge she may possess is the dominant Judeo-Christian Western culture.

However, in the clash of cultures within the home, Ella tries to remain impartial. Ella does not attend mosque, but she does allow George to impose his religious practice onto their children. While the family may be racially/culturally mixed, represented in the images of prayer stickers which litter the parlour contrasted with the children wearing bell bottoms, George's Islamic faith dominates the family. The play opens with the revelation that 12-year-old Sajit, the youngest, has not been circumcised, a ritual signifying belonging to the larger Islamic community. The scene sets up Ella as the sharp-tongued yet yielding Anglo wife, George as the domineering patriarch, and the children as reluctant Muslims. At the same time, the opening scene sets up the central tension within the family demonstrated through the context of Islam. While Ella considers the matter trivial, an irate George exclaims, "All men think I bad my son having this thing, has to be cutting" (Khan-Din 1.1). Of course, when George says "men" he does not mean all men but the small enclave of Islamic men within the local community. George is not concerned about his children belonging to the English community. Rather George strives to maintain his reputation, and to a larger extent, his Islamic self in an exiled condition.

According to political theorist Benedict Anderson, "the members of even the smallest nation will never know most of their fellow members, meet them, or even hear of them, yet in the mind of each lives the image of their communion" (6). This "imagined community" as Anderson famously coined results in a fierce and sometimes brutal nationalism as citizens who otherwise are strangers develop strong feelings of belonging and loyalty. Especially relevant in understanding the diaspora experience, this concept of an imagined community helps to explain the survival of Pakistani-Islamic customs even when existing on the periphery of another culture. The English town where the Khans reside has a local mosque and the suburb of Bradford is nicknamed Bradistan because of its large population from Pakistan. The principles of Islam reinforce a self-perception of exceptionalism as echoed by George. He explains to his son Saleem, "You no English, English people no accepting you. In Islam, everyone equal see, no black man, no white man. Only Muslim, it special community" (Khan-Din 2.3). Nostalgia, a yearning for the past, strengthens ties to an imagined community as well. Psychologist Alexander V. Zinchenko points out, "It is quite natural that immigrants often idealize their past, including its negative and unpleasant aspects. They also often invent nonexistent biographies in an attempt to prove to others and themselves that their life was worth living" (91). As a coping mechanism, an ethnic community "offers a much needed 'resting place,'" escape, or sanctuary that helps to lower anxiety and depression among immigrants. The new community of Pakistani-Islamic immigrants, instead of completely adopting English culture in *East is East*, has created an extension of their home country which simultaneously prevents and facilitates assimilation.

However, the play highlights the reality that though immigrants might be able to preserve their community through language, food, and faith, this preservation falls apart in the second generation. The Khan children resentfully attend mosque, don't speak Urdu fluently, eat pork secretly, and Tariq hates Pakistani music. The eldest son is estranged from the family, an unfortunate casualty of George's tyrannical clinging to traditional Islamic life which even for George is inconsistent, having married someone outside of the Muslim faith. Moreover, though George is seen performing daily prayers, Islam for George is little more than a cultural artefact, and as such, the children fail to view it as a spiritual truth. As a result, the children's nonexistent or impersonal faith speaks to their tenuous relationship with the imagined community of the Pakistani-Islamic diaspora.

There is one exception: Maneer. adopts a pious lifestyle, attending mosque every day, wearing a skull cap, and performing daily chants on his prayer mat. Of the children, Tariq and Maneer represent two extreme responses to the Pakistani-Islamic culture embodied in their father. Tariq completely rejects it; Maneer completely accepts it. Yet, both responses are treated critically by the text. Maneer's siblings tease him about his faith, taking his skull cap, and Tariq jokes that "even if [his] cap is religious, people round here just think [he has] got a tea cosy on [his] head" (Khan-Din 1.2). The comment reflects the need for a broader community to recognize symbols of faith – in this case, the skull cap – to help validate one's belief and culture. In addition, though facetious, the comment reveals how the dominant English culture might translate and undermine the unfamiliar religious symbol, reducing its potency and significance. Tariq's joke speaks to the difficulties of preserving the authenticity of a marginalized faith in a foreign culture. Yet, Tariq also comes under fire by his siblings. Despite Tariq's attempts to be English, mocking his father's traditions with his English friends, sneaking out at night, even proclaiming that he and his siblings should not consider themselves hybridized Anglo-Indian or Eurasian but simply English, Maneer reveals a sobering truth, "No one round here thinks we're English, we're the Paki family who run the chippy ..." (Khan-Din 2.2). Both brothers deny hybridity, and in doing so, avoid an internal conflict of identity, but the text suggests neither will experience resolution or true authenticity until each accepts his bicultural heritage.

The play portrays Maneer's faith as genuine yet still surface-level. Maneer does not know, for instance, the importance of circumcision, replying only that "foreskins are dirty" (1.3); however, Maneer's faith exemplifies another value that the text upholds. In explaining why he follows their father's religion, Maneer says to Tariq, "It's my choice, I like it, I wouldn't force it on anyone, I don't think my dad should either. He's wrong to do that" (2.2). The value of choice is reiterated in the end as well. *East is East* culminates in a violent family altercation as Ella defends her two older sons, Abdul and Tariq, from being arranged in marriage by George. Abdul who has sided with his father throughout most of the play stops George from beating Ella and assumes leadership of the family after the fight. When George exits weeping, a transformed Abdul tells his siblings that their father has "no right to tell [them] what [their] cultures should be" and promises that "things are gonna be different around here" (2.5). In this way, Abdul challenges the authoritative, fixed foundations of culture and faith. With a more accurate, compassionate figure to represent the mixed Khan family, the play concludes with the hope that the Khan children, and their new leader, can take control of their cultural identity, rather than being imprisoned by it, and better navigate the cultural tension that threatens to tear them apart.

While Khan-Din describes the difficulties of living as a Pakistani-Muslim in England, German-born Ruth Prawer Jhabvala's "An Experience of India" relates another kind of diaspora experience – a wealthy white English couple living in postcolonial India.[1] The unnamed speaker is the wife of a successful journalist who grows increasingly dissatisfied when their life in Delhi turns into a replica of their affluent life in the West. Having come to India to "escape from that Western materialism," the blond-haired speaker immediately dresses in Indian clothes, eating rice and curry off leaves with her fingers, in an effort "to be Indian" (Jhabvala 126), but she ventures on her own once her husband ceases to desire what she considers a true Indian lifestyle. The text engages with the stereotype of India as both a spiritual mecca and exotic land for Westerners, but the speaker finds herself in a similar position as many immigrants, dislocated and without community. Yet, unlike other immigrant communities, she does not wish to preserve her cultural identity, and consequently, nostalgia, a crucial aspect of the exiled or migrant identity, factors little in her diaspora experience.

Instead, she attempts to *be* India through two intimate ways: sexually and spiritually. Estranged from her husband, but still financially supported by him, she travels by herself and indulges in numerous affairs, most of which are meaningless one-night stands. After failing to establish any stable relationship with men (and thus India), the speaker tries an alternative way to achieve a sense of place and connection with her adopted country. The speaker witnesses the complete and simple joy of an elderly holy Hindu woman who lives alone on top of a roof, enthusiastically sharing ancient stories from Hindu mythology "as if it was all real and going on exactly now;" the speaker becomes attracted

---

[1] Jhabvala's own cultural history is a testament to globalization and hybridity. Jhabvala was born in Germany to Jewish parents, lived in London during WW II, and moved to India in 1951. She married an Indian architect and resided in India for more than 20 years. She then moved to New York and became a naturalized U.S. citizen.

to "whatever it was she had [because] obviously it was the one thing worth having" (Jhabvala 136). As a result, she joins an ashram led by a guru. The text portrays the sect as a sham, a corruption of the pure faith conveyed by the Hindu woman. The sect is racially diverse, since many Westerners come to India to gain spiritual enlightenment, but the text depicts the guru as possessing the Western ego and ambition that they have come to escape. The guru hassles the speaker to tell her husband about the ashram so that they can receive more attention and power and becomes uncontrollably furious when the speaker refuses his aggressive demands. When the guru rapes the speaker, she responds in laughter. In that moment, she realizes the guru is no different than the other men she has slept with, and the commonness, rather than despairing her, delights her. The text resists the materialistic West/ spiritual East dichotomy, and in doing so, suggests the virtues of any faith, even Eastern ones, are not immune to artificiality and falseness.

However, what is particularly significant about this episode is the speaker's desire to gain completeness or "whatever it was [the Hindu woman] had" and her belief in India's promise of a higher or more authentic spiritual truth, a truth that (it is implied) has been denied to her in a Western Judeo-Christian society. Despite her desire, the speaker, almost rebelliously, never fits into the ashram. She never experiences the peace the other disciples receive upon mediation nor does she express devotion and reverence to the guru, refusing to touch his feet and speaking to him without deference. At the same time, she seeks the "higher" state of spirituality that the Hindu disciples attain, or appear to attain, through listening to and living the holy word. Interestingly, the speaker does momentarily and partially achieve inner peace at the ashram, not through communal meditation but through private moments with nature. She reveals,

> But there were times when I went up to sit on the roof and looked out over the river, the way it stretched so calm and broad to the opposite bank and the boats going up and down it and the light changing and being reflected back on water: and then, though I wasn't trying to meditate or come to any higher thoughts, I did feel very peaceful and was glad to be there (138).

It is one of the few times the speaker feels content in a society that otherwise has fallen short of its expectations. Similar scenes occur in E. M. Forster's *A Passage to India* (1924), a novel that explores colonial relationships in the context of the political and metaphysical, where nature induces sublime, reflective responses from its two female protagonists Mrs. Moore and Adela. For example, as Mrs. Moore watches the moon "a sudden sense of unity, of kinship with the heavenly bodies, passed into [her]" (28). Both texts privilege a spiritual identity that might be sought in foreign cultures and Eastern faiths but is fulfilled through a close communion with nature. The text leaves readers with a deserted woman preparing to roam the streets of Delhi with no place to arrive and no place to return. The speaker loses everything: her husband (and with him, any financial support), her servant, and her apartment. Without a home, she embodies best the diaspora individual who must wander with no direction in an unfamiliar land. Yet, the text refuses to depict the speaker's displacement in completely negative terms. Evicted from her home, the speaker describes a mixture of fear, sorrow, and excitement, her heart racing, calling the inevitable expulsion her next adventure as she accepts that this state of endless travel and endless seeking may very well be a permanent condition, physically and spiritually.

Jamaica Kincaid's female protagonist also is seeking greater understanding in *Lucy*. The Antiguan-American writer has become a relevant voice in postcolonial literary studies because, like contemporary Salman Rushdie, she possesses an interstitial perspective that informs her critical eye towards both the East and the West, and *Lucy* exemplifies the immigrant's insider/outsider position that is both unsettling and liberating. Unlike Rushdie, Kincaid's texts have become infamous for its bitter tone. Ramón E. Soto-Crespo argues, "Kincaid writes about mourning in such a way as to suggest that it is less a psychological phase to be superseded than a political condition of existence" (343) where mourning for the diaspora writer is a connection to a "decaying past" (372). *Lucy* certainly expresses a deep grief. Kincaid constructs a postcolonial context for the coming-of-age story of a 19-year-old who must shed layers as both a colonized West Indian woman and as a West Indian immigrant living in the U.S. to fully begin the process of self-development. The text presents two distinct homes for the titular character – American and Caribbean – where the West commands the dominant position. However, Lucy, who migrates to the U.S. to nanny for an affluent family in New York City, is too self-aware to accept either home without skepticism because all models of home available to her, foreign and native, are just re-articulations of control and ownership.

Lucy is not especially religious; however, the textual description of Lucy's Caribbean upbringing includes a type of Christianity in stark contrast to Western incarnations. Lucy, who is also the narrator, relates to readers a disturbing story about a schoolmate whose father "had dealings with the Devil" and became possessed after snooping into her father's business. Lucy would overhear her cries from being beaten by whatever possessed her, and eventually the girl leaves the island "where the Devil couldn't follow her, because the Devil cannot walk over water" (21). The childhood story is told objectively with no suggestions that Lucy doubts the existence of a devil, the devil's ability to walk on water, or the possibility of possession; for Lucy such incidences and beliefs are a matter-of-fact reality. More significant, the text does not encourage readers to doubt Lucy's story either. Though readers might reason that the girl's cries are rooted in some other cause – a sickness or abuse – the text provides no alternative.

Lucy's Christian upbringing in the West Indies, influenced by local folklore and obeah, is unfamiliar to mainline Christianity practiced in the U.S. which, while diverse in practice, shares an intellectual tradition that has largely disengaged from medievalism and superstition. Thus, the faith that has informed Lucy's worldview is a hybrid of Christian and West Indian practice, and within the narrative, strengthens the initial difference between Lucy's two worlds. Lucy continually marvels at her employer Mariah's Western world which seems weightless: Mariah dances and twirls "without knocking over anything" (26); she feels alive by "some flowers bending in the breeze" (17); and the "right thing always happens to her" (26). Lucy's repeated mantra – *how could someone be this way?* – voices the incredulity of difference Lucy experiences in her new home. While Lucy defines life as "heavy and hard" (25), a description that also defines her understanding of faith as judgment, with a devil that is very real, Mariah enjoys a position of privilege. Whatever faith Mariah may have (the family does not say grace at meals or attend church), it is certainly benign and not an integral part of her worldview. For Lucy, the Western world as interpreted through Mariah is sanitized and, consequently, un-relatable.

Neither the culture of Mariah nor her mother is sufficient for Lucy. In one instance, Lucy recalls the words of her mother: "You cannot escape the fact that I am your mother, my blood runs in you" (90). As Lucy realizes that her mother's love was "designed solely to make [Lucy] into an echo of her" (36), she no longer sees her love as unconditional; rather she sees her love as a vicious tool in cultural reproduction. Mariah, meanwhile, embodies a multitude of symbolic representations in *Lucy*. She is a white colonizer, a white feminist, and a white mother. All of these roles position Mariah above Lucy. As a benevolent master, Mariah buys Lucy clothes, takes her to the museum, and kisses her good night. Though Mariah tries to redefine the employer/employee relationship through a loving friendship, Mariah fails to realize that a friendship based on a master/slave hierarchy is no friendship at all. Lucy never loses sight of this fact. Veronica Gregg attributes their failed friendship to Mariah's inability to understand the colonial world that has shaped Lucy, while "Lucy studies Mariah as conditioned by history and language, blind to their power ..." (38). No matter how kind Mariah may be to her, Lucy still feels like a "dog on a leash, a long leash but a leash all the same" (110).

Even still, Lucy does not continue to practice her Christian faith in America as she did in Antigua. By the end of the novel, Lucy reveals that she has not attended church since she arrived in New York a year ago, yet still believed in God because "after all, what else could [she] do" (146). Lucy, in fashioning a new identity apart from the world of Mariah and the world of her West Indian mother, decides that she cannot ask God for help in coping with two conflicting realities, none of which are home for her. She explains, "But no longer could I ask God what to do, since the answer, I was sure would not suit me. I could do what suited me now, as long as I could pay for it" (146).

Like the children in *East is East* and the female speaker in "An Experience of India," Lucy awakens to the freedom of choice diaspora can bring, including the freedom to maintain, reject, or reinvent spirituality. In this case, Lucy makes a deliberate choice to be independent of all guidance and controlling influence, whether it is her mother, Mariah, or a Christian God. Not exactly rejecting Christianity, Lucy seems to acknowledge that there might be negative consequences to her extreme independence, as well as limits, and, in this way, separates herself from the carefree independent spirit Mariah had previously enjoyed. Moreover, the text approves Lucy's attempt to forge an entirely new identity. Eventually, Lucy quits her job and moves out of Mariah's home. Living on her own and writing the first entry in her new diary, Lucy declares that she desires to "love someone so much that [she] would die from it" (164). Lucy's first entry implies a redefinition of home, love, and identity un-rooted from cultural paradigms of control and judgment; Lucy's definition involves an annihilation of self (rather than a reproduction of self) which for Lucy is the only idea of home worth striving for, and, ironically, reproduces a Christian ideal of sacrificial love.

Home is not merely a geographical place of birth or settling. It is a state of normalcy one hopes to maintain regardless of geography. Native religion for the diaspora individual can help reproduce a state of normalcy in a foreign place, but contemporary diaspora literature reveals efforts to carbon copy culture will only result in frustration, a feeling of loss, and failure. Instead, the diaspora experience must reconsider cultural hybridity as a welcome expression of freedom. For the second and third generation in the West, hybridity can be a painful aspect of self-actualization, especially when Western cultures carry a sense of modernity and progress. Sunaina Maira's study on

New York City college age Indian-Americans in the late 90s speaks to the difficulties of identification. In one interview, Radhika asserts her American national identity over her ethnic one, clarifying, "I define myself as an American with an Indian cultural background, but don't ever call me [Indian] because I am not Indian" (Maira 3). Radhika's comments rehearse a notion of choice rooted in her own negative experiences, such as racial teasing as a child, and her criticism of oppressive practices in South Asian culture, which Maira points out exist in the West but may appear less explicitly (11). At the same time, Maira observes the nuances of a then rising subculture of "desi" dance parties that infused hip-hop and techno with Bhangra and Bollywood music, and while this shared space allowed for American and Indian cultures to intersect briefly, it ended once the party was over. Maira concludes that "hybridity … is not always easy to live, for social institutions and networks continue to demand loyalty to … competing cultural ideals" (45). Negotiating cultural identities can be overwhelming, and as *East is East* suggests, religion can become an explosive marker of compromise, but if the second and third generations of the immigrant-diaspora community can transform their cultural struggle into a cultural emergence, then hybridity can be viewed less as "conflicting selves always canceling each other out" (Lahiri) and more powerfully as act of creation, turning faith – typically a sign of domination – into an affirmation of individual choice.

References

Anderson, Benedict. 1983. *Imagined Communities*. London and New York: Verso, 2016. Print.

Bhabha, Homi K. 1990. "The Third Space: Interview with Homi K. Bhabha." Ed. Jonathon Rutherford. *Identity: Community, Culture, Difference*. London: Lawrence and Wishart. 202-221.

Forster, E. M. 1924. *A Passage to India*. New York: Harcourt Brace.

Gregg, Veronica. 1999. 'What a History You Have': The Mistress and the Servant in Jamaica Kincaid's 'Lucy'. *Journal of West Indian Literature* 8.2 (): 38-49.

Hall, Stuart. 1996. "Cultural Identity and Diaspora." Ed. Padmini Mongia. *Contemporary Postcolonial Theory: A Reader.* New York: Oxford University Press, 110-121.

Jhabvala, Ruth Prawer. "An Experience of India." *Out of India.* New York: Simon & Schuster, 1986. 125-146.

Khan-Din, Ayub. 1996. *East is East.* London: Nick Hern Books, Kindle edition. Kincaid, Jamaica. *Lucy.* New York: Penguin, 1991.

Lahiri, Jhumpa. 2006. "My Two Lives." *Newsweek* (March).

Maira, Sunaina. 2002. *Desis In the House: Indian American Youth Culture in NYC.* Philadelphia: Temple University Press.

Ramón, Soto-Crespo E. 2002. "Death and the Diaspora Writer: Hybridity and Mourning in the Work of Jamaica Kincaid." *Contemporary Literature* 43.2. p342-376.

Tucker, Brian J. 2010. You Belong to Christ: Paul and the Formation of Social Identity in 1 Corinthians 1-4. Eugene, OR: Pickwick.

Zinchenko, Alexander V. 2011 "Nostalgia: Dialogue Between Memory and Knowing." *Journal of Russian and East European Psychology* 49.3. 84-97.

Death in Diaspora:

Reincarnation, Oblivion or Heaven?

Bobby Bose

I left Calcutta (now Kolkata) to study theology in the UK in the early 1980s and soon I found myself involved in the ministry among South Asians. It was there I first met my American wife-to-be serving among the same community. After my study, I joined as a full-time staff with a London local church to serve among the South Asians and served there until 1992. While I was there, a South Asian Christian school teacher asked me to do a memorial service in honor of her mother who had just passed away. Assuming my hearers to be broadly Christian, I presented a message of hope in the Lord Jesus Christ to comfort the grieving family and friends. However, after the service, a heated discussion arose as to the veracity of the Christian truths I had shared. I found out that school teacher's husband, a Hindu, believed in re-incarnation and her two grown sons held more of a Secular Humanist perspective. Some of her friends were Muslims, while others present believed in Purgatory. The universal experience of the death of a loved one had brought together these differing perspectives and I was unprepared.

Later on, for my PhD research, I investigated views held by Hindu, Muslim, and Modern Secularist on the "State-after-Death" and sought to contribute to Christian conversation in pluralistic contexts about death. This chapter is a brief summary of dissertation and book with the same title. I believe a person's view on the "State-after-Death" greatly influences their acceptance or rejection of the Gospel of Jesus Christ and this topic is crucial for the South Asian Christians and all involved with South Asians. In diasporic settings, the issue of death is further complicated as many prefer to die in the land of their birth and elaborate rituals associated with death in some cultures. All religious systems and cultures have developed ideas on the state of the human 'person' after death. A belief in life after death is almost universal yet there is a dearth of Christian literature that deals with the topic. I found almost no one has examined "State-after-Death" in comparison to people of major South Asian religious groups.

What happens after death is an intriguing yet non-threatening topic for discussion. It is an essential part of the Gospel and must be communicated thoughtfully in pluralistic contexts. Among many conflicting views about life after death, it is crucial that South Asian Christians are informed about views of Hindus, Muslims and Secular Humanists, and effectively communicate Christian worldview on death while communicating the gospel of Jesus Christ. Following a method of doing theology in pluralistic setting developed by E. Stanely Jones (Van Engen et al. 1999), in this paper I present other worldviews on death and Biblical understanding, to suggest a more effective model of a theology of "State-after-Death" for pluralistic contexts.

Hindu, Muslim, and Modern Secular Views on Death

According to the tradition of the *Upanishads* and later writings, the predominant Hindu view of "State-after-Death" is reincarnation with varying interpretations. Death is a painful predicament for both the victims of death and the surviving community. It is not considered the end of life but a passage to re-birth. It is considered a break in the series of events called life, necessary and meaningful in the cycle of birth, death and re-birth. The Hindu re-birth cycle is based on the principle of Karma (deeds). Good deeds help one to be re-born as a

Brahmin (priest), *Kshatriya* (warrior) *or Vaishya* (merchant or farmer), while evil deeds lead to rebirth as a *Shudra* (menial laborer) or an *outcaste* or even as an animal. *Karmic* view holds that gods are the highest form of existence, followed in order by humans, animals, and plants and atoms of matter are the lowest.

For Hindus, the Soul (*atman*) of humans is immortal and indestructible and when death comes, only the physical body dies. The soul is eternal and considered either a part of or the same as *Brahman*, the impersonal ultimate Reality; and if different from *Brahman*, possibly of the same essence as *Brahman*. While the physical body dies, Rambachan shows that the so-called Subtle Body (*suksma sarira*) carries the memory of *Karma* from one life to the next as the Subtle Body separates from the physical body at the moment of death (1997, 66-86). The way of salvation from this seemingly endless cycle of birth and rebirth is through Self-Realization, that is, the discovery of the Self that is hidden in the heart, through the process of spiritual discipline in the present life. There are three paths of spiritual discipline to escape from this cycle of re-birth: the way of good deeds (*Karma Marga*), the way of knowledge (*Jnana Marga*), and the way of devotion (*Bhakti Marga*).

If there is no judgment or reward of the eternal Soul itself for the deeds done in this life, then what particular aspect of an individual human person is being judged? Perhaps the Hindu way of asking this question would be: Exactly what dimension of an individual is subject to the deterministic consequences of *Karma*? Is it only the so-called "subtle body" that faces the consequence of actions of the previous life to the next in the cycle of re-birth? Swami Adiswarananda notes that all Hindus will attain Self-Knowledge ultimately, even though they may take many detours of multiple births in the process, whether higher or lower on the ladder of existence (1986, 170-171). Perhaps, this is why many urban Hindus, vying to succeed in the fast pace of today's world, leave very little time for practicing the three religious ways of escape from the cycle of re-birth and have accepted Modern Secular notion that death is the end of all existence.

There are two main implications of the Hindu perspective on death. First, after-death, the whole being of an individual person does not face the full consequence of actions done in one's life. The result is that the whole being is not considered responsible for those actions. If, on one hand, the Self is the primary "I" of a person and the Self does not face the consequence of that person's actions, then, in essence, the responsibility of the primary "I" for every action is being ignored or excused. If, on the other hand, the Self is not the primary "I" of a person but is a part of or is *Brahman* present in a human being, then what is the primary "I" of a person that is responsible for and must face the consequences of that person's action? Is it the physical body that is destroyed at death and/or the subtle body that includes the senses, the mind, and the intellect? If the Self is not the primary "I" of a person, then why did *Krishna* advise *Arjuna* not to mourn for the Self, since the Self is not killed when the body is killed but is "leaving aside worn-out bodies, To other, new ones goes the embodied (soul)" (*Bhagavad Gita* 2:17-22)?

The second implication is that, whatever the primary "I" of a person is, the Self or some aspect of the body, the succession of lives resulting from multiple births lessens responsibility for actions, and promotes a lackadaisical attitude towards this life. Even further, it obliterates a sense of accountability in the present life because of the option that the consequences of human actions can be faced in the next life. The Hindu belief that ultimately all will attain Self-knowledge and salvation in the end through the detours of many lives, may give people the idea that ultimately it does not really matter how unrighteous one lives in the present life.

The Muslim perspective of "State-after-Death" is in many ways similar to Judeo-Christian views, with one life here on earth, then death and finally resurrection on the Judgment Day, a day of cosmic upheaval. All dead will be judged according to their deeds during life on earth, however, minute these may be and then sent to either an everlasting paradise of pleasures or a hell of continuous affliction and suffering. Though human beings are not considered inherently evil or misguided,

Islam recognizes that all people err and that each individual alone is responsible and accountable for one's own deeds at the Judgment. Some Muslims believe that judgment begins on the first night in the grave after death where two angels question them about their beliefs and depending on their response are placed in a pleasant state or a situation of torment in the grave itself.

Muslims believe the deceased remain in the grave until the day of resurrection in an intermediate state, during which prayers are said and alms are given on behalf of the dead to add to their tally of good deeds. The concept of *Barzakh* defined this intermediate state, but what happens to the soul in *Barzakh* is not discussed much in the Qur'an and there is a lot of speculation about it in the Islamic traditions, with varying degrees of authenticity and reliability. The themes of joy and torment to be experienced at the time of final judgment is prefigured and repeated in a variety of ways from the very beginning, as one follows the sequence of death and after-death events, beginning with the kind of welcome the grave will offer to the deceased.

For a Muslim, faithfulness in religious duties will be rewarded on the Judgment Day in the Garden, a place of beauty and physical satisfaction. However, delinquency in religious duties and unrighteous acts will be punished on Judgment Day in the Fire, a place of roaring flames and torment. Muslims believe that varying levels of the Garden and the Fire exist for varying degrees of success or failure in one's deeds in life. As there are no sure means of forgiveness in Islam, there is also no clear assurance of salvation after death, though there is a vague hope for Allah's mercy because of allegiance to Prophet Muhammad.

The *Hadith* consider Prophet Muhammad (PBUH) and his power to intercede unique compared to other prophets in that only his intercession will be accepted by God on the Day of Judgment. Perhaps this power of intercession of Muhammad provides Muslims with a general sense of assurance that all will be well in the end because of their faith in Allah and his last prophet. Of course, in the twelfth century, the great Islamic theologian, Al-Ghazali, thought that some of the descriptions of heaven or hell seem to have chiefly moral meaning in order to emphasize the importance of the 'straight path' by which Allah guides the faithful. While the Qur'an affirms the eternality of both heaven and hell, most Muslims, without doubting the eternality of the Garden, seem to think that "it is not only possible but even likely that at some future time all sinners will be pardoned and the fires of judgment will be extinguished forever" (Smith 1986, 201). Muslims hope that Allah will be merciful to them because of their allegiance to the prophet Muhammad, provided they live a good life and practice religious duties.

There are two main implications of the Muslim perspective on death: First is a positive one that Muslims have some fear about the judgment of God after death, be it immediately after death or at the final Day of Judgment. This fear of judgment of God after death motivates them to live a religious life (praying five times a day, fasting in the month of Ramadan, giving alms, etc.) and avoiding evil deeds, according to the standards of Islam. Another implication is that they depend entirely on their individual good works for a blessed hereafter. Also, no one can be sure whether his or her good deeds will be good enough in God's sight for paradise. Due to this ambiguity, Islamic traditions have tried to strengthen the hope of Muslims by emphasizing the power of Muhammad's intercession for them to assure them all will be well in the end.

For *Modern Secularists,* death is denied or ignored, controlled, and managed. "Here and now" is what matters and any thought about an existence after death is totally shunned and rejected as "pie in the sky." The common refrain of this humanistic, naturalistic perspective is that when you are dead, that's the end. Our biological life is what matters and any concept of human essence beyond the physical realm is considered absurd and outside the public arena of inquiry. Though this notion is not usually considered a religious perspective, it has become a primary idea in pluralistic contexts. This is embraced by a great number of people, even by some religious groups. Thus, the Modern Secular perspective must be recognized as a religious position that is equally influential and controlling as is any other religious perspective.

Aldwinckle shows us how strong the influence of this Modern Secular perspective is, even within the Christian church, particularly in the West, where many tend to downplay the importance of a life after death (1972, 19). This neglect is reflected in their day-to-day behavior with a narrow concern only for this earthly life. While Aldwinckle sees Bertrand Russell, along with Freud, as primarily responsible for bringing about this perspective (1972, 24), Toynbee traces the roots of this thinking to the Epicurean school of Greek philosophers (1976, 6). However, Longenecker derives this Secular perspective from three sources: "Buddhism or Confucianism (its Eastern heritage); from Stoicism or the Epicureans (its Classical heritage); and/or from naturalistic or religious humanism (its Western heritage)" (1998, 14). Hick shows the weakness of the Modern Secular perspective in that with no life after death, it does not provide any hope for a large majority of the human race, of both past and present worlds, who have not enjoyed or do not enjoy the basic amenities of life that the people of the affluent Western societies enjoy (1976, 152-153).

Aldwinckle, following Bonhoeffer, shows another weakness in that life is fast and frantic in the Western countries and in the urban centers of the world because Modern Secularists have only a limited time to work for and enjoy everything life provides. They lack hope of life beyond death and, with only this limited life are frantic to make the best use of their short time. There are, however, some who, instead of a philosophy of despair and denial of death, believe in an existence beyond death, even in some form of reincarnation or a general heaven.

Christian View on Death

This section considers contemporary Christian theologians who have either dealt with the question of "State-after-Death" and/or have responded to the challenge of pluralism in regard to death. Although Dietrich Bonhoeffer, Paul Devanandan, Stephen Neill, Hendrik Kraemer and M. M. Thomas did not deal with death at great length, they faced the challenge of religious pluralism. But the pluralist theologian John Hick and the reformist Catholic theologian Hans Küng do stand out among Christian theologians of the Twentieth Century as having courage and insight to discuss death in dialogue with world religions.

Early ideas of death begin at Gen. 2:17ff. as God pronounced the first sentence of death on Adam and Eve as punishment for their disobedience. Adam and Eve were created with the ability to choose "to die" or "not to die." They chose death through their disobedience, resulting in the fall, after which the whole of humanity suffered the curse of death. The Old Testament shows that "State-after-Death" is a critical component of God's universal rescue mission of humanity from one form of final destiny to another. The Old Testament focuses mainly on Israel's earthly life in which God revealed himself to his people as they were called to obey, serve, and worship God only, though they often failed. Yet in spite of the difficulty of tracing the growth of the understanding of life after death in ancient Israel, we observe a progressive revelation of the concept of "State-after-Death" in the Old Testament as part of God's universal mission.

Sheol and similar terms generally mean "the underworld," or the realm where the deceased go deep down, under the earth. Israelites responded negatively to neighboring Near-Eastern pluralistic views of death by choosing the unique term *Sheol* with its distinct monotheistic theological meaning for the underworld. They did not absorb the polytheistic assumptions of surrounding non-Yahwist peoples. In the OT, the underworld is a real and literal place away from God, a place of no return, of darkness and gloom, yet not totally outside of God's control. Finally, with the help of Phillip Johnston's survey of underworld references in the OT, we conclude that it is mainly the destiny of those under God's judgment, the ungodly and sinners, and not the general destiny of all human dead, whether righteous or unrighteous (2002).

Several texts in the Old Testament point to an alternative to *Sheol*, a hope for the godly or the righteous through a continuity of fellowship and communion with God, even beyond physical death. In particular, Enoch and Elijah, different Psalms, Proverbs, and the classic passage of Job 19:25-27 all indicate a hope for the righteous and the faithful beyond death. OT references explicitly deal with resurrection from the dead within the progressive revelation of the Scriptures like Gen. 22, Deut. 32 and 1 Sam. 2, Hosea 6, Ezekiel 37, Isaiah 26, and finally Daniel 12. In these "signposts", a term borrowed from Martin-Achard (1960), there is the promise of resurrection from the dead. These "signposts" become clearer (from implicit to explicit) as we move through the OT narratives. These indications of resurrection hope, in the midst of neighboring pluralistic views, show that "State-after- Death" is a critical component of God's mission to provide an alternative to *Sheol*.

In the New Testament, the truth of resurrection from the dead is fully revealed through the death and resurrection of Christ. Jesus promises eternal life for believers and the opposite for unbelievers and reasons convincingly with the Sadducees about the truth of the resurrection, miraculously raises dead people, and predicts his own death and resurrection. The resurrection narratives of Jesus offer three predominant themes: the empty tomb, the witness of women, and the appearances of the risen Jesus, convincingly proving his bodily resurrection. Believers have new hope because of Jesus' resurrection, and there is continuity as well as a discontinuity with the physical body. While unbelievers will be consigned to *Hades* immediately after death, a state of temporary punishment, before experiencing eternal suffering in the fires of *Gehenna* after the final judgment.

In the Gospel of John, resurrection and eternal life are dominant themes. There will be a general resurrection of all people, the righteous and the unrighteous, the former for eternal life and the latter for condemnation. Jesus predicted his death and resurrection in his saying concerning the destruction of the temple and its rebuilding in three days. Resurrection from the dead shows most clearly in John's account of Jesus' response to the charge that he was making himself equal with God because he claimed to raise the dead and give life just like God does. Lazarus' resurrection is not only a sign for the immediate death and resurrection of Jesus but, most importantly, it gives Jesus' clear teaching in his dialogue with Martha on what happens after the death of a believer. Jesus takes authority over death and through Jesus, believers will triumph over death. In John's first letter, the theme of resurrection is implied throughout.

The narratives of Jesus' resurrection in all four gospels confirm the historicity of the event and affirm the ultimate destiny of believers in Christ. They will be bodily resurrected in the end and will continue in resurrected life forever. As for the unbelievers, there is no mention of *Hades* and *Gehenna* in John's Gospel, as a place of punishment, but it mentions perishing, death, and condemnation/ judgment, while the letters mention death (not just physical death) as a final destiny only once (1 John 5:16).

In spite of the pluralistic contexts of the Greco-Roman world of the NT, God revealed his unique message of hope after death to his people, available because of Jesus' death and the resurrection. This message was radically different from the existing pluralistic views. For the early disciples of Jesus Christ, amid their mixed religious environment, the issue of "State-after-Death" was an important and fruitful area for conversation. The same is true for the present-day South Asian diaspora Christian church, as we engage with people of other faiths.

The centrality of the theme of resurrection permeates all of the letters of Paul, most importantly in 1 Thess. 4:13-5:11, 1 Cor. 15, and 2 Cor. 4:7-5:10. A Pharisee prior to his conversion, Paul would have believed in bodily resurrection from the dead and, therefore understood Christ's resurrection from that perspective and applied that belief to the future resurrection of the believers. For Paul, when believers die they are consciously present in the spirit with Christ in a temporary intermediate state, until their bodies are raised up by Christ at his return and are transformed. Thus, for Paul, there is a continuity as well as discontinuity between the resurrected body and the physical body of a believer. The believers' transformation will include the revivification of the material body at the resurrection. There may have been some development in Paul's thought regarding the resurrection of believers within the progressive nature of God's revelation but his underlying theology of the resurrection of the body for those who believe in Christ remains constant.

Like John, Paul does not deal with *Hades* and *Gehenna*, but does refer to other terms related to unbelievers' final destiny such as the term, *death*. For Paul, death is not merely physical or bodily death but also death of any relationship between God and humans, as death *reigned* through one man Adam (Rom. 5:17) and no one can escape that destiny. But God himself has made a provision of grace through one man Jesus, who has *conquered* death and can reestablish that relationship. Paul also speaks of God's *wrath* and righteous *judgment*. In 2 Thess. 1:6-10, Paul foretells the coming judgment and wrath of God on the unbelievers. Paul also states that the unbelievers' final destiny will be the exact opposite of that of believers when Jesus returns. Thus, for Paul, if the believers will be raised from the dead, be transformed, and have *eternal life* when Christ returns, then the unbelievers will face *everlasting destruction* (and separation) from the presence of the Lord and from the glory of his power.

In the Book of Revelation, we see God is going to judge the kingdoms of this world and establish his rule and as a result there are two different destinies one for the righteous and the other for the unrighteous. As with the Gospels and Paul's letters, the message is clear. Believers no longer need fear God's judgment or the punishment of *death* and *Hades*, because of the risen Jesus, who, having conquered death, has the keys of *death* and *Hades*. Symbolic language in the Book of Revelation describes the reward for overcoming believers in their final destiny. They will have authority over the nations just as Jesus received authority from the Father, and Jesus will acknowledge their name before the Father and his angels. They will be pillars in the temple of God and will never leave it, and Jesus will give them the right to sit with him on his throne, just as Jesus sat down with his Father on his throne. In spite of the symbolism, we can safely conclude that these are powerful descriptions of the believers' blessed hereafter at Christ's return.

As far as the unbelievers' final destiny is concerned, as they refuse to worship God and the Lamb, they will meet the "second death" in a fiery lake of burning Sulphur where worshippers of the beast will be tormented, with smoke rising forever, and the devil, beast, and false prophet will also be tormented forever (Rev. 14:9-11; 20:7-15). However, the Lamb (Jesus) who was slain will redeem many people from every tribe, language, ethnic group, and nation with his shed blood (5:9-10). Revelation 6:9-11 seems to suggest that believers who have died are resting "under the altar" in the presence of God in a temporary intermediate state and are awaiting full bodily resurrection.

In the final three chapters of Revelation, God is in control, Satan is bound and eventually punished (along with the unbelievers), and the believers are rewarded and blessed. In Chapter 20 there is a possibility of an initial resurrection for some believers, those who were martyrs because of their faith, whereas the rest will be resurrected in the general resurrection along with the unrighteous even though, ultimately, all believers will be rewarded and blessed. But the unrighteous unbelievers after their resurrection will face God's judgment and will have no escape from the fiery furnace of "second death" where they will suffer *eternally*. Thus NT gives a hopeful message of "State-after-Death" which God revealed to his people and which is quite *dissimilar* to the surrounding pluralistic religious views of the Greco-Roman world.

Suggestions and Recommendations

Interpersonal dialogue is the first step for effective communication of the Gospel to those of other faiths. To converse about death with people of the other religious faiths, Christians should explore the following suggestions: First, know your audience and what they believe about death. For Secular Humanists, the primary hurdle is to communicate that something happens after death. Their perspective has its roots in Classical Greek philosophy which says that biological life is all there is and when that life ends there is nothing more. The Greco-Roman world during the early church period had the same perspective which led to a state of hopelessness. As a result, they also accepted the so-called contrasting view of "transmigration of souls." Conversation about "State-after-Death" is less threatening and existentially more real to a Secular Humanist than the question of whether or not God exists. Only if people accept the possibility of existence after death can they consider the possibility of some form of accountability for one's life after death to a higher supernatural power. God's judgment is critical to the Christian Gospel and Christians must discuss the final judgment and also of God's forgiveness and offer of eternal life through the work of Jesus Christ.

One weakness of no-life-after-death theory is that it provides no hope for a large majority of the human race who do not live this life in comfort. Another weakness of the notion "death is the final end," in that, no one knows when they are going to die and so they are afraid of death. This perspective can push people, in frantic defiance, to try to get as much as possible out of this life in a short period of time. When they fail to squeeze the best out of this life in a short period of time that then leads them to despair. This is where we as Christians have an opportunity for conversation with the hope of eternal life.

Some of those in their hopelessness may seek an alternative to annihilation in some form of reincarnation with no accountability to God. Instead of a philosophy of despair and denial of death, some secularists even believe in a general heaven. In such cases, Christians need to be available among them to hold conversations about judgment and eternal life through Jesus Christ. Aldwinckle has shown how many Christians in the church, influenced by the Modern Secular perspective, promote "an exclusively this-worldly version of the Christian faith" with no thought for "State-after-Death." He rightly argues that it is not a case of "either-or" but "both-and" (1972, 23). Only when we are assured of eternal life in Jesus Christ, we can live this life fearlessly in service for God and his created humanity.

Second, in discussing "State-after-Death" as part of our communication of the Gospel to Hindus who believe in some form of more than one life on earth, the first hurdle would be to persuade them to believe in one life on earth. There is no point in talking about judgment after death and punishment for sins, if they expect to escape judgment and punishment by repetitive cycles of life. Even if they ignore the prospect of death in their day-to-day lives, Hindus recognize death as an existential reality and admit that their views about "State-after-Death" influence their present living. While Hindus find it easy and non-threatening to talk about what they believe may happen after death, Christians must keep in mind that such perspectives of "State-after-Death" are closely related to their views of God as impersonal ultimate reality. However, they may find talking about what happens after death easier than comparing which view of God or the ultimate reality is more plausible.

Christians could raise questions with Hindus about exactly what dimension of an individual is subjected to the deterministic consequences of *Karma*. Is it the "subtle body" that faces the consequences of actions from the past life into the next in the cycle of re-birth? Or, after-death, does the whole being of an individual person face the full consequence of actions done in one's life? Perhaps this is why many Hindus have more or less accepted the Modern Secular notion that death is the end of all existence. Some Hindus see the cycle of re-birth as a form of judgment and punishment of their *Karma* rather than a second chance and may strive to escape that cycle of re-birth. The doctrine of Karma and rebirth does not appear in Vedic literature, but in Upanishads (Pathickal 2012, 33). They seek salvation by meditation, good deeds, or sincere devotion to a personal deity.

Christians need not shift from *Christocentric* to *Theocentric*, or even to *Ultimate-Reality centered*, as John Hick did. We believe in a "State-after-Death" that leads to eternal life through Jesus Christ in the presence of God who is *personal* and *wholly other* than his creation. Also, by eternal life, we do not mean eternally being merged into some impersonal ultimate reality, which remains an important distinctions between Christianity and other faiths. Those who see multiple lives as a better option than the one life on earth of Christian faith, we need to talk about Jesus' own teaching and predictions about resurrection, and the historicity of his own bodily resurrection, and his visible ascension to heaven after one life on earth. We need to share not only the good news and promise of eternal life with God for believers according to the Christian Gospel but also the judgment of God and consequent punishment if we reject the Gospel of Jesus Christ in this life in creative and loving manner, without sounding judgmental or putting other faith systems as inferior.

Third, since the Muslim views of judgment, future resurrection of the dead, and heaven and hell as reward and punishment, are similar to Jewish and Christian view of death, it is less threatening as a start-up conversation with Muslims. Muslims who choose suicide as part of terrorism, believe God will reward them for their "courageous" acts. Their expectation of paradise appears far better than their present life, so in that sense suicide is not a selfless act. Muslims fear the judgment of God and believe final destiny depends entirely on their individual good works. In conversation, we may challenge their vague assurance of salvation or confidence in others to intercede for them.

Conclusion

Let us return to the introduction of this chapter and reconsider the memorial service preaching. If I were asked to take the same service again, after completing this study, I would present the message quite differently from what I did then. First, I would give a longer introduction on the possibilities of where the departed loved one might be after death, according to pluralistic religious and secular perspectives. My hearers must see that I take their and others' perspectives about ultimate destiny quite seriously even if these viewpoints are not held by the people who were present at that memorial service. If some present held these perspectives, they would also recognize my interest in their viewpoints and that I care about them as people.

Next, I would sensitively reason to show the pointlessness and the inconsistencies of some of these perspectives. I would deal with the inconsistency of universalism, which claims all will be well for all of humanity in the end by pointing only to God's mercy and neglecting his justice and righteous wrath. In the end, I would point them to Jesus, who (a) through his response to the Sadducees, (b) through his predictions of his own death and resurrection, (c) through raising Lazarus and others, and (d) through his own death and resurrection proves the validity and hope of the Christian Gospel of Jesus Christ.

References

Adiswarananda, Swami. 1986. "Hinduism" in *Encounters with Eternity: Religious Views on Death and Life After Death*. Christopher J. Johnson and Marsha G. McGee (Eds.) New York: Philosophical Library.

Aldiwinckle, Russell. 1972. *Death in the Secular City*. London: George Allen & Unwin.

Bose, Bobby. 2016. *Reincarnation, Oblivion or Heaven? A Christian Exploration*. Carlisle, UK: Langham Global Library.

Hick, John. 1976. *Death and Eternal Life*. New York: Harper & Row Publishers.

Johnson, Philip S. 2002. *Shades of Sheol: Death and Afterlife in the Old Testament*. Downers Grove, IL: Intervarsity Press.

Longnecker, Richard N. (Ed). 1998. *Life in the Face of Death: The Resurrection Message of the New Testament*. Grand Rapids, MI: Eerdmans.

Martin-Achard, Robert. 1960. *From Death to Life: A Study of the Development of the Doctrine of the Resurrection in the Old Testament*. John P. Smith, trans. London: Oliver & Boyd Ltd.

Pathickal, Paul. 2012. *Christ and the Hindu Diaspora*. Bloomington, IN: WestBow Press.

Rambachan, Anantanand. 1997. "Hinduism" in *Life after Death in World Religions*. Harold Coward (Ed). Maryknoll, NY: Orbis Books.

Smith, Jane Idleman. 1986. "Islam" in *Encounters with Eternity: Religious Views of Death and Life After Death*. Christopher J. Johnson and March G. McGree (Eds.) New York: Philosophical Library.

Toynbee, Arnold and Arthur Koestler (Eds). 1976. *Life after Death*. New York: McGraw Hill Book Company.

Van Engen, Charles, Nancy Thomas and Robert Gallagher (Eds.). 1999. *Footprints of God: A Narrative Theology of Mission*. Monrovia, CA: MARC.

Conclusion

Sam George

South Asian Christians have successfully transplanted themselves across the globe—some of them maintain ties to churches or institutions back in South Asia, while others join local as well as international ecclesial structures. Many are revived in their Christian faith, while others have embraced Christianity at overseas locations. These are clearly evident in cases of technology-enabled dispersion of Telugus worldwide in recent decades as well as medical professionals or the indentured laborers of the past. Many Indians pursue education abroad or stateless Nepali-Bhutanese who seek refuge in foreign countries. Parents seek marriage alliances from abroad for their daughters and families live transnationally. They occupy closed Anglican churches in the United Kingdom and host weekly house meetings under great personal risk in closed countries. Among the forcefully displaced on account of the civil war in Sri Lanka, trafficked Nepali minors and persecuted Pakistanis, many have become followers of Christ in foreign lands. The faith, resourcefulness and leadership of displaced South Asians even in dire circumstances are very inspiring and commendable.

The Christian immigrants who go to post-Christian West are unable to associate with churches in host countries and often discriminated against on account of race or ethnicity. Most South Asians Christians are mistaken for Hindus or Muslims by Western Christians and in other parts of the world, many of whom are unaware of the sizable Christian population in South Asia and its long history. Their distinctive Christian practices appear foreign to host nation Christians some of whom are reluctant to rent facilities for worship in a strange language and customs. A larger number of the South Asian migrants are Christians or become so after migrating to foreign lands. When some host nation churches are struggling for survival, these immigrant Christians are bringing fresh energy and enthusiasm to Christian faith everywhere.

Diasporic Diversities: Many Colors

What is evident in these divergent narrative of this volume is that each presents an insider perspective of their own respective communities in different locations of the world and they affirm the categorical definition of diaspora developed by scholars such as Safran (1991) and Cohen (1997) by meeting the basic prerequisites for diaspora: an ethnic consciousness, an active associative communal life, real or imaginary contacts with the land of origin and relations with other groups of same ethnic origin spread around the world. What has become obvious in these narratives is that diasporic reality is a "social construct founded on feeling, consciousness, memory, mythology, history, meaningful narratives, group identity, longings, dreams, allegorical and virtual elements" (Shuval 2000, 43). This diasporic consciousness is one of ambivalence and contradiction, ready to embrace change and create new realities for families, churches and societies. These essays also confirm that migration is truly a "theologizing experience" on account of the "intensification of the psychic basis of religious commitment" as evident in renewed role played by Christian faith in diasporic settings (Smith 1978, 1175).

The migratory displacement is not just geographic, but also social, cultural, economic, political and religious. It comes with the loss of order, relational networks, and the world that was familiar with its symbolic meanings that guided daily lives of the migrants. The impact of this human and sociocultural displacement is both traumatic and transformative. They suffer from the guilt of abandoning family members, reminiscent of the past and at the same time fearful of ambiguous futures. It involves grieving the past and renewed courage to face indeterminate prospects ahead. They strangely feel closer to the land they left behind that is thousands of miles away while remaining distant and disconnected with those who live next door or colleagues at work. At the places of settlements, migrants seek to break the bondage of the hegemony of the majority while resisting and creating homogeneity simultaneously among themselves.

The pain, loss and uncertainty arising out of displacement often initiate an existential search for answers within religious realms. It is not surprising that religious attachments frequently intensify subsequent to immigration to a degree that surpasses the devotion while living in the native land (Hirschman 2004). A study by Hagan and Ebaugh (2003) suggested that the risks and the experience of a lack of control during immigration create a stronger reliance on religion giving adversity a spiritual tone and meaning. Many indications have been made by several contributors to this volume about the intensification of religious consciousness in diasporic setting and how faith is an inimitable resource in migrant wanderings in life.

The diasporic realities compel people to question age-old assumptions that they have relied on for generations and the conceptual boundaries are traversed continuously in order to accommodate new contextual realities. The border crossing involved in diasporic living forces one to reconfigure boundaries repeatedly through maintenance, conflicts and negotiations. The uprooting, relocation and transplanting to new soils in foreign lands results in a deep crisis of identification, belonging, meaning and ultimately belief about God. All of these deeper quest, longing and inner transformation in the migratory wanderings and diasporic living has profound influence on how migrants perceive their mission in life.

Diasporization introduces new parameters into identity formation process and develops a new knack in boundary crossing activities. One's identity, meaning and life mission can no longer be shaped exclusively by ethnicity or culture, but they look beyond the confines of color of skin, birthplace, nationality, vocation, language and the like. They possess an innate propensity to fathom beyond dichotomous archetypes and willing to take greater risk to wrestle in crafting novel ways of being, belonging, knowing, learning and relating. They develop new intuitive sensibilities as well as cultural competencies that go beyond taxonomic and rigid categories in order to negotiate intricacies of inhabiting the diaspora space. The spaces they occupy direct them to negotiate in between spaces home and abroad, center and periphery, us and them in order to live simultaneously in multiple worlds with its own cultural currencies. Thus, they become natural translators, interpreting one world to other and vice versa for sheer survival, which eventually spills over to reimagining God and the mission of God in the world. Being pulled between the adopted homeland "here" and ancestral homeland "there", they develop a new Christological vision for earthly life in Christ and an eschatological vision of home in heaven.

An excellent case in point is Apostle Paul, whose diasporic life played a crucial role in the development of the early Christianity because his life, identity, sociocultural realities, interpretation of scripture, mission and writings cannot be fully grasped without taking seriously his diasporic location (Charles 2014; Wallace 1998; Wright 2005). Calvin Roetzel argues that Paul's social location in diaspora Judaism is crucial "to understand the dynamic of Paul's theology" (1992). Paul grew up in diasporic setting in Tarsus, read diaspora Bible, was educated in Greek language, was a Roman citizen, trained under a leading Jewish teacher of his time in Jerusalem, influenced by Hellenistic rhetoric and Stoic philosophy, moved around as an itinerant across many diaspora communities, engaged diaspora Jews and ministered to Gentiles, wrote epistles in Greek etc. - all of his life pervades notions of diasporic realities. As a diaspora figure living "in-between" social realities and religious ideals, Paul's life-transforming encounter with Jesus Christ ensued in significant restructuring of his sense of identity, intercultural skills, ultimate allegiance and mission in life.

Likewise, the modern diaspora Christians are at the forefront of expansion and transformation of Christianity as they employ multiple strategies to navigate between different identities and cultures. As they adapt, accommodate and redefine life in new contexts, they also interpret Christ in new ways and gospel diffuses across cultural lines to diasporic communities and host nations. Their identities are complex and plural, no essentialized to fit some fixed, rigid, permanent, distinctive and predefined notions, but being forged by incessant exchange across cultures and interactions with people who are unlike themselves. Their social, spatial, relational, temporal and theological insights are shaped, differentiated and interrelated by different crossings and exposures.

Emerging Themes: A Coat of Many Colors

The differences of ethnic, linguistic and cultural matters become unambiguously noticeable as people migrate overseas and this study confirms the resurgence of ethnic and religious identities in diasporic locations. It demonstrates across languages, cultures, doctrinal beliefs, generations and regions of origin and destinations. The ethnic and religious identities in diaspora are intricately intertwined and the future generations are challenging assumptions and established institutions of early immigrants, forcing them to either assimilate with majority Christian identity in host nation or adapt for relevance and effectiveness of ministry.

By traversing the global accounts of diaspora narratives of different South Asian Christians, it is obvious that transplantation and preservation do not occur uniformly. The locality and cultural context in new homelands or places of settlement determine many practices and religious fervor. For example, religious restrictions or educational levels of some South Asian Christians in the Middle East are different than that of those who have chosen to settle in Australia. The proximity to their homeland and nature of migration such as labor migrations also significantly smudge various expressions of lived religion. Inability to permanently settle or buy property in a particular region like the Persian Gulf forces South Asian Christians to maintain closer ties than those who moved to Europe or North America.

In diasporic contexts, religion takes new forms and provides new meaning that might not have existed prior to migration. It gains some new functions and offers new challenges as a result of dispersion. All immigrant religion serves as a glue to the ancestral homeland and a means to define themselves in adopted homelands. The inherited identities that religions offer for emigrants through cultural preservation and linguistic identifications. Yet, religions undergo major transformation subsequent to relocation and influence of culture and religions of the host societies. They suffer many losses and also establish many gains in social, cultural and spiritual realms.

Transnational ties that diasporic communities maintain appear repeatedly in many chapters and how South Asian Christians maintain close links to native Christians with whom they feel a greater emotional affinity. Such feeling might arise out of a sense of wanting to give something back to religious bodies or institutions which have come to mean so much to the immigrants or a spirit of missions to evangelize the "heathens" back home. They achieve this by providing financial support or going on mission trips, while others serve actively in governing bodies of churches and mission agencies to have a significant impact on people in ancestral homelands. Other forms of transnational interactions in the form of music, faith practices and itinerant preachers exert decisive spiritual influence on both ends of diasporic linkages.

It can be inferred that future generations who are born and raised in foreign countries, with limited interaction with ancestral homelands and having lost the linguistic and cultural competencies in diasporic locations, are developing a new understanding of their hybrid self-perceptions and prefer to be identified as World Christians in their adopted homelands. They have multiple cultural heritage, complex life journey and experiences, and who do not fall into existing categories of being a particular kind of a Christian. They possess special insights and skills being in the frontiers of Christian faith and topple prevailing dominant notions of faith.

Diaspora communities break exclusivist and ethnic elitism among Christians by acting as a corrective to the tendency to domesticate God trapped within a culture and geography. Human dispersion acts as a catalyst for cross cultural diffusion of the gospel and migrants performs the function of missionaries in the frontiers of Christianity. No particular church, place or culture owns Christianity entirely and at different epochs in history, different people and places have become its chief representatives. Moreover, diaspora functions as a divine strategy to fulfil the universal missionary mandate and inclusion of all nations in the redemptive plan of God. It shows that God is sovereign over human dispersion and the migration of people bring them to direct access to the gospel without any sociocultural and religious constraints, which might not have been possible prior to displacement.

Conversion is another repeated theme across many chapters, not just those from other faith backgrounds who have embraced Christianity in other countries. Conversion is the appropriation of Christ into thought, life, culture and mind. Even Christian undergoes a conversion subsequent to migrating to foreign countries. Conversion is "turning" what is already there to Christ, not adding something new to something old. At overseas locations, embracing Christian faith has helped many to break out of shackles of ancestral faiths and cultural bondages of South Asia, both where Christianity is majority and minority. Christianity also experiences a conversion from its archaic forms and the host cultures as new converts as well as future generations act as catalytic agents for this metamorphosis.

Unity in Diversity: One in Christ

This volume has attempted to portray some of the great diversity within South Asian Christians in diaspora, yet it has barely touched upon the colossal complexities within these communities. This diversity is result of complex history of Christianity in South Asia – ranging from Apostolic traditions to Colonial influences to modern missionary movements and the development of indigenous Christianity, multifaceted socio-cultural settings of the subcontinent, very spirited discourses on varying theological persuasions, widespread dispersion of people over a long period of time and not to mention complexities generated through diasporic contexts, disparate identifications and discrete representations. As much as this volume endeavors to paint a narrative of a collective whole, it juxtaposes many competing and contradictory ideas and perspectives, while trying to weave through ambivalent notions of identity, belonging, faith practices, beliefs and transnational linkages of a lived religion in a global context and some if its many theological and missiological implications.

The dispersion of this diverse populace to far-flung corners of our planet has not only amplified the differences within South Asian Christianity exponentially but also exposes the very core of the Protestant Christianity, particularly its spread and growth through repeated divisions and its constant evolution. As we commemorate the 500th anniversary of the Reformation in 2017, one must reorganize that there are nearly 50,000 Christian denominations in the world today (CSGC 2015) and this fragmentation is the result of new theological ideas as well as mission concepts that advanced the gospel across cultural lines all over the world. At the beginning of the 21st century, Christianity is most global and diverse than it has ever been and is strategically placed to spread to all peoples everywhere while holding some great potential for confusion.

Some of the theological concepts and ideas that emerged from the Reformation that ushered the splintering and great gospel mobility are: the doctrine of Christian freedom, masses gaining access to Scripture, Bible translations, the rise of vernacular, interpretive pluralism, the priesthood of all believers, cross cultural mission, context matters, and others. The ensuing and related ideas of protestant work ethics, economics, rise of individualism and ties to local politics also had a far reaching influence upon the development and expansion of Christianity. All of these ideas cannot be unpacked at this point conclusively and I only make an essential argument here to justify my usage of Diaspora Christianities and the need for establishing unity across diversities produced by diaspora congregations all over the world. Thus Christianity is not a solitary static edifice of doctrine, but a constantly moving community of faith under the Lordship of Christ in all its cultural diversity.

Some of the above ideas bred conscientious objection to church leaders and belief based upon personal convictions grounded in

Scriptures. The translation and availability of Bible in local languages proliferated new ideas and empowered masses to take into their own hands all religious and spiritual matters without depending upon ecclesial authorities. The elitist and exclusivity of clergy class are congruous to Brahmanical orders of majority South Asian religions and the radical idea of all being priests in the service of God and fellow humanity, unleashed the massive potential trapped within church pews. Going abroad also liberated people from social and religious obligations that curtailed them freely exercising their new founded identity as servants of a missionary God and call to serve fellow immigrants and others in their host countries. The power of the vernacular in knitting the immigrants together in diasporic settings and effectiveness of ministry in heart languages cannot be overstated. The geographical and cultural uprooting provides great impetus to spiritual transformation and great momentum to faith itself.

For this and other reasons, I argue that Christianity of South Asian diaspora must be presented in plural form (Diaspora Christianities) rather than singular (Diaspora Christianity). I approach the study of South Asian Diaspora Christians from the distinct vantage point of World Christianities of the early 21st century that takes into account great diversity of people and cultures of the world (McLeod 2014). Walls is accurate in his assessment that Christianity is more culturally diverse than it has ever been (2002, 68). The current state of human mobility is proving to be more consequential than the Reformation itself in transforming Christianity and the contemporary diaspora Christians are accelerating the creation of new representative Christianity and its advancement. Christianity has been quintessential indigenous religion, continually adapting across cultural lines as it believes in a God who incarnated into a particular time, place and person. Jesus took flesh lived among humans within a particular geographical, cultural and religious boundaries. Thus, Christianity is autochthonous in nature by remaining local globally. Its adaptability and translatability has provided great momentum to Christian expansion in the twentieth century but has also created much perplexity and pain in form of cultic practices and erroneous theologies.

Christianity is pluralistic at its core or in other words comprise of many different kinds of culturalized Christianities and this is visibly amplified in diaspora contexts. Since Christianity is a translatable faith and Christians must be continuously engaged in the task of translation, never more pertinent than in diasporas, that these diverse lived expressions can be rightly called as Diaspora Christianities. This does not mean Christ is divided or 'divide and grow' as the best strategy for Christian expansion. The plurality within Christianity is normative and there exists a need to acknowledge divisions created by the sociocultural and linguistic difference that has grown exponentially over the last century. At the beginning of the 21st century, Christianity has taken root in every nation in the world and when Christians from majority world relocate to former heartlands of Christianity, they are not only reviving Christianity in their adopted homelands but also adding to the diversity of expressions and globalizing national Christianities everywhere.

It is pertinent at this juncture to briefly reflect on Apostle Paul's exhortation to the Corinthians: "One of you says, 'I follow Paul'; another, 'I follow Apollos'; another, 'I follow Cephas'; still another, 'I follow Christ.' Is Christ divided? (1 Cor. 1:12-13). Paul decries division within the Corinthian church and extreme individualism voiced as "all things are lawful" (6:12; 10:23) that is detrimental to communal life. Paul employs two dominant imageries – the body and the building – to counteract anti-communal forces that are ripping believers apart and reinforcing their collective identity. The "you" in 3:9 and 3:16 are plural and reflects corporate identity of the people of God. It is unavoidable to compare this analogy of the Temple and God's presence to Church and indwelling of the Holy Spirit. Again, usage "God's spirit dwells in you" is more accurately translated as "the Spirit which dwells among you", thus establishing church not as a collection of Spirit-filled individuals, but an organic whole unified by the Spirit and disproves any tendency toward factionalism (Levison 2006, 195).

Pauline epistles clearly takes on the challenge of unity amidst many disparate peoples and cultures as Christianity moved beyond the confines of Jerusalem and as a Jewish sect by emphasizing a common identity, body, mission and Lordship of Christ. "In Christ" is one of often repeated phrase in Pauline corpus and important concept to understand the basis of unity amid diversities (Schnelle 2003; Dunn 1998; Thompson 2014). Paul presented his case for inclusion of Gentiles converts without circumcision, insisting that both Jews and Gentiles are justified by faith in Jesus Christ (cf. Gal. 2:16; 3:26). While insisting on continuity of his Gentile community with Israel (table fellowship and spiritual inheritance), while at the same time allowing discontinuity in (descendants and incorporation through circumcision). Paul redefines the people of God as those who have identified with Christ, "put on" in baptism (Gal. 3:27) and envisions one community where old identities are subordinated to the new identity of those who are in Christ. He breaks down barriers of ethnicity (Jew/Gentile), social (Slave/Free) and gender (male/female) identities while establishing a new collective identity in Christ (Gal. 3:28). The collective consciousness is obscured in English translation in Paul's usage of "you" and the plural "you are" (este) includes all who are baptized into Christ (3:27), indicating a solidarity of all believers in Christ. To become "one in Christ", the church must overcome all forms of divisions while not obliterating our uniqueness. We must allow room for diversity of people within a church and not make it a balkanized community of separate identities. Thus, life in Christ is not private matter nor is church for dispensing spiritual services for personal consumption and satisfaction. To be in Christ means to be in the company of others who are in Christ with whom we share a common identity, life, mission and destiny. That is why it is said that 'to belong to Christ means you belong to everyone who belongs to Christ.'

Homogeneity or Heterogeneity: One Body with Many Parts

In the missiological circle, Donald McGavran's Homogenous Unit Principle (HUP) is widely known and lies at the heart of the church growth movement of the 1970s. He developed the concept based upon the Indian system of caste, seeing people coming to Christ and still remaining within specific caste based groups. Moreover, behind his work in India, there is the American culture with the individualistic worldview and the ethnic superiority of people. This led him to conclude that people become Christians crossing no or least amount of racial, linguistic, or class barriers. Though it was a helpful concept in missions back then, it is accused of cultural ghetto mentality in churches, erecting boundaries to prevent cross cultural diffusion and cultural captivity of the gospel.

Hence, I make a slight twist to HUP as Heterogeneous Unity Paradigm. Of course, it is major redefinition conceptually and is a major paradigm shift. The new HUP holds immense potential to understand increased intercultural penetration we are seeing in the world resulting out of unprecedented human mobility and diasporic interplays reshaping Christianity everywhere. Any kind of geographical displacement of people, whether it be voluntary or forced, creates a greater level of receptivity towards new ideas, beliefs, and lifestyles. They ask new questions which they would not have raised before moving to new places. They question assumptions that were taken for granted for ages before. Exposure to other people, cultures and ideas compel diaspora people to reconsider some of their presumptions and beliefs about the origin, meaning, purpose and ultimate destiny of human life which broaches into questions about God.

The loss and dislocation contests for a theology of otherness and diversity while mounting a new basis of unity beyond social or cultural commonalities. When known and familiar world is left behind and replaced by diasporic settings of unfamiliar and strange where one lives as an 'other'. The diasporic living in two worlds – one that they left behind yet feels strangely connected and one that they adopted yet feels estranged. The separation from home and hearth coupled with sojourning in the land of another, never feeling settled or secure, produces angst of disorientation, rejection, discrimination and alienation. The assimilation into dominant cultures of host nations and hybridized self-conceptions create much pain, confusion, anxiety and a deep yearning for belonging. It is in this new, strange and often oppressive contexts that identity of an alienating otherness of diaspora is forged and at the cusp of expansion of theological understanding of people, cultures, gospel, church and Christ.

As Avtar Brah remarks, "All diasporas are differentiated, heterogeneous, contested spaces, even as they are implicated in the construction of a common 'we' (1996, 184). The rules of this solidarity has to go beyond economic, sociocultural and political realities and the creative dynamics of displacement invites the diasporic subjects to renegotiate, reappropriate and reimagine ethnicity/race, caste, class, gender, education, wealth and power differentials in terms of the Body of Christ, faith practices, common mission of God in the world, and hope of eternal life. The collective identity in diaspora is constantly produced and reproduced anew as a result of differences and transformation when encountering the other. The complexities inherent in diasporic conditions, where cultural, sociopolitical and economic identities are in perpetual flux, forces the diasporic subjects to reconceive meaning and purpose of life in new ways, which were unknown to them in the old life and cannot be done with the simple old line of imagination as well as vocabulary. The rhetoric of mission of God in diaspora spaces concerns with inclusion, equality and mutuality and calls for fresh conceptualization and reframing our theologies of Christ as the head of the global church, healthy appreciation of others in the body of Christ who are unlike me, our common eternal future and oneness in the body of Christ.

The diasporic space also provides a site of resistance to hegemonic and homogenizing forces and practices that threaten to nullify diversities. In an age of global diasporas, our ecclesiology and missiology have to progress beyond the least common denominators of social and anthropological uniformity and find ways to include common vision across differences. How can we be a local church with a high awareness of the global church and immense cross-cultural competency to welcome and celebrate all forms of diversities everywhere? How to breakout of narrow, ethnocentric and enclave mentality to develop and embrace a theology of otherness? How do we see Christ as the head of not only local church, but of the global church? How can we express solidarity with fellow Christians all over the world? Maybe that is why God is unscrambling nations and scattering people everywhere, that we will see, learn and experience afresh that Christ is the Lord of the universal church, helping us experience the fullness of the body of Christ in Jesus and give us a glimpse of our eternal home in heaven.

The new life in Christ is not about cultural uniformity, which comes from proselytizing, but always about fresh appropriations or translations of the Christian faith. The distinction between the convert and proselyte, is crucial, as the latter simply and wrongly is forced to repeat a foreign cultural form of belief and practice (Walls 2002, 68). This carries much importance for the practice of cross-cultural ministry. Thus conversion leads to the embodiment of faith in diverse cultures and results in translation. Theologically, God is a translator, centrally as Christ took on human form. Translation is linguistic and cultural, and is always taking place (Sanneh 2009). This conception of translation is very different from "contextualization" and is much more enriching for the wider church, yet also profoundly challenges existing paradigms of theology. It is clearly evident from diverse narratives of this volume that Christian faith is "both captive to and liberator of cultures". Thus the translation of the gospel into a culture never occurs without a critique of culture. Transmission is certainly not an easy or uncomplicated process, but it ultimately produces a dynamic of theological integrity.

The notion of hybridity that was theorized by Homi Bhabha (1994 and 2006) are helpful to understand diasporic struggles of assimilation, authority, change, tradition, subordination and resistance in diaspora contexts. The diaspora paradigm forces us to look beyond the immigrant generation and into subsequent generations and their "in between" space and arbitration of existence in the interstices of life. Likewise, Stuart Hall argues that diasporic experience "is defined, not by essence or purity, but by the recognition of a necessary heterogeneity and diversity; by a conception of identity which lives with and through, not respite, difference; by hybridity" (1992, 310-14). He saw the subversive force of this hybridization lies in its capacity to deconstruct the discourses of the majority and powerful by decentering, challenging and recreating the master codes of the dominant culture and theologies, leading to making something new. It destabilizes unitary narratives by questioning how we do church and mission in the diasporic world and host nations which are permanently altered by the presence of diaspora communities from around the world. Thus, diaspora spaces marked by movement across boundaries are a fertile ground for creation of new ideas, complex identities and fresh theological articulation to deconstruct old paradigms and reconstruct new possibilities.

Finally, Walls caution may be pertinent as we realize the ever growing need for unity amidst our great diversity of Christianity in the twenty-first century. He reminds us that "The Ephesian Moment is whether or not the church in all its diversity will demonstrate its unity by the interactive participation of all its culture-specific segments, the interactive participation that is to be expected in a functioning body." (Walls 1998, 72-84). Christians worldwide can ill afford to express themselves in terms of disjointed Christianities. Our basis of unity is not doctrines or organizational; neither it is cultural or programmatic, but the Lordship of Christ and realization of the global body of Christ. The current global dispersion of Christians is not only advancing Christianity in unexpected ways but is stretching our minds to wrap around a more fuller version of the body of Christ by bringing us face to face with Christians from all over the world.

The Church of Jesus Christ is not a fixed homogenous group but a community composed of people whom we did not choose but united together by the Holy Spirit as one body with ethnic or social distinctions and we must come against forces that divide us. Whenever Paul speaks of the church as the body of Christ he employs the imagery of one body with many members – "we, who are many, are one body in Christ" (Rom. 12:5) and "the body is one and has many members" (1 Cor. 12:12). Paul argues that baptism into the one body is the basis of unity and partaking at the table of the Lord's Supper is an expression of the unity while joining in the mission of God is the activity of the unity and hope in eternity is our eventual destiny of the unity of the church. The dialectic between the local and the global church prohibits an insular focus of the local congregation being obsessed with its own cares or preserve continual homogeneity, but to intentionally develop great diversity within and greater cooperation with other churches in the region and around the world. Diasporization is breeding heterogeneity and helping local churches to become more global and to reflect the universal church. The reality of unprecedented human mobility is moving the church closer to the "full stature of Christ" (Eph. 4:13) through greater unity and maturity, beyond our idiosyncratic cultural Churchianity. The worldwide scattering (diaspora) of the gathered and gathering (ekklesia or church) of the scattered are creating greater momentum in evangelization and advance of the gospel to the ends of the earth. May this "Ephesian Moment" of diasporas help the global church of Jesus Christ to realize a greater understanding of the body of Christ with all of its diversities and leverage it for the mission of God in the world.

References

Bhabha, Homi. 1994. *Location of Culture,* London: Routledge.

_____, 2006. Cultural diversity and Cultural differences in *The Post-Colonial Studies Reader,* Editor Bill Ashcroft, London: Routledge.

Brah, Avtar. 1996. *Cartographies of Diaspora: Contesting Identities,* London: Routledge.

Center for the Study of Global Christianity. 2015. Status of Global Mission AD 1800-2025. http://www.gordonconwell.edu/resources/documents/StatusOfGlobalMission.pdf (Accessed Jul 14, 2017).

Charles, Ronald. 2014. *Paul and the Politics of Diaspora.* Minneapolis: Fortress Press.

Cohen, Robin. 1998. *Global Diasporas: An Introduction.* Seattle: University of Washington Press.

Dunn, James D.G. 1998. *The Theology of Paul the Apostle.* Grand Rapids: Eerdmans.

Hagan, J. and Ebaugh, H. R. (2003), Calling Upon the Sacred: Migrants' Use of Religion in the Migration Process. *International Migration Review,* 37: 1145–1162.

Hall, Stuart. 1992. The Question of Cultural Identity in *Modernity and Its Futures*, Eds. Stuart Hall, David Held, and Anthony McGrew, Polity Press, Cambridge, 310-14.

Hirschman, C. (2004). The Role of Religion in the Origins and Adaptation of Immigrant Groups in the United States. *International Migration Review*, 38: 1206–1233.

Levison, John R. 2006. The Spirit and the Temple in Paul's letter to the Corinthians in *Paul and His Theology*, ed. Stanley Porter. Leiden: Brill.

McLeod, Hugh. 2014. *Cambridge History of Christianity: World Christianities 1914-2000*. Vol 9. New York: Cambridge University Press.

Safaran, William. 1991. Diasporas in Modern Societies: Myth of Homeland and Return, *Diaspora: A Journal of Transnational Studies*. (1) 83-99.

Shuval, Judith. 2000. "Diaspora Migration: Definitional Ambiguity and a Theoretical Paradigm, *International Migration: Quarterly Review*. 38: 41–56

Smith, Timothy. 1978. Religion and Ethnicity in America, *The American Historical Review*, 83 (5): 1155.

Thompson, James W. 2014. *The Church according to Paul: Rediscovering the Community Confirmed to Christ*. Grand Rapids: Baker Academic.

Roetzel, Calvin. 1992. Oikoumene and the Limits of Pluralism in Alexandrian Judaism and Paul" in *Diaspora Jews and Judaism*, Andrew Overman and Robert MacLenan (Eds), Atlanta: Scholars Press.

Sanneh, Lamin. 2006. *Translating the Message: The Missionary Impact on Culture*. 2nd Edition. New York: Orbis Books.

Schnelle, Udo. 2003. *Apostle Paul: His Life and Theology*. Grand Rapids: Baker Academic.

Wallace, Richard. 1998. *The Three Worlds of Paul of Tarsus*, Routledge, New York.

Walls, Andrew F. 1997. *The Missionary Movement in Christian History: Studies in the Transmission of Faith*. New York: Orbis Books.

_____, 1998. *Cross Cultural Process in Christian History*, New York: Orbis Books.

Wright, N.T. 2005. *Paul in Fresh Perspectives*, Minneapolis: Fortress Press.

Appendix

Mathew Thomas

Top 25 Migrant Destinations from Southern Asia in 2015

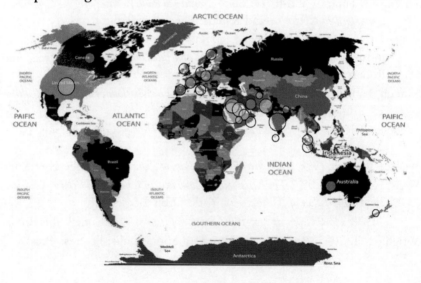

Rank	Destination Country	Total Migration	Bangladesh	Bhutan	India	Nepal	Pakistan	Sri Lanka	Maldives
1	United Arab Emirates	5,427,275	906,483		3,499,337	43,809	863,858	113,788	
2	India	4,982,222	3,171,022	6,647	NA	542,947	1,106,212	155,195	199
3	Saudi Arabia	4,766,699	967,223		1,894,380	381,102	1,123,260	400,734	
4	United States of America	2,603,711	186,028		1,969,286	74,904	325,419	48,074	
5	Pakistan	2,001,486			2,000,908		NA	578	
6	Kuwait	1,783,655	350,229		1,061,758	22,678	312,434	36,556	
7	United Kingdom	1,741,553	230,143	463	776,603	54,695	540,495	138,752	402
8	Oman	1,446,537	346,068		777,632		284,460	38,377	
9	Qatar	1,145,017	160,183		645,577	151,314	133,212	54,731	
10	Canada	1,007,247	51,227	2,519	621,469	9,830	175,204	146,998	0
11	Malaysia	729,644	358,432		132,699	205,021	26,858	6,634	
12	Australia	620,392	37,092	3,829	389,992	32,872	43,949	112,120	538
13	Nepal	476,778	233	28,740	446,491		1,268	46	
14	Bahrain	469,371	78,396		302,635	3,789	74,710	9,841	
15	Italy	405,168	97,036	35	136,403	1,775	84,792	85,093	34
16	Singapore	370,812	80,747		150,082		129,253	10,730	
17	Afghanistan	348,369					348,369		
18	Germany	176,681	7,576		68,291	3,924	50,174	46,716	

19	France	126,117	4,995	87	48,061	1,325	23,779	47,864	6
20	Spain	103,396	10,033		33,483	3,136	56,116	628	
21	New Zealand	85,712	1,530		69,800	1,465	2,961	9,956	
22	Maldives	85,300	53,565		22,120		167	9,448	
23	Bangladesh	73,490			34,431	39,059			
24	Switzerland	68,875	2,114	72	19,081	953	4,451	42,139	65
25	Greece	52,203	9,812	2	10,152	50	31,295	889	3
Total		**31,097,710**	**7,110,167**	**42,394**	**15,110,671**	**1,574,648**	**5,742,696**	**1,515,887**	**1,247**

Source: UN Migrant Stock by Origin and Destination 2015, United Nations Department of Economic and Social Affairs

Index